ROCK AGAINST RACISM

Photograph: Red Saunders

Photograph: Sarah Wyld

Anti Nazi League

Edited by
Roger Huddle & **Red Saunders**

★

Reminiscences of RAR

Rock Against Racism (1976-1982)

REDWORDS

Reminiscences of RAR: Rock Against Racism 1976-1982
Edited by Roger Huddle & Red Saunders
First published by Redwords December 2016

This extended edition published January 2021

Set in ITC Franklin Gothic
Design and production Roger Huddle
Printed by Halstan Press, Amersham HP6 6HJ

Paperback: 978-1-912926-88-6
Kindle: 978-1-912926-89-3
e-pub: 978-1-912926-90-9

Redwords is linked to Bookmarks: the socialist bookshop
1 Bloomsbury Street, London WC1B 3QE

bookmarksbookshop.co.uk

Frontispiece: Part of the demonstation on its way from Trafalgar Square to Victoria Pary 30 April 1978

The publication of edition of the book was made possible by the funds raised through **gofundme**. Thanks to everyone who donated.

ROCK AGAINST RACISM

the writers, fighters & rockers

Roger Huddle (Introduction)
Jeff Allen
Phil Allsop
Attila the Stockbroker
Roger Barrett
Bob & Roberta Smith
Chris Bolton
Geoff Brown
Selwyn Brown
Alex Callinicos
Steve Cedar
Gurinder Chadha
Jerry Dammers
John W Dennis
Shaun Doherty
John Ellis
Tim Evans
Jim Fagan
Colin Fancy
Kim Farnell
Jerry Fitzpatrick
Paul Furness
Rachel Gallagher
Jacquie Garstin
Dav Gilchrist
Darla Gilroy
Paul Gilroy
Debbie Golt
Vivien Goldman
Nick Grant
Roger Green
Ruth Gregory
Carol Grimes
Nina Hammill
David Hinds
Mike Hobart
Paul Holborrow
Trudy Howson
Bob Humm
Jon Langford
Graham Larkbey
Richard Lees
Bob Light
Liz Mackie
Hassan Mahamdallie
Gered Mankowitz
Judith & Derek Merrill
Wayne Minter
Sharon Moore
Steve O'Donahue
Prav Parmar
Sam Pattinson
Mark Perryman
Balwinder Rana
Jack Robertson
Tom Robinson
Keith Rusby
Nina Saunders
Red Saunders
David Seymour
Michael Shann
Neil Spencer
Virginia Turbett
Kate Webb
Lucy Whitman
Dave Widgery
Bernie Wilcox
Polly Wilson
Jo Wreford
Sarah Wyld

Mike Simons (Timeline)

Khadijah Ibrahiim (poem)

Dedicated to David Widgery (1947-1992)
& to all those who stood against racism and fascism during this tumultuous period

Park Ban Protest, Ealing Town Hall, 7 November 1978

Roger Huddle

Introduction: Reggae Soul Rock 'n' Roll, Jazz Funk Punk – Our Music!

'Don't forget: Rock Against Racism is *political* and you'll have to fight hard for it – but remember – it's always worth it'. *TH Gig Guide*

After the victory of Labour in 1974, hopes were high that real change could be won. There was a level of optimism because the Tories had gambled the election by asking who ran the country, them or the trade unions. The Tories were defeated. However, as the oil crisis of 1973 deepened and the Labour Government showed more willingness to do the bosses' bidding than defend the jobs and conditions of ordinary working people, there was widespread misery and disillusionment. On the back of this the Nazi National Front (NF) tried to build an organisation.

They were traditional Nazis so it was racism, anti-Semitism and a hatred for union organisation. There are all kinds of reasons why Nazis hate trade unions, the key one is that unions can organise along class lines and are for unity against the bosses. For the Nazis this is betrayal of country and race. White race, nation and state are 'as one' in Nazi thinking. But their strongest and most violent weapon is racism. By the middle of 1976 the NF were doing very well in local elections, blaming the crisis on black and Asian immigrants and lefties in the unions. They had some action on the streets but they had learnt from the past and were concentrating on presenting the average 'concerned white nuclear family' as suffering most in their propaganda. This had to be combatted.

I was asked to join the newly established *Socialist Worker* print shop in 1971 by an excellent designer and friend, John Finn. Somehow the organisation had found the money and the skills needed amongst the membership of the International Socialists to start printing leaflets, pamphlets and, most importantly, their paper and magazine themselves. I had joined the International Socialists (later the Socialist Workers Party) in 1966 while still an apprentice compositor. In the basement at 6 Cottons Gardens was the plate making room and printing machine, on the ground floor the typesetting and design studio, editorial offices up a floor, at the top our bookshop. All this was squeezed into a broken down four storey, toilet on the roof, set of nineteenth century workshops in Shoreditch, London E2. Five years later I had become a typographer and graphic designer. We taught each other (there were four designers) but John was the central influence on us all. I learnt my craft in an exciting and turbulent few years.

● *SW* print shop around 1978. Includes Ruth Gregory, Bob Humm, and Syd Shelton. In sunglasses is John Finn. I'm at the back. Almost everyone in the photograph was involved in producing and printing TH in one way or another on their own time.

In 1974 the Right to Work Campaign was formed to try and unite those in work with those without work, mainly young school leavers, to fight rising unemployment together. Its main campaign tool was organising long marches to Labour Party Conferences, or from depressed areas to the TUC in London, using the unemployed marches from the 1930s as a guide. But this was a fighting campaign rather than a passive one. The idea was to link the marchers with workplaces along the route that were facing or fighting closure to see if solidarity was possible. But between 1973 and 1976 unemployment had trebled, and the campaign was faltering with a general feeling of ineffectiveness. Although I'd first seen Red Saunders with CAST (agit-prop theatre group) in the mid-sixties and knew him by sight, it wasn't until a Right to Work Conference in Coventry in the early summer of 1976 that we got talking. Red had joined another agit-prop group, the Kartoon Klowns, and they were there promoting their 7 inch single about the Trico equal pay strike. I got a lift back to London and we became friends.

Later in the year I was asked by John Deason, secretary of the Right to Work Campaign, if I could talk to Red about organising an entertainment for that year's march to the Labour Conference in Brighton. It was ridiculously short notice, but we met anyway to talk about the possibility (just a disco was the outcome) but we agreed that left benefits were unimaginative, unorganised, tired and needed a massive jolt. We talked about the gains the NF were making and their

Men in shades: Red Saunders and Roger Huddle snapped by Syd Shelton at the Radical Wallpaper stall at Unity in the Community, Hackney 1981

openly racist and Nazi politics. I think that was the first time we talked about R&B, blue beat, soul, jazz, and so on being described as 'our' music, the music we both loved: all that the Nazis characterised as 'jungle' music. We talked about the possibility of combating racism with a concert of some kind.

During 1976 racist attacks increased both indirectly and directly: in May there were vile racist articles from the Daily Mail and Express over expelled refugees from Malawi. This led on to the murder in June of Gurdip Singh Chagger by racists in Southall. Nazi Kingsley Read declared 'one down, a million to go'. Then, in August, Eric Clapton, while on tour, paraded his racist filth from the stage in Birmingham. At the end of August the police went on a rampage attacking the Notting Hill Carnival. This was against a background of the first massive cuts to the NHS by Labour Minister Dennis Healey, under instruction from the International Monetary Fund, and a real fall in wages as the Social Contract between Labour and the union leaders began to bite.

Eric Clapton's rant in support of the infamous racist Enoch Powell and his ideas on immigration and repatriation, was from a man who had made his fortune by doing versions of black blues music, and had had an enormous hit that year with Bob Marley's 'I Shot the Sheriff', which in Bob's hands is a revolutionary song.

Red later phoned to read me a letter he had composed in rage against Clapton and asked if I'd sign. I did, along with members of the Klowns and it was sent to *New Musical Express* (NME) and the rest of the music press. The letter also said that we wanted to start a campaign called Rock Against Racism (RAR) and if anyone was interested, to get in touch. We put the PO Box number for 6 Cottons Gardens. Over 300 letters came back during the following few weeks (no email or mobiles in those days). We knew we had to do what we said. How?

We held the first RAR gig at the Princess Alice in east London on 12 November 1976 with Carol Grimes and the London Boogie Band.

As Red, myself and other supporters were involved in graphics, photography, agit-prop theatre, music and revolutionary politics, we went for the idea of RAR gigs immediately, coupled with visual images influenced by all the best in our tradition: the Constructivists of the 1917 Russian Revolution, the photomontages of John Heartfield, Dadaism, Pop Art and the anti-Vietnam War Movement in the US. It was very important that we pitched our propaganda with a highly visual language. Dave King, a brilliant designer, who Red knew through the Sunday Times colour magazine, was asked to design a logo and the RAR star was born. Later he also designed the Anti Nazi League (ANL) arrow.

Because of our tradition in left politics, we wanted to produce some form of newspaper/magazine that held the group together and made noise. We came up with the idea for Temporary Hoarding. This would carry posters, news from RAR groups and a gig guide so that supporters could do their own RAR gigs. At our second gig in December 1976 at the Royal College of Art (RCA) we asked the bands Matumbi, Limousine and Carol Grimes, to come back on the stage for a session together to finish. Other musicians who had been backstage or in the audience joined them (black and white united). This was the beginning of trying to make sure that gigs ended with a show of unity on the stage. See Paul Furness about having punk bands and reggae sound systems at the Leeds RAR Club.

During 1977 there were open street battles with the NF, in Wood Green, north London and, much more seriously in Lewisham south London. It was obvious that a much wider united front was needed and the ANL was launched.

The struggle against the NF was aided fantastically with the ANL alongside RAR. We succeeded because we knew that the majority of ordinary working people were not automatically racist, we knew the importance of music in the lives of young (and not so young) people, and that through the organisations and institutions of working people, and through rebel music, we could fight racism. The pessimism felt by many about their futures and the general state of the country meant that if given a purpose, both black and white would unite over the overriding threat of the Nazis – or if nothing was done, sink further into despair. Our simple one purpose campaign, 'Reggae, Soul, Rock 'n' Roll, Jazz, Funk, Punk: Our music' united thousands across communities along with NF=No Fun and NF=No Future. The ANL slogans were simply Never Again and Stop the Nazis. The most extraordinary group to come from a sort of marriage between RAR and the ANL was School Kids Against the Nazis (SKAN), with its badge of a yellow and red target pierced by an arrow, worn on many lapels and school uniforms.

Who was in charge?

From the beginning a fluctuating group would meet every week at Red's photographic studio in Soho, in London's West End. Constant were myself, Red and Robert Galvin, a solid group of students from the RCA, including Wayne Minton, John W. Dennis, Darla-Jane Gilroy and Rick Fawcett. Later Kate Webb, Syd Shelton, Dave Widgery and Ruth Gregory. There were others who just came for a week or two, or now and again.

I was a part-time DJ at benefits, trade union socials, and socialist parties calling myself the Night Train. Lionel, a comrade and friend, asked me to play at a benefit for a Gay switchboard he was setting up called Icebreaker. Red and myself went to the gig and the live music was the Tom Robinson Band, and that was where we met. Tom not only became a firm supporter of RAR, but would also come to meetings when possible.

At these meetings we discussed strategies, gigs and organising conferences for as many people as we could involve. RAR was a truly grass roots campaign. RAR groups all over the country were autonomous but led by people in general agreement — like Derek and Judith Merrill in Southall, Paul Furness in Leeds, Richards Lees in Hull, and Kim Farnell in Birmingham. This was an ad-hoc democratic structure. We had conferences but these were mainly jamborees and bonding days. I remember giving a talk on Gil Scott-Heron and jazz to a totally bemused young punkish audience, very embarrassing but no one booed. The doers led. That's that. If you want someone in charge, it was Red, who had enormous energy, vision and a total commitment to a united front. RAR progressed with an office staffed by Kate Webb, John Dennis, and Wayne Minter in Clerkenwell. In all other localities' supporters ran RAR. One of the purposes of this book is to give voice to as many of those people as I can.

I was, and still am, a black music fan, in all its forms from jazz right through to hip-hop. So punk came as a massive shock. I can honestly say I was never a punk but I understood it, knew its energy and knew that is was a committed revolution in popular music. Alongside punk there was a developing black music being made in the cities of the UK: Aswad, Steel Pulse, Matumbi, and Misty in Roots, plus many others. We knew instinctively that these two forms of music, punk and reggae, would be central to our campaign. Both had broken away from the tired lyrics of the 'pop song' and were writing words that came from their lived experience. With the despair and pessimism of the Sex Pistols (*Pretty Vacant*) to the anger and fight back of The Clash (*White Riot*), the fury of Steel Pulse (*Klu Klux Klan*), Misty In Roots (*Ghetto of the City*), and the simple assertion of dignity from Aswad (*I a Rebel Soul*), the sounds for change were everywhere. Black bands played for RAR but years of suspicion within ethnic minority communities, alongside the rise in racism, meant that many didn't work as closely with us as we would have liked. Also stop and search laws made it problematic for black youth to travel outside their home areas. We know now that many individuals were onside and came with their mates to the carnivals and gigs. The last Carnival in Leeds with Aswad, Misty, Au Pairs and The Specials was the most mixed carnival we held.

A story from the Carnival in Victoria Park

I was part of the stage management squad, left back in Victoria Park to get everything ready for the Carnival when it arrived. The whole process had been hand to mouth, guerrilla tactics, never telling any of the authorities what we wanted or what we were doing. This means that to repeat the Carnival today would be absolutely impossible.

We had no contact with the march on its way from Trafalgar Square, so we had no idea how many would come.

For the whole week before it had rained. Victoria Park was sodden. People from Bethnal Green ANL had spent the night guarding the stage. I am not superstitious but the rain stopped and the sun came out as I introduced X-Ray Spex at noon. There were about six people in the park, including two children and a man walking his dog. During her first song, the demonstration arrived. I stood at the edge of the stage amazed, watching the park fill with 80,000 people who had just walked six or so miles. This is important because media pundits always say that the crowd only came for the music. No, they came to march and to chant and to rock against the NF and racism.
Straight away the fence at the front of the stage collapsed. People were passing out. We had insisted on no professional security so we were on our own. The stage was in front of an empty open-air swimming pool in the park. We were using the locker rooms as changing rooms. In fact, I last saw the park keeper disappear into a room full of ganja smoke. We carried the barely conscious young people around to the poolside where we laid them down. Out of nowhere appeared an elderly grey-haired man in a St John's Ambulance uniform. 'Do you need any help?' he said. As far as I can remember he stayed most of the afternoon reviving young dancers, and sending them back into the bouncing fray. But, like I said, I'm not superstitious.
Those few years of intense struggle against the NF and racism were exhilarating and extremely hard. During the worst of times we needed to mobilise on the streets on a weekly basis against a march, or threatened march, by the Nazis. In schools, colleges, workplaces and in our communities we confronted the racists, and drove the NF back into the sewer.

● Red Saunders makes a fine point about politics and art with Roger Huddle at the Jeremy Deller exhibition in the William Morris Gallery, 2014.

Reminiscences of RAR

For me the book had to give space to revolutionaries, anti-racists, the music fans and the once angry youth. We are all an older generation now. I do hope that younger readers find the stories here inspirational, interesting and helpful in the struggle against racism today. I have not altered in my political beliefs over the last fifty years, and I think this is obvious. But I did want everyone to say what it meant to them, irrespective of political alliances, or even no politics. I think that this book reflects, from all those involved, a true expression of the unity, in society and culture, that came to the fore during those years. In can be

said that because I was a member of a revolutionary organisation and Red was not, the united front began with us. A roots movement was the aim. And what still unites all the contributions to the book is our stand then and now against racism.
Individuals together can make history and in that struggle to change society, they themselves are changed. These few years were all that: a struggle that stopped the rise of a Nazi organisation, that went to war on racism and in the struggle through the music, diverse cultures and the unity, we danced, sang and fought for something better.
But it is also important to remember black and Asian communities were attacked, many RAR or ANL badge wearers were beaten, we came up against the police time and again, punk gigs were destroyed. Some people lost their lives.

As long as fascist groups exist, there needs to be opposition. What forms that opposition takes is not predictable. Music and cultural campaigns could exist but whether RAR as it was will come into existence again I doubt it.
Are there any fundamental differences in today's society that could prevent another movement such as Rock Against Racism from happening again? No. Racism still exists, capitalism remains to oppress and exploit. Of course, the struggle can appear at any time and it can take a cultural form.
I wanted to produce this book because it's a story needed to be told by the participants. It is a history book, but told in fragments. It has stories, memories, all from the same time, being told from 71 different perspectives. And out of this, even with the contradictions of some accounts, I'd like to think we get an accurate narrative of the period. Mike Simons has put together a timeline as a guide. So if you are reading someone's reminiscences and want to fit it in context, that's the place to go.
There are many RAR members, street fighters and dance floor rockers who, for one reason or another, are not included here. We are both sorry to have missed you. Nevertheless, it has been wonderful to contact so many of our friends and comrades and fellow anti-racists for the book. I thank you all. Good or bad, like the late seventies, it was wonderful to go through the making of the book.

Roger Huddle
November 2016

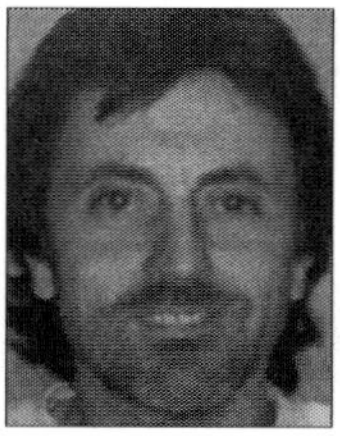

Jeff Allen

RAR stage manager. Victoria Park/Brockwell Park & other RAR concerts

I first met Red Saunders at the photographic studio in Gt. Windmill Street, Soho, he shared with Gered Mankowitz and Gil Galvin – my girlfriend Jacky was the studio manager and she had arranged the use of the studio for a photo shoot for East of Eden the band I was drumming in at the time.

Red, a charismatic mountain of energy, was the driving force behind the RAR project. He was an award winning photographer for the *Sunday Times* colour magazine, as I recall, and Gered, a leading pop/ rock photographer (The Rolling Stones, Jimi Henrix, The Who et al). Other friends, activists, RAR people I remember include Roger Huddle from the SWP, Pete Bruno, Jo Wreford, Sid and Ruth, Dr David Widgery, Kartoon Klowns theatre group, Paul Foot and many more.

I was seconded as a RAR stage manager at one of the early get togethers – (in my kitchen in Stoke Newington) – as the only professional musician in what was the 'RAR ad hoc committee' – and probably the only one there with experience as to the mechanics of staging an open air music event such as we were contemplating.

I remember

David Widgery saying 'bless your pointy cowboy boots' as the meeting moved on to the where, why, when, and how of what was to become the biggest festival-sized concert in London since the Rolling Stones in Hyde Park.

An extraordinary bunch of friends and colleagues with a mission to make a reality, Red's idea of a grandiose musical statement against the prevalent racism in the UK linked with the Anti Nazi League's fight against the National Front

I remember

— Discussing sound requirements with Roger Barret from Star Hire our stage and PA supplier and proposing a system for a potential audience of 10-15,000.

I later remember us looking out at 80,000 plus and thinking 'oh shit!'.

I remember:

— Going to fetch Steel Pulse from the tiny dressing room area and being knocked sideways by a heavy cloud of weed when I opened the door.

I remember:

— Bernard Rhodes The Clash manager being a complete arsehole saying he was just there to cause trouble. He had arranged for Jack Hazzan and his film crew to take over the stage to film The Clash set as part of the 'Rude Boy' movie he was making – a heads-up as to what was on the agenda from Bernard, or Jack, would have gone a long way to us helping them rather than looking to throw them off the stage.

I remember

— X-Ray Spex with Poly Styrene being great, in fact all the acts were fantastic: Tom Robinson, Steel Pulse and of course The Clash with Jimmy Pursey guesting, helped I'm sure by the vibe from such a massive trouble-free audience – un-policed as I remember.

Not much more can I remember I'm afraid except the pride I felt and still feel in being involved in something that really did make a difference.

I am still flaying about on drums whenever an opportunity arises. Playing with a variety of people since Mick Taylor, who I was managing and drumming for, got back involved with the Stones. After finishing a Rita Coolidge tour I have been in Germany with some Local Heroes playing Bob Dylan songs! Back next week to do some more with old rocker Zoot Money. Still have the Sensible Music as a base with the recording studio, equipment hire and event production. Intending to grow old as disgracefully as I possibly can.

Best

Jeff (September 2016)

Phil Allsopp

A view from Middle England

Phil Allsopp teaches history in a secondary school in west London and is a member of the Socialist Workers Party, which he joined in 1981.

I grew up in a small town in the Midlands called Leamington. Today it is a successful and quite prosperous town marketing itself as being in 'Shakespeare Country'. But in the 1970s the town was still mainly industrial, being home to a number of sizeable factories including a Ford's foundry and Automotive Products which made brake linings for the car industry in nearby Coventry. Already the recession in the industry was affecting the local economy and what with the effects of the mid-70's oil crisis hitting car sales along with the imposition of austerity after the Labour Party went 'cap in hand' to the IMF in 1976, the full employment of the 1960s and early 70s was over and unemployment was beginning to rise.

In 1976 a local resident made headlines nationally by putting a sign outside his house saying 'For Sale – To an English Family Only'. His name was Robert Relf. He had, of course, no intention of selling his house to a white family or anyone else. Relf was a hard-core Nazi who had a long history in far-right organisations and wanted to become a martyr for his 'defiance' of the Race Relations Act. Supported by the most of the mainstream media, Relf's case led to his arrest and his refusal to take down the sign led to prison. Two Nazi groups, the National Front and the British Movement used Relf's case to demonstrate through multi-cultural areas of the Midlands. 'Free Relf' became a rallying cry of the far right in Britain – and my hometown became the focus of attention.

As a local school student at the time, I was already well aware of racism within the community and the effects of it on some of my school friends. By 1976, Leamington had become home to a large community of mainly Sikhs from the Punjab region of India, a working class com-

munity which largely lived in the older, poorer part of town and worked in the local factories. Relf and the National Front clearly wanted to divide the working class using racism at a time when many people were starting to feel less certain about the future.
As well as being at school I managed to get a Saturday job in a local small independent record shop, which was a great job for a 16 year old; I spent most of my wages on records! By 1976 my interests were wide and varied but when a band from London called the Sex Pistols made headlines by swearing on TV and were splashed all over the newspapers, it sparked my interest and I was soon listening to this new band and the others that came in their wake. The shop I worked in started specialising in 'punk rock' as it became known. Punk was amazing as the bands played in small venues all over the country, in contrast to the super groups that dominated the older rock scene, like Led Zeppelin and Pink Floyd. Getting to see such bands would have meant paying loads of money to sit in a massive venue and being subjected to long self-indulgent guitar solos by bands with little interest in their fans. Punk was different. For a start it was small, loud and pretty amateur. When I saw The Adverts, TV Smith appeared pretty drunk and spent most of the time lying on the floor singing incomprehensibly into a mic. But these gigs were amazingly emotive. The atmosphere created by loud bands playing in night clubs with small audiences packed in the front of a dance floor meant that you felt like part of a movement. Interjected into that was the politics of a country ill at ease with itself and the changes it was going through. Punk reflected this as the beginnings of industrial decline and the end of the post-war boom fused with tension over issues such as Ireland and migration. Punk declared the dream of the 60s had ended; 'no more Elvis, Beatles or the Rolling Stones' sang The Clash on the song *1977* which reflected the hopelessness of being young and 'on the dole'.

I can't exactly remember when I first heard about Rock Against Racism (RAR). The magazine *New Musical Express* had pioneered punk rock from 1977 and it also promoted RAR. This also inspired many of the customers of the record shop. We had a regular crowd who had been energised by punk and came every Saturday to see what new singles and albums we had, what gigs we'd heard about or had tickets for, or just to chat and catch up with the latest band we'd seen. In the context of Leamington in the 1970s, Rock Against Racism really made sense and became an important part of the movement.
The conflicts in wider society also affected the punk scene. In the early days, some of the bands used the Swastika as an anti-establishment symbol – much of the impulse behind punk was despair at a system that seemed totally out of touch with young people. Using Nazi signs like this was dangerous, but for young people who'd grown up in an era

when most older people could still remember the Second World War displaying the swastika was designed to shock and be rebellious. Real life Nazis in the National Front tried to use the symbolism to ingratiate themselves with punk.

I remember at gigs by The Clash, probably the most political band of the era, seeing small groups of youths doing Nazi salutes. Their first single was called *White Riot*, and despite the band's intentions, was taken by some to be a call for white people to make a racist stand. I remember a long discussion with an Irish friend when I revealed I'd seen Belfast-based Stiff Little Fingers, as he believed the band to be racist UVF supporters based on misjudging a track called *White Noise* which compared racism against Asians with racism against the Irish using overtly racist language. When I saw Sham 69 most of audience were skinheads (punks tended to have short hair, but not shaven heads) with Doc Marten 'bovver boots' intent on having a fight. Again some shouted support for the NF or did Nazi salutes from the audience. I don't recall the band doing much about this at the time. As far as I remember, singer Jimmy Pursey ignored what was going on and just got on with a pretty raucous gig. The Stranglers were avowedly anti-RAR for some reason. They were also disliked by the *NME* and had a reputation for sexism. But I do remember seeing them playing in Coventry supported by Steel Pulse, an amazingly hypnotic reggae band from Birmingham who included a song supporting RAR in their set! It's also worth mentioning that the music played between the support bands and waiting for the main acts in most punk gigs was mostly reggae, which introduced the music of Jamaica to a largely white audience.

In 1978 I saw The Clash at the Top Rank in Birmingham. It was probably the most violent gig I went to with a number of fights in the audience and Suicide, an electronic band from New York, playing through a shower of beer glasses and bottles. In their song (White Man) in Hammersmith Palais, The Clash sang about the problems in gigs at the time: 'punk rockers in the UK / They won't notice anyway / They're all too busy fighting / to get a good place under the lighting'. About third down on the list of support bands was a group introduced as The Coventry Specials (which, given we were in Birmingham, may have been a mistake) playing a mixture of punk and ska. Despite the atmosphere, they were amazing. They were also overtly multi-cultural being made up of black and white band members and singing about issues of racism. Within a year they'd be at the forefront of a massive ska revival connected explicitly with Rock Against Racism.

A massive turning point for Rock Against Racism was getting The Clash involved. They were, for most of us, the epitome of a punk band. The first time I saw The Clash in early 1977, it was electric. The dance hall was packed for one thing, with everyone pogoing (jumping up and down) to the music. Their first album released shortly afterwards was an amazingly abrasive statement of politics, nihilism and anger, with a punk version of a popular reggae tune thrown in for good measure. The Clash headlining the 1978 RAR carnival in Hackney – an area that was known for having an NF problem – really helped turn the tide on racism among young people. Not only did we have The Clash supporting Rock Against Racism, but they were joined on stage by Jimmy Pursey of Sham 69. This completely undermined the far right supporters that had attached itself to the band and made the NF completely uncool.

When a young man called Satnam Singh Gill was murdered in a racist attack in Coventry city centre on a busy Saturday afternoon, I joined thousands of others, including large numbers of local Asian youths, to oppose racism. The protest was met by the National Front in Pool Meadow bus station in the city centre and there followed a full-on riot. The NF needed police protection to make their way out of town. Coventry became the focus for anti-racists and Rock Against Racism organised a festival at a local stadium headlined by The Specials.

● The Clash

It was events like this that built the anti-racist movement and gave young people the confidence to challenge the threat of the National Front. The Specials song *Concrete Jungle* summed up the fear: I have to carry a knife / because there's people threatening my life / I can't dress just the way I want / I'm getting chased by the National Front. Many black and Asian people felt under attack. In isolation, anti-racists felt scared to confront the racists. Getting together gave us strength and the confidence to fight back. Rock Against Racism made young people confront some of the realities of the world around them, and by getting the bands we were listening to and being influenced by to make clear anti-racist statements, we felt we could challenge the racists head-on.

For me the legacy of Rock Against Racism is that it was not enough just to play music that reflected the world you live in. Punk did that in many ways. But it wasn't until it fused with Rock Against Racism that punk became effective in challenging some of the things that needed changing. It's still good to get out those old records and spend a few hours down memory lane from time to time – but more importantly it's good to use the history of the times to inspire us to keep fighting back today. Things may be different now, but many of the issues haven't gone away – there's still a world to win.

Attila the Stockbroker

Launched into public consciousness by the legendary Radio One DJ John Peel in 1982/3, performance poet/songwriter Attila the Stockbroker has spent 35 years touring the world, doing over 3,000 gigs in 24 countries and releasing about 40 CDs/LPs/EPs and seven books of poetry.
In 2015 he published his autobiography – *Arguments Yard: 35 Years of Ranting Verse and Thrash Mandola.*

RAR and its sister organisation, the Anti Nazi League, came about as a result of four main factors. These were the punk explosion and the resultant politicisation of the music scene: the powerful links between punk and reggae epitomised by the likes of The Clash, The Ruts and Misty in Roots: the massive growth in support for the fascist National Front in the late seventies: and the obscenely stupid behaviour of two members of what was by then seen as music's 'old guard'.
In 1976 David Bowie had given a magazine interview saying he was sympathetic to fascism and had later made a Nazi salute at Victoria Station on arrival back from a tour. Even more astonishingly, given that he was/is a blues guitarist and had just revived his career with a cover of Bob Marley's *I Shot the Sheriff*, Eric Clapton interrupted a concert in Birmingham to make an infamous speech supporting the racist Tory MP, Enoch Powell. All this in a year when the National Front was at its political zenith, achieving 200,000 votes across the country in local elections. What absolute cretins.
The impact on many music fans, and especially people involved in the developing punk scene, was enormous. I had never had any time for Eric Clapton, but I loved Bowie's early stuff, and his references to 'supermen' and the 'homo superior' – which at the time I had passed off as arty, sci-fi posturing – now took on a new, sinister meaning. The National Front of course tried to cash in, and for a time after this I hated Bowie

with a vengeance. There is no doubt that both he and Clapton soon realised how contemptible their behaviour had been and recanted, but the damage had been done, and to their immense credit, some people responded straight away.

Photographer Red Saunders (of whom more later), Roger Huddle and Dave Widgery, among others, orchestrated a host of letters to the music press in protest. They then started putting on concerts under the banner of Rock Against Racism, the first of which was at the Royal College of Art in December 1976 and featured reggae band Matumbi and singer Carol Grimes. Allied as it was with the developing punk scene, the RAR movement quickly spread all over the country.

At Kent University we took up the cause with gusto by mid 1977, ordering loads of copies of the RAR fanzine *Temporary Hoarding,* plus badges and stickers, and a group of us started planning gigs, using RAR's format and inviting all kinds of bands (mainly punk and reggae) to play side by side. As the slogan went: 'Reggae, Soul, Rock 'n' Roll, Jazz, Funk, Punk – Our music!'

Our sporadic events were incredibly successful, even though many just featured Brighton and Kent coast bands (The Depressions, The Provokers, The Infested among others) and lesser known reggae bands like The Enchanters (from the legendary Ruts/Misty in Roots 'People Unite' collective in Southall). At these gigs I met RAR activists from other areas and went to the events they were organising elsewhere: as a white 19 year old from the Sussex coast I learned a lot, very quickly. Rastas and punks joined together at the gigs – People Unite indeed!

It was a heady time. I immersed myself in the new music and learned an awful lot about organising gigs, which would stand me in very good stead a few years later, when I needed to promote my own. Our Brighton Riot Squad gig happened that summer. Then, on 13 August 1977, Max and I, along with Joby & the Hooligans and members of various other Brighton punk bands, travelled to south east London to join thousands of others opposing a huge National Front march at what came to be known as 'The Battle Of Lewisham'. It was a defining moment in modern British anti-fascist history: the Front had never been stronger, and they came to Lewisham boasting that they would control the streets of London and, in the words of wannabe Fuhrers John Tyndall and Martin Webster, 'kick their way into the headlines'...

'Black and White, Unite and Fight! Smash the National Front!'

'Punks and Teds and Natty Dreads, smash the Front and join the Reds!'

Multicultural Britain turned up to stop the fascists in their tracks.

At Clifton Rise bricks rained down on the 'master race' from all directions and when a wedge of anti fascists split their so called 'Honour Guard' from the rest of the march.

Leaving the coach loads of bigots who had travelled down from NF strongholds like Leicester confused and isolated, the result was never in doubt. They got battered. Mainly, I am happy to say, by locals who were angry beyond belief that scum like that had dared to set foot there in the first place.

In the aftermath of Lewisham the Anti Nazi League was formed, to play the same role in everyday political life that RAR did in the music scene, and all kinds of local ANL groups were set up: Teachers Against the Nazis, Football Fans Against Nazis (I was in there!), Left Handed Vegetarians against the Nazis....

Then came the huge RAR/ANL Carnivals. The first one took place on 30 April 1978 at Victoria Park in east London: The Clash, Tom Robinson Band, Steel Pulse, X-Ray Spex and my soon to be mentor Patrik Fitzgerald (plus the Ruts and Misty in Roots playing on a flatbed truck – I remember that very well) with more than 80,000 people there to listen and celebrate. We marched to Victoria Park from Trafalgar Square, some 6 miles, and when we arrived they told us people were still leaving the departure point. The second one was on 24 September 1978, at Brockwell Park in south London: Aswad, Misty, Elvis Costello and Sham 69, and even more people!

RAR and the ANL, plus Thatcher appropriating the Front's rhetoric at the 1979 General Election ('we are being swamped by an alien culture') saw to it that the NF would never again be the electoral force they had been – although the fascists didn't go away, far from it. On the very day of the second Carnival, they organised a march through the East End of London which we didn't even hear about till afterwards, because the Carnival organisers took the decision not to tell us: this caused serious and lasting divisions in the anti-racist movement. Fascists were already causing trouble at RAR gigs, especially in London, and as the British Movement took over from the National Front as the main rallying point for the boneheads, Nazi violence at gigs would become a real problem.

By this time I was absolutely determined that one way or the other, music and words would be my living as well as my life. My academic work suffered enormously because of all my other activities – including standing unsuccessfully for Union President – but in the summer of 1978, in between the two RAR carnivals, I did my final exams at university and, somehow, got a degree. A Desmond.

● Extracted from *Arguments Yard: 35 Years of Ranting Verse,* Cherry Red Books, 2015.

Roger Barrett

Roger and Maddy, from the beginning, RAR's passionate road, and sound crew

Star Hire began life in Baldock, North Hertfordshire in 1976 as a touring audio company and quickly picked up work with a number of artists on Island Records, which led to the company becoming the dominant audio supplier to reggae bands in the UK, both Jamaican and home grown. Owned and managed by working class northerners, the company also worked on a lot of demos and protest marches, with a nifty line in guerrilla tactics to get substantial PA systems onto trucks in the middle of street protests.
An early client was Aswad and their manager, Michael 'Dreads' Campbell, introduced Star Hire into the RAR team on the basis that they had 'set up a tour and needed a bit of help…' which led to Roger Barrett meeting the RAR team at their offices over a bookshop just along from Finsbury Park.

● I thought the concept of the Militant Entertainment tour was great but the practicalities were challenging, to say the least. We carried all the sound, lights and 3 crew in one small truck and it was nothing short of exhausting, but an amazing experience. The truck was so over-loaded we had to go very slowly round roundabouts to prevent it falling over. There was a very 'collective' approach to things, which included having 4 bands play each show for 4 nights, then another 4 bands for the next 4 nights etc. Great in theory but totally confusing for the crew! Of course, some shows were great because the band sequence was as it should be and other nights, bands that should have been support acts had the uphill task of following a set that should have been the finale.

That all paled into insignificance against the energy generated by the crowds and the tension when the NF turned up – Red Saunders doing a truly stunning job of bouncing around on stage as a huge teddy boy and getting violent skinheads 'on message' – something I'll never forget.

It is hard to appreciate now just how many NF logos were graffitied across the UK and we carried a big box of giant size marker pens and some spray cans – we all knew how to add to the NF logo so it changed to read No Fun and we must have changed 100's as the tour progressed.

● X-Ray Spex opening for Carnival 1978 Photograph: Andy Wilson

If the Militant Entertainment tour were to happen now, it would be recorded in minute detail and circulated through all the wonders of Social Media – in 1979 there was none of that, not even a mobile phone between us and so we had very little advance info as to what we would be walking into at each venue. Many of the venues have faded in my memory to a blur of doors, stairs, small stages, over-crowded dressing rooms and the like but the instant antidote is Syd Shelton. His iconic images, especially with The Ruts onstage at West Runton pavilion (long gone as a venue) trigger quite detailed memories. Other than the stuff that Syd captured, key memories include constantly falling over the Leyton Buzzard's plastic palm tree and (more seriously) having the privilege to mix sound for most of the acts that appeared. Of course, as a small business we were actually getting paid for working on this tour, although not very much and not very regularly. Getting enough cash to keep going was a constant battle and one of the key unsung heroes was a young accountant called John Ellis who worked tirelessly to collect, track and distribute funds as well as being in many ways the glue that kept the team together. This very challenging working environment was to prove the foundation for an almost 30 year relationship between John's small accountancy firm and Star Hire (now Star Events). Largely thanks to John's advice, Star Events has traded without a break for 40 years, managing not to go out of business even once, bucking the fashion of much of the event supplier industry in the process.

Having squeezed and shoe-horned our way into small clubs and gigs up and down the UK, the finale in the Great Hall at Alexandra Palace was the entire opposite: we struggled to find enough gear to fill it for the enormous crowd that turned up, and to this day I can't hear a Tom Robinson song without remembering that day. It was all the more special for the appearance of Jimmy Pursey with Sham 69 (edgy or what, at a RAR gig!) and Alex Harvey, still one of the finest rock performers of all time – fortunately the big fire that almost destroyed the whole place was sufficiently long after RAR were there that we couldn't be blamed!

Life sort of returned to normal after that finale, although it wasn't long before we were doing a gig in Glasgow when we got the news that the NF had failed to get a single MP elected but that Thatcher had won, a bitter sweet victory if ever there was one. Little did we know that Thatcher's election would see us out on the street many times, rocking against sexism, blood sports et al and doing countless benefits for the miners.

Along the way we provided sound for the massive Specials gig in Leeds that marked the end of RAR and then went on to work with Artists Against Apartheid, covering both the quarter of a million people AAA festival on Clapham Common and the iconic Smiths gig at Brixton Academy. Plus 12 years providing all the sound systems to the Notting Hill Carnival, which should be the subject of another book!

● Fast forward to 2008 and Star Hire (the sound company) had become Star Events Group (the stage company) and we were back in Victoria Park, relishing the opportunity to provide the stage for the RAR 30th anniversary gig. It is a matter of great personal regret that I'm writing this just after the rubbish 'leave' vote and the racist aftermath, showing just how much there still is to do before we can say we live in a country we can be proud of. The fight goes on.

Bob & Roberta Smith / Artist

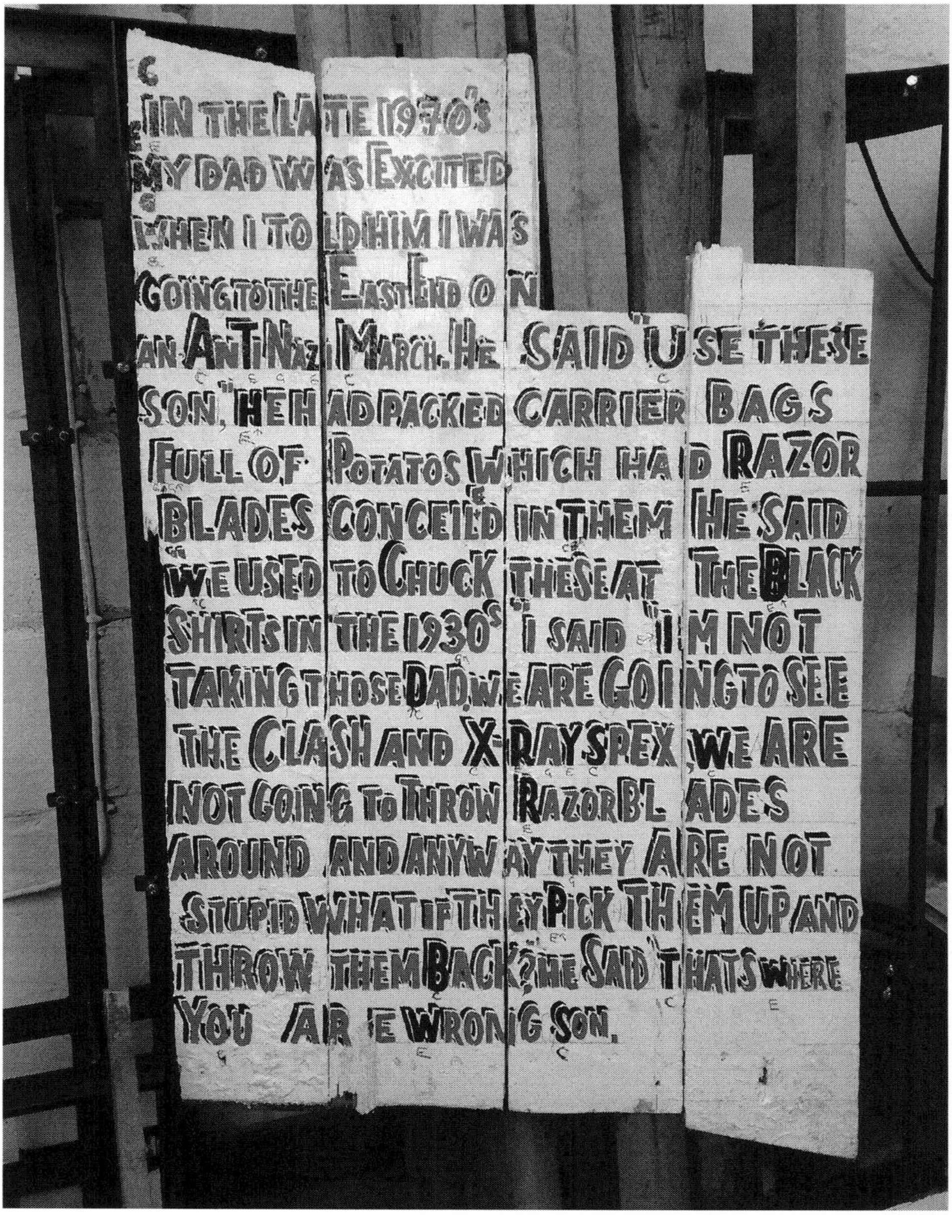

Chris Bolton

at the time Sound Man with Misty in Roots

RAR Central London Poly, 28 February 1978:
Misty in Roots and Sham 69

The event had a build-up. Through attending RAR meetings at Red's office in Soho we were aware of the situation of Sham 69 and their BM followers and of how organised racists could disrupt gigs.

We went to see 999, who had a Southall following, and a guitarist John Watson from Southall at Barking Assembly Hall near West Ham with a view to booking them to play in Southall. In Barking there was a regular punk show but we saw an organised attempt by an organised group of thugs to destroy something that was being created. They started attacking any black people in the hall and anyone else with them. But you have to stand up and be counted and the racists were taken by surprise as people did stand up and the racists were chased out of the hall.

This was one of many examples from which we knew there were organised racist groups making attacks. The Mangrove restaurant was another. There were attacks on Acklam Hall and the Albany in Deptford. In Southall a Billy Bean campaigned to 'Save our Southall'. There were attacks on the Bengalis in the East End, who racists saw as easier targets than the Panjabis in Southall. I was once on a cross-Channel ferry when working for EMI and on that ferry were a group going to attend a fascist gathering somewhere in Europe. They were led by a man whom I saw a few weeks later leading a group of racists in Brick Lane.

We realised that there were the same sort of people among those who supported Sham 69. Punk though expressed the rebellion of rock'n'roll. Like reggae it was rebel music. Punks felt safe in reggae. RAR created a self-defence mechanism and said to the racists you push one way we push the other harder. There were other organisations that helped. *Searchlight* provided information on fascists and the Anti Nazi League was an important factor; members would turn up to protect the community.

When Jimmy Pursey asked for help and to do a RAR gig we needed to meet him. We went to Surrey, to Walton & Hersham (hence the Sham!) to meet Jimmy. Walton on Thames is the rich part; Hersham is the ghetto next door near to Feltham prison. Pursey lived on a council estate there. We asked him why he wanted to do the show. He seemed to be a desperate man. He wanted to make money but felt he was under pressure from the record company. He needed to lose the tag of being a fascist and feared it would blow whatever he was trying to do. He wanted to put a stop to this and he needed to break away from that.

The night itself probably had more build-up than any other show. We made sure we brought with us good security and took a large team of people with us. The event was a very well organised one, as there were people outside the venue who could recognise troublemakers. Once inside any potential troublemakers were politely asked if they could go one way and were isolated. There were some very large people on security who were very efficient, lovely people who were very interested in Nazis and very professional in dealing with them. We had a genuine united front and this is what RAR did, it united people.

That gig protected that cherished item in our lives – music. Jimmy came on stage with Misty and sang *Exodus*. It stopped dead that particular round of attacks but did not stop it forever. On 4 July 1981 as we were going to a gig in Euston, we saw a coach load of skinheads with flags going the other way. They went to the Hambrough Tavern in Southall for on Oi gig but were met by an Asian hockey team with their sticks and the Hambrough Tavern was burnt down.

Since the first edition of this book Chris Bolton died June 2019

Chris at a Southall gig alongside Misty 1978. Photograh: Red Saunders

Chris was a co-manager of Misty in Roots, and an organiser with People Unite community based arts group, when he and his friend Clarence Baker came to give their support to RAR back in the winter of 1977. A cultural warrior, an activist always on the front line, a working class boy from Southall in West London. He was a lifelong trade unionist and socialist, clear and knowledgeable about his politics, an internationalist with a passion for African and Caribbean music which he centred his life around.

I'd been told he was terminally ill so went down to Bognor Regis to visit him, it was clear he was frail and very weak. It was a beautiful sunny day I took him out for fish and chips on the sea front and we sat and chatted on a about the old days and RAR times we had shared.

He was still raging against the injustices of the world we live in, still ridiculing 'our leaders'. These are some Facebook comments after his death 'great story teller, a wonderful father, down to earth, 'a life lived well', 'he leaves a huge hole', 'multi cultural man, a real gent.'

He was a natural for RAR and what a committed fighter who loved **unity** culture, he wanted passionately to wipe the stain of racism and facism from this world to the very end of his life. RIP brother.

Red Saunders

Stop the NF Nazis!
ROCK AGAINST RACISM
Anti Nazi League
Stop the NF Nazis!
Stop Nazis
Anti Nazi League

Geoff Brown

Manchester Anti Nazi League organiser in 1978, now a historian 'from below', writing about the fight against racism and fascism in the 1970s.

Above: Geoff in 1978. ● Previous page: Bands on the streets at the Northern Carnival Manchester, 15 July 1978. Photo John Sturrock

After being battered at Lewisham in July 1977, the NF decided to make their come-back 'up north', choosing the small ex-mill town of Hyde. On the day, only the NF leader, Martin Webster, marched, accompanied by over a thousand police. I was in front of him, alongside Ramila Patel, who carried a placard denouncing Webster. Everything moved to a higher gear when the Anti Nazi League was set up a few months later, out regularly confronting any attempt by the NF to organise. We talked to local people where the Front were trying to hold meetings, asking them to help with scrubbing out Nazi graffiti, borrowing a ladder to get to the ones that were high up. The Nazis still tried to build their base. They had a public meeting in Bolton Town Hall behind a wall of police after a backroom deal between Labour and Tory councillors let them have a room.

I spent a lot of time distributing leaflets and badges. We measured our sales of badges by the bucketful. Then we got a badge machine and folk made their own. Eventually you couldn't walk across the middle of Manchester without seeing people wearing ANL and RAR badges. I used to joke that I worked the day shift and Bernie Wilcox, Manchester RAR organiser, worked the night shift and we saw each other at shift change. Around Easter 1978 the date was set for the first Carnival in London, 30 April, and we began to organise transport, posters, leaflets, selling tickets. The demand went through the roof. There wasn't a corner of the Manchester area where there wasn't going to be a pick-up point. The coach companies, always hard nosed when it came to money, liked what we were doing. I booked the last coach the night before the carnival. About 2,500 came down from Manchester in 50 coaches and minibuses.

On the way back Bernie and I decided we wanted a carnival in Manchester. I was going to Poland at the end of July so I wanted it before then, ten weeks away. No one said this was unrealistic, everybody was keen on the idea and things fell into place. Roger Huddle came up to help sort out the venue. One look at black and white kids playing football in Alexandra Park decided it. The organisers of Deeply Vale festival near Rochdale were planning for the following weekend after our date, which cut our costs putting the stage up in Alex park then taking it down for Deeply Vale. As ANL organiser I spent much of my time in the campaign against the National Front candidate in the Moss Side by-election which was taking place on the Thursday before the carnival. We agreed with Tosh Ryan, who controlled fly posting for gigs in the city that we wouldn't compete, but he would get our posters up. A bigger problem was getting permission off the council to use the park, but we had very solid support from the unions, including the secretary of the North West TUC Colin Barnett who was well connected. The negotiations were with the Director of the Parks Department and concluded with permission for one concert on Saturday afternoon. Then Graham Parker and The Rumour, on their way to support Bob Dylan at Blackbushe aerodrome, did a practice session with a few thousand people listening on a beautiful evening. Their sound system – much bigger than ours – could be heard by the Parks Dept director in his back garden 2 miles away. The rumpus that followed was only resolved when it became clear that anyone who decided to pull the plug would have thousands of local Buzzcock fans looking for them.

Below: Colin Barnett, secretary of the North West TUC, leads the march through Hume, on the way to Alexandra Park Manchester, 15 July 1978.

On the day I was up at six with others making sure that the car park in front of Strangeways prison stayed free of cars for the rally at noon. We had about 15,000 there. The police tried to take control but we pointed out to them that nobody was in control of this huge crowd which was going to march off to Alex Park whatever anybody said. We had half a dozen flat back wagons which we had kitted out with small electric generators. Each one had a band so that a good part of the crowd danced the four miles from Strangeways to the park. The

Left: Ramila Patel, Bolton Asian Youth movement and SWP member, carries placard that reads, 'Webster marches alone because of the united opposition of tens of thousands of working people. Black+White Unite+Fight Smash The Nazi Front'. Below: Ramila and Geoff speak at Northern Carnival 40th anniversary meeting.

concert went as planned and afterwards my main job was collecting money and giving some of it to kids who had missed their coaches. By the time it came to organising for Carnival 2 in Brockwell Park in September, the only question we had was how much bigger it was going to be than Carnival 1.

The National Front didn't disappear overnight, but they were never again a serious problem in Manchester. Kids from every school in the city had been at the carnival and back home they would ask the local playground Nazi where was he on Saturday? and he wouldn't have an answer. The NF organised an all-white youth football team called the Lillywhites in Tameside playing in a Sunday League. We went up there a couple of times on a bus driven by a sympathetic driver and occupied the pitch. Together with getting as many complaints to the council as we could about the use of the pitch, this soon led to the team disappearing. The success of the carnival gave our side such a boost that whenever the NF tried to organise something, we could always put out a call and be sure that people would turn out in numbers. We wore the NF down so that eventually they gave up, reduced to a bunch of racists getting drunk in a pub.

Selwyn Brown

Keyboards: Steel Pulse

Rock Against Racism – it is humbling to think we played a part in such an important movement at a crucial stage of all our lives and looking back, Rock Against Racism very much helped to reshape the way people across the UK viewed racism and gave a voice to those who otherwise felt silenced, especially with the way racism was tolerated in so many aspects of our society....in the workplace, education, the police, media, parliament and much more. So many great emotions come to me whenever I recall the times we toured, performed and hung out with all the bands and artists involved with Rock Against Racism and the Punk Rock movement. There was a great camaraderie that existed amongst all of us, created out of the collective desire to create a better world by breaking down racial/social/cultural/religious barriers. Looking back at that time, my overriding feeling is one of determination by all the bands, organisers, music fans to establish a force of resistance against a system built on divide and rule and scare mongering, pretty much the same thing happening now worldwide. Obviously the stand out events were the Victoria Park concert in London and the Northern Carnival in Manchester, both held in 1978. I remember thinking at the time 'wow, I've never seen so many people gathered together in one place'. As time has passed I've met many people who come up to me and say 'I was at Victoria Park' or 'I'll never forget the Northern Carnival'. Just shows the incredible impact the RAR movement had and the enduring commitment of people to continue the fight against racism.

We're living in times now where this evil has raised its head again, not just nationally but worldwide. Looking back again I recall how nervous we were when we played at our first punk event. That simple act of black artists sharing the same stage as white artists was something that the Punk Rock, Roots Reggae, Two Tone and Rock Against Racism era helped to establish as the norm. Up to that time this was very much a rarity and would be unthinkable now. Forty years on, even with all the struggles that exist in our world, we can still proudly say we live in a multicultural society and Rock Against Racism truly played a major part in achieving that ideal.

● Dr David Widgery speaking to the picket outside Bethnal Green Hospital in September 1978, protesting against closure of the casualty department. Photograph: Colin Knowles

Alex Callinicos

teaches International Political Economy at King's College London and edits International Socialism. Back in the late 1970s, he edited the old monthly *International Socialism* (which Roger Huddle then designed) and then *Socialist Review* (to which David Widgery often contributed).

David Widgery

Every radical movement needs its philosopher, and Rock Against Racism was very lucky in its – David Widgery, East End GP, unrepentant and rebellious revolutionary Marxist, and omnivorous lover of a bewildering variety of cultural forms – though he said 'R&B remains the root: passionate, sexy and highly political,' (210).[1]

Dave himself wondered 'whether Rock Against Racism was the last gasp of the 1960s' (115). No one I knew during our time together as fellow members of the International Socialists and the Socialist Workers Party better embodied the spirit of that much-mythologized decade. Dave subverted the old cliché that if you remember the 1960s, you weren't there. He had experienced it all – I remember him reminiscing one terrifying and hilarious evening at Alastair Hatchett's and Elana Dallas's house in Highbury sometime during the early 1980s, while, very drunk, showering the rest of us in abuse – and seemed to have forgotten nothing. More than anyone else I have known, he embodied the revolutionary energy of those years, which informed his many activities and writings.

Partly through his omnivorous reading and partly thanks to his avidity for experience, Dave seemed to have developed the intuitive skills of a cultural historian. He could spot unexpected connections with sometimes astonishing insight – indeed, more than anything else, he was a connector, of people, ideas, struggles, and art-forms. The essay Dave wrote for the *London Review of Books* about John Lennon gets him better than anything else I have read. [2]

But when he says Lennon's originality lay in 'his response to the very specific origins: the anglicised R&B, the intensities of the grammar art schools of the time, the insubordinate popular culture of the north

---

1 References in the text are to David Widgery, Preserving Disorder: Selected Essays 1968-1988 (London: Pluto, 1989).

2 David Widgery, 'Lennonism', London Review of Books, 21 February 1985, http://www.lrb.co.uk/v07/n03/david-widgery/lennonism

of England' (75), he might – leaving aside the Beatles' Liverpool that he so brilliantly evokes in the essay – have been writing about himself, another English grammar school boy who found in African-American music the language in which to express his rebellion against postwar Britain, 'a strange world of fretwork radios, college scarves, white bread and deference' (xvii).

But it would be a huge mistake to confuse Dave with one of the cultural critics or academic theorists he despised (this comment on the high theory of the post-1963 *New Left Review* conveys his considerable talent for invective: 'the paper emporium of a coterie of Marxist swots at the mercy of their own intellectual crazes, and prizing theory more as evidence for their own cleverness than for its possible relevance in the struggle for socialism.[3]) He was a revolutionary socialist through and through, an active Marxist with a strong sense of the continuities of working-class struggle. Here he is in 1974 on Sylvia Pankhurst, the suffragette turned communist active, sixty years earlier in the same East End that he served and wrote about:

> My interest, affection, it's hard not to call it love for Sylvia Pankhurst has grown over the past five years spent practising as a doctor not half a mile from her home in the Old Ford Road. East London is different now, studded with tower blocks and fenced with corrugated iron. But curiously the same. Still solidly proletarian, still the sweatshops and street-fights and rent strikes and plenty of old lady patients who remember 'our Sylvia' with a twinkle. Still the migrants, speaking Bangladeshi rather than Yiddish, still the dole queues, longer now than ever. And still a revolutionary socialist minority, of which I'm part, spouting at street corners, dishing out leaflets, spreading union membership, occupying hospitals due for closure. (55)

I first encountered Dave a little earlier as another of that minority, in Hackney and Islington IS during that epic year of working-class revolt 1972. I remember him – a slight frail intense figure, bearing the marks of the childhood polio to which, strangely enough, I too had fallen victim – spouting away on a soapbox in Chapel Market when we campaigning against the Tory Housing Finance Act. I never knew him well, though. Our main dealings were on paper. As a young and inexperienced editor of a new monthly, *Socialist Review*, I published the wrong article on the first Carnival in Victoria Park, and was thoroughly cuffed in a letter by Dave and others from RAR.

On the whole, though, our dealings were amicable. Dave wrote some important articles for the same *Socialist Review* – I especially remember a magical piece for another early issue marking the 10th anniversary of 1968 that expressed what it felt like to be politically

3 David Widgery, The Left in Britain 1956-68 (Harmondsworth: Penguin, 1976), p. 513.

active that year: 'It was as if an international political pageant was being acted out – the ideas we had treasured in pamphlets and argued about in tiny pub back rooms were now roaming, alive, three dimensional. Marxism had come out of the cold'. [4]

Dave wrote like an angel. His ridiculously early death in October 1992 at the age of 45 deprived us of one of the very best socialist writers. As an editor, though, I sometimes had to tone down the enthusiastic and sometimes arcane lists reflecting his vast eclectic reading that pepper his sentences. Standing at my shoulder (occasionally literally), I had my friend and mentor Chris Harman – Dave and he shared a slightly wary respect for each other, but Chris was the master of a much plainer and less ornate prose style. Dave seemed to bear what he probably thought of as mediocre pruning cheerfully. For the rest of his life, like many others I would be the recipient of occasional notes from him, scratched out in doctor's scrawl (what we lose with email), full of suggestions, praise, or thanks. It was like being touched by the energy that seemed always to flow through him.

But this energy wasn't direction-less. Dave was deeply committed to the unifying principle of the SWP's interpretation of Marxism – articulated by Tony Cliff starting from his path-breaking critique of state capitalism in Russia – that socialism is the self-emancipation of the working class. This wasn't a bloodless theoretical axiom for Dave. His profession required a continuous daily commitment to working-class people in all their variety.

His last book *Some Lives!* (1991) brilliantly portrays the London that we now know but that was only beginning to take shape then at the end of the Thatcher era – a capital city polarized between the City and the super-rich on the one hand and on the other hand what are still some of the poorest areas in Britain. But the book is also, as its title implies, a series of portraits of the people of the East End, in all their quiddity, simultaneously affectionate and unsparing, perhaps as only a socialist doctor could write. The political commitment informing this writing was expressed practically in Dave's campaigning to defend the National Health Service against cuts under both Labour and Tory governments. He would have loved Bethnal Green's insurgency against New Labour in the era of the 'war on terror'.

Dave's Marxism was, compared to most of us, catholic. In tracing the genealogy of the tradition of socialism from below, he would cite not just Cliff, but Cornelius Castoriadis, Raya Dunayevskaya, and, of course, his beloved C L R James. Dave was a self-confessed aficionado of the duplicated sectariana produced by the far left (in those far-off days the Gestetner played the role, much more laboriously, that blogs and social media do now). But he combined this with a rare

4 David Widgery, 'Ten Years for Pandora', Socialist Review, no 2, May 1978, https://www.marxists.org/archive/widgery/1978/05/10years.htm

generosity of spirit. *The Left in Britain* weaves together Dave's own vivid and thoroughly biased narrative with many different, often discordant voices. He was a consistent advocate of the women's liberation movement and strongly supported what we now know as LGBT+ liberation.

Running through all this was, I think, a conception of socialist revolution as a process of total liberation, one that working-class people would experience directly in all aspects of their lives, and one that they would represent to themselves and others visually, musically, and in writing. Dave had no patience for the argument made most eloquently by Trotsky that a genuinely liberated art would have to wait till the construction of communism. Revolutionary art was itself a medium of liberation in the here and now. He also thought that how socialists communicate needed to be transformed in ways that participated in these aesthetic innovations. These ideas at least in part informed Dave's approach to RAR. They sprang from debates that go back much further, to William Morris, Mayakovsky, the Surrealists, and the Situationists (of all of whom Dave was a fan – he claimed to have joined IS because we published an obituary of André Breton). They're unlikely to be resolved any time soon.

So, like all the best Marxists, Dave was unorthodox. But he also understood that the best heresy is a creative continuation of orthodoxy. I'm proud to have published in *Socialist Review* in 1979 Dave's review essay on the third volume of Cliff's biography of Lenin, *The Revolution Besieged*. Calling for a 'post-electronic Leninism' (53), Dave portrays Lenin's tradition as a victim of the isolation and decay of the workers' revolution of October 1917 under the pressure of counter-revolution and foreign intervention:

> The blossoming-blighting process which Cliff documents froze over Leninism and only mass revolutionary working class action is able to melt it from its icy limbo. Lenin is therefore trapped in his moment, surrounded by a thicket and awaiting political rescue: 'An old communist conceives an embryo of longing'.[5] One day his Modern Prince will come. Until he is woken with the proletarian kiss, the problem is not that Leninism has failed, but that it has not been tried. And 'alternatives' to Leninism are often old reactions in new disguises, forms of terrorism, reformism and anarchism which were politically surpassed by Marxism a century ago'. (52)

In another frozen moment, amid the triumph of Thatcherism in the late 1980s, Dave reaffirmed his own idiosyncratic Leninism:

> It was certainly being, and remaining, a member of an organized Marxist grouping, as well as my professional work as a doctor,

---

5 I haven't been able to trace the source of this quotation. Hugh MacDiarmid?

> which put me, and kept me, in direct contact with the realities of working-class life... Without 1968 and the SWP I would, no doubt, in the conventional manner of the educationally upwardly mobile, be ensconced in the Department of Community Medicine of a cathedral town with my children down for public school and a sub today to the SDP [the right-wing breakaway from Labour that helped to form the Liberal Democrats]. (xiv)

These words were written not too long before Dave died. He was a one-off, a unique talent and personality, whose quality his writings can only imperfectly convey. But he was exemplary in his commitment to revolutionary Marxism and human liberation. One of the many reasons why RAR was so memorable is that it gave this extraordinary figure the best platform of his life, one for which his abilities, tastes, and experiences had all thoroughly prepared him.

● David Widgery: Hard/Nice Times

Steve Cedar

was a worker who became unemployed and then a student, and then unemployed again before becoming a worker again, and at the time of RAR and the ANL, a student activist in the SWP. He studied at the now defunct North East London Polytechnic (NELP), in a building that is no longer there, like the Princess Alice pub where the first RAR concert was held, and the last time he was in Stratford or Forest Gate, was unable to recognise it. He has lived in Catalonia for 31 years, leaving Britain after the miners strike in search of another life, and he found it, has a partner, Lidia, and a revolutionary daughter, Itziar, and he is still fighting fascism, which is yet again stretching its talons across Europe. Never again, No pasarán! Here or anywhere!

RAR: the first concert

The Princess Alice, an unremarkable pub in Forest Gate, E7, an unremarkable district of East London, was the venue for the first ever Rock Against Racism concert, organised by 3 or 4 unremarkable lefties from the area, myself included, perhaps in terms of musical taste, the most unremarkable of them all.

My knowledge of music was zero. My taste for music, the subject of ridicule among my comrades in the Outer East London District of the SWP and other social movements, was unremarkable. I liked Andy Fairweather-Low and Alan Price, and Vivian Stanshall and Bonzo Dog, Humble Pie (I was more accepted there) and John Lee Hooker (*Simply the Blues* was my first album I bought, 1971 I think) and Paul Simon. 45 years later I still listen to most of the above, but with a bit of Nitin Sawhney and Wookie and anything Spotify thinks would be of interest to me, with some 14th-century medieval music taking a leading position. So you could safely say I was "pre-punk" in taste, and "post-punk" in attitude. Being a revolutionary aged 21 meant you had to at least pretend to be serious and not influenced by bourgeois distractions like pogoing or spitting at each other or ripping off your T-shirt in the mosh pit (my daughter taught me that word in 2012), so you would think I was not that well qualified to go into show business, even though starting at the bottom.

But In other ways I was highly qualified to help organise a RAR rock concert – I fucking hated racism in all its forms, and even I, whose only social activity at the time was selling papers and then going to the pub, had heard of Eric Clapton's disgusting comments about foreigners touching his wife and of David Bowie's irresponsible antics at London Airport dressed in Nazi gear and seig-heiling from a limousine. He at least had the dignity to admit he was being a tosser at the time. And of course these comments and actions, far from being just the ravings of eccentrics with artistic license, actually had an impact on what went on in the streets and districts of towns and cities with the increase in racism, racist attacks and even racist murders, aided and abetted by the politicians who were quite happy to continue dividing and ruling, history repeating itself with the rise of fascist organisations like the National Front, and in East London they had their leader in Hoxton, and active groups in most districts. There was an unreported urban warfare taking place, and every Saturday or Sunday often involved some kind of altercation with fascists in the high streets around paper sales, and of course the daily harassment of black people on the streets and in the communities by police, racists and institutions. In some aspects little has changed, but because of our struggles then I am sure responses to racism today are far more unified and coherent.

● Carol Grimes outside her Yellow House where she lived in a flat upstairs in the 60/70s next to The Mangrove on All Saints Road.

So I was very proud to form part of the organisation of the first ever RAR concert in that pub. To be honest, I don't remember much about the concert. I remember the rubbish lighting and rubbish sound system, but the reggae band was good and Carol Grimes topped the bill and sang some great classic rock. I spent most of the time with a pint in my hand and an eye on the cash till, and I reckon about 200 people came to the event, a great success seeing as the posters advertising it were hand printed on a stencilling machine in our living room in Plaistow, as everything was in those days, from demos to public meetings. We also made a healthy profit with more than enough to pay for the drinks we bought for the bands (cans of light ale and cheap whiskey, I remember it very clearly), and that's where my memory becomes sharper. Every story of success has its down side. After the concert we were tidying up and the landlord came upstairs to check on everything and when he saw the cans of beer and empty whiskey bottles went totally apeshit. He wanted to break my head open with one of the empty bottles and take all our profits for 'corkage', a new word for me then, which meant the difference in his earnings due to the gift for the musicians. I pleaded total ignorance and made sure I got well behind Bob Light and Pete Goodwin, two of the other organisers of the great event. We calmed him down eventually by me accepting a lifetime ban from the Princess Alice and appealing to his Irish origins in the search for solidarity with a movement that was against racism and the British Empire, but I think the lifetime ban was what clinched it. So I walked the mile home clanking with change in a metal cashbox, feeling proud to have launched my showbiz promoting career for a worthy cause.

Little did we know what would become of RAR. At times we felt like corks floating on the ocean, the waves carrying us one way and then the other, dragging us along with them, always trying to keep up with events and responding to the fascists in the best way we knew, mobilisation. I think the RAR movement opened up politics and political action to hundreds of thousands of young people who would not have been involved through the traditional politics of the left. Fortunately some videos have been preserved of the amazing concert in Victoria Park in East London the following year where 100,000 of us marched from Trafalgar Square to the East End. I remember the faces of the pockets of fascists standing outside a pub in Roman Road with their jaws dropping. We had beaten them. NF = No Fun, NF = No Future, Black and White Unite and Fight, Smash the National Front, and always with the soundtrack in the background of Steel Pulse, Tom Robinson, the Clash, X-Ray Specs, Aswad, The Specials, and loads of groups I never knew or remembered the names of but who formed part of the Rock Against Racism movement and part of my lifetime DNA.

A European-wide RAR wouldn't go amiss today.

● Carol Grimes at the 30th Anniversary of RAR, Hackney Empire, 2006
Photograph: Jess Hurd

Gurinder Chadha

Film director

In 1976 I was a London school girl. I had no idea who Eric Clapton was. I used to watch Top of the Pops avidly. I was suspicious of Glam Rock, Heavy Metal, all kinds of rock. It represented 'them', people different to me, not nice bands that my parents liked like The Beatles or Cliff Richard. I liked the Jackson 5, never dreaming of ever seeing someone like me on there. The only Indian I had ever seen on Top of the Pops was Biddu singing backing vocals on the Carl Douglas song *Kung Fu Fighting*. Hoo ha!

My parents owned a shop so most of my days were either at school or helping in the shop. I hated being in the shop, you never knew when a racist might come in and, at best, call you a Paki and brazenly steal something, or, at worst, try and hurt you. Once a group of young English boys came in, mooned my Mum and ran off with crates of beer. Years later this mooning moment found its way into my first film, *Bhaji on the Beach*.

At that time, I was always amazed at how my parents took this in their stride, even though we often heard of other Indian shopkeepers being brutally hurt and hospitalised. It had happened to our Surjit uncle who had a shop he ran with his wife in Lewisham. The day the NF marched through that part of London he and his wife were beaten up. We went to visit them and my Dad said: "This is life here, what can we do?".

● 2 Tone

I was enraged but helpless: do we put up and shut up like that generation? Britain was tense, years of immigrant-bashing had succeeded in wearing down my parents. The ugly rise of racism on the street being supported by the police meant we were islands on our own, no wonder Indians took to owning shops where they felt they could have some control over their lives as isolated units.

Then at school I heard someone talking about a new group called Rock Against Racism. I was suspicious of white male Rockers with long hair and I thought this was a bizarre idea. Why would those white, long-haired Rockers stand up for people like me and my parents?

But by now punk had changed the musical landscape. I was put off by the more aggressive bands like the Sex Pistols – why would they want to put safety pins in their noses, that's got to hurt right? But other bands like The Clash seemed to be different, they used black music – reggae – and paid homage to it openly. Something was changing. I began reading about RAR and how they were planning a march from Trafalgar Square to Victoria Park to stand up to the National Front in their own back yard. I was intrigued. I wanted to go and see what this was about. I told my parents I wanted to go on the march. They went apoplectic. No way, they said, you will be provoking the National Front thugs who are violent and know no limits to decency. Why would you put yourself in their way? You are asking for trouble. You will be beaten up and arrested. Your place is here with us in the shop.

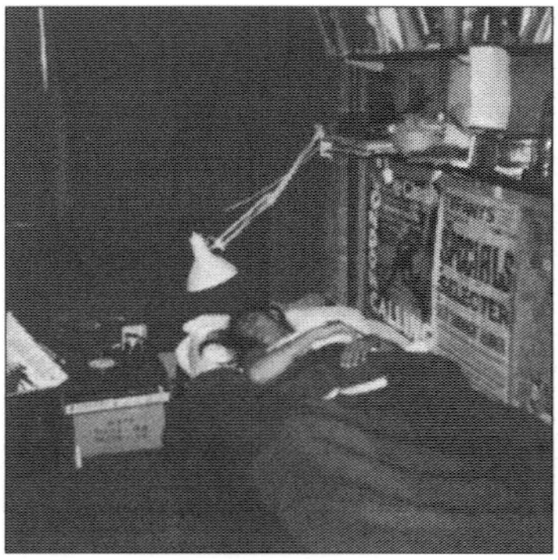

● This was my bedroom at UEA, with my beloved original two tone tour poster from 1979, The Clash and London Calling and Third World Poster. You may be able to see The Specials LP on the deck too, very cool!

Part of me agreed with them, I must be mad putting myself in the way of all that aggression, but I also felt I was on the brink of a new way of thinking, a possibility to climb out of this sheltered trench. Here were all these bands putting themselves out there, speaking out about racism, even if nothing came of it, it was worth at least checking out. So I [misdirected them] compromised. I told my parents I was going to C & A to get a new wrap-around jacket and promptly headed out. I was too scared to go to Trafalgar Square so I went straight to Victoria Park, on my own. I arrived in the vast empty park while The Clash were doing a sound check. Wow, Joe Strummer showed up, I thought. Then the band finished and I wandered round for a bit but nothing was happening. No crowds, no audience building, nothing. After a couple of hours of hanging around I thought to myself, it was a good try but nobody cares enough to come out, or maybe like me they were intimidated by the threat of violence and stayed away. Either way I proceeded to the gate to make my way home.

As I approached the gate I started to hear this bizarre sound, a kind of high-pitched buzz that was growing louder and louder: what was it? Should I run away from it? But then I heard music too and chanting. I headed for the gate and found an old box to stand on. When I looked down the street what I saw changed my life forever. From that moment I became the political filmmaker I am today.

What I saw were hundreds and hundreds of people marching, side by side in a display of exuberance, defiance and most importantly, victory. I couldn't believe my eyes, these were white, English people –

many with long hair like the rockers I could never relate to – marching, chanting to help ME and my family find our place in our adopted homeland. I didn't know any English boys, I went to a girls' school, so the sight of them along with all the other women and Black and Asians in that moment made me feel I belonged. I had found my tribe, my kindred clan.

When I got home I told my parents where I had been and what I had seen. In a strange way my Father was actually quite proud of me, he said: "you took a risk but you stood up for what is right". In years to come, those sentiments found their way in the final father-daughter scene in Bend it like Beckham.

I wore my RAR and Anti Nazi League badges proudly, I went to meetings, to marches. And I was proud when the Asian community stepped up and defended Southall when the racists thought they could march down my Southall Broadway. When their HQ, the Hamborough Tavern, was set alight, the NF had to retreat. We had stood up to them and the tragedy of Blair Peach's death was yet another turning point as the whole community came out and mourned this New Zealander's tragic death, defending our streets at the hands of the British SPG police group.

The music was still important along with the political voices, RAR continued to organise and inspire. So when The Specials came along I really found my groove. A band of black and white musicians performing ska together and singing about OUR England. Jerry Dammers said anti-racism was intrinsic to the formation of The Specials. This further consolidated my political, cultural and musical education.

I followed The Specials to many concerts, I was there at the Top of the Pops studio when they performed the number 1 hit, 'Message to you Rudy'. I became friends with Terry who was intrigued by me, a rarity for him as an Indian girl pogo'ing in the front of their gigs. As teenagers then, once over a cup of tea, I told him how as a young Indian girl I was trapped in my own world before I had been led out by RAR and the music. He replied he had felt the same growing up in Coventry – that was an eye opener for me. We remain friends till today.

I owe a lot to Rock Against Racism. It gave me the confidence to find a voice, but also made me feel I was part of something bigger. All my 8 feature films to date are about difference, prejudice and what the possibilities are for us as a human race, without division based on prejudice and hate.

Jerry Dammers

founder and main songwriter of The Specials and 2 Tone Records

I think my first memory of attending a Rock Against Racism gig was the reggae band Misty in Roots at the Butts technical college in Coventry, in around 1977. I remember the excitement and positivity of that gig. My mate Stan Dombey actually still owes RAR the entrance fee, because he didn't have a ticket, but somehow climbed in an upstairs window, and later unfolded himself to emerge from the absolutely tiny 'dumb waiter' lift that bought the food down from the kitchen into the students' canteen. Such was the buzz about the gig that it could not be missed. I think I probably remember the slow and heavy 'See Dem a Come (but We Nah Run)' a song in defiance of the National Front, British Movement and racist Babylon in general. Anyway I eventually had that record, and I think it was a bit of an influence on *Ghost Town*.

That gig was in the students union. Little did I know that several years later we as The Specials would be playing an anti-racist festival at the sports stadium attached to the same college, to protest at the appalling racist murders in Coventry of Satnam Singh Gill and Dr. Amal Dharry. Those were some of the darkest days in Coventry's history and I can only hope our little festival achieved something to try and counter the disgusting events in some small way. What made it worse was that there were rumours that there was supposedly going to be some sort of pathetic "march" by the National Front/ British Movement outside the stadium, the very idea of which showed their truly vile colours given the tragic circumstances. As far as I know nothing remotely resembling a march actually materialised at all.

We would also eventually, as The Specials, play with Misty in Roots at the huge Leeds Carnival Against Racism in 1981, and we closed the show with *Ghost Town*, which had just been released. The atmosphere was incredible, one of the most exciting and effective concerts we ever did, and so sad that it was also our last in this country I think. I remember that day; the vibe out front and backstage was fantastic, with Misty in Roots and so many other bands, and people, coming together to express their disgust at that ugly and xenophobic aspect that sadly persists in some English people, for some incomprehensible reason. I remember seeing the NF counter demonstration as we drove into Leeds on the coach, and it was rather a dark and ugly vision, which actually felt quite evil. I don't know why but to me it looked like a sort of giant slug, bristling with union jacks, moving very slowly down the street. I personally don't remember seeing any youngsters at all; they seemed more like a lot of sad old men in grubby car coats. I don't think its any exaggeration to say that practically all young people at the time would have much preferred to be raving at the gig than to be involved in anything like that, and that was the power of Rock Against Racism. It would be nice to think there could be such a mass expression against racism today, because it really seemed to work and was very successful. The miserable National Front was consigned to the dustbin of history.

Rock Against Racism had been an influence on The Specials from the start of the band, an influence on my decision to try and make the band specifically multiracial, playing a truly integrated mix of punk and reggae, and to deliberately recruit members from the communities of both those very different types of music. A bit mad musically, I don't think that had actually been tried before in one band, although punk and reggae bands regularly played alongside each other at RAR gigs, which in itself was one amazing achievement of Rock Against Racism. I actually talked our way onto a trial spot on The Clash On Parole tour, without their manager Bernie Rhodes ever having actually seen The Specials. I think he was so intrigued by the concept; he wanted to see if it was actually possible. Luckily The Clash liked us enough to offer us the whole tour, but the music wasn't really properly integrated, until after the Clash tour, when we went back in time, to the more up-tempo ska rhythm, and my mad idea finally came together properly. Sometimes you maybe have to look back into the history of radical ideas to find new ideas for a particular time. The hey day of the most exuberant ska had come at the same time as Jamaica's independence from its colonial master Britain, and I don't think that was a coincidence. Somehow we were able to harness that exuberance

again, hopefully to some extent in the service of anti-racism, which seemed appropriate to the music.

Some sixties white artists who had played black music, sadly went on to claim that it was them, as white artists, who had made the black artists famous. Maybe it was in response to Eric Clapton's famous outburst, which had given birth to Rock Against Racism, that I had come to hate that attitude – obviously it was actually the other way round: it was the black originators who had made the white artists famous. I have always at least tried to express my gratitude to the original Jamaican musicians who invented ska – without them there would have been no Specials and no Two Tone. There had been multiracial bands before in Britain like The Equals, Greyhound, Hot Chocolate, Heatwave and others, but sadly maybe not as many as there could have been, and I think that is probably still true today. I think Rock Against Racism also influenced me to some extent to write specifically anti-racist lyrics in songs such as 'Doesn't Make it Alright', and that continued through The Specials with songs like our Jamaican guitarist Lynval Golding's 'Why?' written following a racist attack on him.

I probably responded to Rock Against Racism partly because I had been involved in anti-racism from years before, when I had campaigned against Apartheid, specifically against the South African Springboks' rugby tour which was the first demonstration I ever went on, when I was about fifteen. I had put stickers around the school and managed to recruit a posse of about two others to come on the demonstration. An old school friend maybe remembered that when years later in 1983 I met him in the street and he told me about a concert at Alexander Palace celebrating the 65th birthday of someone I had never heard of – Nelson Mandela. The anti-racist theme influenced by Rock Against Racism continued after the Fun Boy Three had left The Specials, when I wrote my song *Free Nelson Mandela*, inspired by a song Julian Bahula sang about Mandela, which I heard at that Alexander Palace concert. My song then became known around the world. That in turn led to Dali Tambo, the son of the leader of the ANC Oliver Tambo, asking me to organise Artists Against Apartheid in Britain. We held a series of concerts, based to an extent on the Rock Against Racism model, and that series of concerts grew into the largest Anti-Apartheid demonstration ever held anywhere at the time – the 200 thousand strong Clapham Common concert in 1986. That in turn led to the two Wembley Stadium Mandela concerts that were seen by millions of people around the world. I think it is highly likely all that would not have happened in the way it did, if it hadn't been for the inspiration, success, and not to mention the support, of Rock Against Racism. That organisation and Red Saunders, as well as the Anti Nazi League, do deserve a share in some of whatever credit may be due for all that stuff happening in Britain.

John W. Dennis

Full-time RAR Organiser 1978-81

Nazis Are No Fun – RAR

The summer of '76 was a long, sweaty, drought-dry meltdown. When black youth at Notting Hill Carnival claimed their birthright as British citizens and fought back against the police oppression of the SUS laws, it was the wake-up call Britain needed. The poor always pay but this was fightback time.

The strike-back, for union rights and a living wage, by Asian women at the north London factory called Grunwicks, fed the furnace from which punk music and militant reggae sounds blasted out. Remember, this was just two short years after the miners had brought down the Tory government and there we were back on the streets fighting the Labour government's police and poverty assault.

But twelve thousand workers blocking the streets of north London in solidarity with two dozen Asian women workers at Grunwicks, and the black community defending itself, fired us up and set the tempo for the anti-racist agenda for the next five years.

In those days, as politically active students, we were rarely in college. If we weren't occupying it in protest against the cuts, we were out filming the Notting Hill Carnival fight back from the roof of a café on the Portobello road. Or we were on the picket line at Grunwicks and our mates were filming the police Special Patrol Group revenge-riot on the mass picketing. Our project was to become the "Nazis Are No Fun" movie/badge/t shirt.

When Rock Against Racism launched in autumn '76, we were busy with the student fight back against the cuts in education and occupied the Royal College of Art for a month. Red Saunders and friends' letter to the music press about the wave of racism endorsed by Eric Clapton's approval of Enoch Powell had caught the ant-racist mood and zeitgeist of the mid 1970's. Together with Roger Huddle's love of black music and organisational clout within the SWP they managed to get RAR off the ground. In the aftermath of the anti-cuts campaign fellow post-grad student Wayne Minter and I joined the SWP and it was there that we heard about RAR. We were inspired by the militant dynamism of the punk and reggae mix as the kick-starter for an anti-racist campaign that was well set up to take the swastika out of punk.

In the summer of '77 we were arrested on the shoot at the Battle of Lewisham against the National Front, and charged along with five local kids with organising the riot, yep this is true! When the cops broke into the squat, where the local campaign against the NF was based, an hour before the battle, we managed to video them breaking in. Someone offered to let them in but they smashed their way in anyway. We were on the top floor because it was a good vantage point to shoot the battle and kept the video going while the cops piled into the room and lined up around the walls unsure of what to do while I was filming them. Finally we were carted off to jail for the day but kept the camera rolling until we got to the cop shop and we were charged.

● John Dennis

Eventually the court case came around and we were discharged because the video, which the police gave us back, was shown to the court and clearly supported our claim that we were trying to cooperate and were hardly likely to be the main organisers of the battle. So, well tooled up with old school video cameras, we were out capturing the riots during the day and showing the assembled clips at local RAR gigs in the evening. In the autumn of '77, we managed to persuade our student union at the Royal College of Art to let us have the auditorium for our first RAR gig. We booked 999 to headline and Misty in Roots, The Members and John Cooper Clarke in support. This was achieved after a brain numbing number of phone calls using 2p coins in the phone box across the road from the Albert Hall. We were amazed when the venue was totally sold out to the punks who hung out in the Kings Road and west London. We gave every one of them a Nazis Are No Fun (NANF) badge and treated them to the video and media assault of the same name, while they moshed to the bands. The fire fighters' strike was under way at the time so we invited them along from the local fire station and donated the proceeds of the gig to their fighting fund. The punks loved them. One fire fighter got up on stage in his yellow plastic trousers and spikey hair. All he had to say was "I'm a fire fighter and I'm on strike" and the whole place erupted.

The best put down of the night was when John Cooper Clark was being heckled he came back with " I can't understand you mate. Your mouth's full o shite" in his best Salford accent.

The story of the design of the NANF badge in the summer of '77 Queen's Jubilee and The Pistol's *Never Mind the Bollocks* album, is interesting. The slogan for the badge derived from the NF letters scrawled on a wall in west London street. The N placed above the F as per the original badge pictured. Some smart anti-Nazi added the letter "o" to the N and "un" to the F. So I nicked it for the badge and added "Nazis are" and the RAR star. We manufactured one thousand badges. So popular were they that RAR Central, as it was referred to, decided to put it into production along side the RAR Star. For some reason it was decided to drop the red and black punk colours and separate the N and the F. For me the original design is still the best.

At the momentous Carnival against the Nazis we were flogging the badge and the T-shirt of the movie. The badge was to become the second largest income generator for the campaign, bested only by the original RAR star. With the success of the Carnival, RAR had arrived nationally and internationally. We all got very creative and political on the Nazis ass. More Carnivals across the UK, the Militant Entertainment UK tour, The Southall Kids are Innocent gigs with the Clash and Pete Townshend, and the Nazis crashed and burned at the election in '79.

With the success of the first carnival RAR took off with a burgeoning cohort of militant grass roots activists across the country. That, plus an emerging international profile meant that the demand for more info on how to put on RAR gigs, more mailouts of badges and the RAR magazine *Temporary Hoarding* stretched to the limits the resources of the RAR office. Kate Webb, who had boldly volunteered to run the office, was overwhelmed by the response. I was taken on full-time to help take the load off and work on the organisation of the second Carnival with Jerry Fitzpatrick of the Anti Nazi League. It was at that point that I left the SWP.

Carnival Two

When the ANL proposed a second Carnival in '78, there was some trepidation about raising the stakes on the success of the first Carnival. There was a line up to secure and a little matter of ensuring that RAR got the billing we wanted on the publicity and posters for the event. The significant size of the RAR star on the poster advertising the event indicates that that was sorted and when we secured Elvis Costello, Aswad, Sham 69 and Misty in Roots on the bill we just knew it would be a success. Many visits to Brockwell Park in Lambeth later and the day arrived with much anxiety about security. Costello didn't want any photographers on stage and there were the usual rumours about the NF making a showing after a march they had announced to spoil the day. In the run-up to the event Jerry and I had gone down to the Reading Festival to try make sure Sham 69 were going to do our gig. We blagged our way back stage but couldn't find Jimmy Pursey anywhere. But we did run into one of his road crew who was a British Movement supporter who harangued us for twenty minutes and said Jimmy would never show. Sham 69 eventually pulled out of the gig on the rumours of an NF visit but the irrepressible Jimmy Pursey snuck in with Costello and got to do a couple of numbers. We agreed with Costello that only the RAR photographer could have access to the stage but forget about securing RAR's media rights.

This was a problem that was overlooked at the time but was one that any savvy cultural campaign today would nail. It has been an issue that has rumbled on down the decades and has surfaced most recently in what was tagged "RAR Wars" bringing the campaign into disrepute over copyright issues. More about RAR's Punkoid (old hippies who were very born again punks) faction later.

In the event the NF didn't turn up at Carnival 2 and the entire 100k+ crowd had a good time. The film director of the film *Bend it Like Beckham* Gurinder Chadha has a wonderful story of her as a teenager ducking out of home on some pretext, going to the Carnival, seeing the floats arriving and being blown away by the whole spectacle. An experience shared by many people that day and equally proudly remembered.

Militant Entertainment Tour

It was clear that RAR was growing at a pace that no one predicted. There were RAR groups all over the country working with local bands and booking nationally recognised bands for them to support. We tried many different ways to consolidate that enthusiasm into a coherent organisation. It was in the nature of the beast that most of them failed. In the end the most outrageous and wildly ambitious project galvanised RAR groups across the country and established RAR as a national campaign able to organise a major event independently from the ANL. The March-April '79 plan was to arrange a tour that would include as many of the RAR groups as possible providing the local support bands. We secured the headline bands, national publicity, logistics and funding. We managed to get over 20 known bands to commit to the project. Wayne Minter came on board full-time to travel around the country to do the preliminary recce of the venues and liaise with the local RAR organisers. Kate coordinated the RAR groups from the office and I did the co-ordination of the bands and publicity from London. Resourcing such a crazy project with so few working full-time on it, amazes people to this day. Then we all went out on the road. We rotated the bands every 3 or 4 gigs and we had some amazing co-incidences. The biggest was Stiff Little finger's album, *Suspect Device*, went number 1 when we were in

Glasgow. They were so popular that we did two nights there.
The maddest bit of all was booking Ally Pally in London for the final gig of the tour with 11 bands and Tom Robinson headlining. The only way for us to deal with the awful acoustics there was to turn up the volume and jam pack the venue with people. We did both. I missed most of the acts because the budget for the whole shebang was tight so I spent most of my time with John Ellis (RAR's accountant) in the box office making sure we held on to every penny.

Southall Kids Are Innocent

The day after the Ally Pally gig the police Special Patrol Group ran riot on 23 April '79 at the anti-racist demo in Southall west London. They killed Blair Peach, an antiracist activist, and nearly killed Clarence Baker, the manager of Misty in Roots. We were all so knackered after the tour that I don't think any of us got to the demonstration that day. When we heard the news, we were all in deep shock and crashed after the elation of the tour. The police had also ransacked the People Unite Centre, which was where Misty In Roots were based. A demonstration to remember the life of Blair Peach and to put pressure on the police to hand over the murderer was organised. Misty played on the lorry at the head of the march.
Fortunately, Clarence recovered and it turned out that Pete Townshend of the Who had been a great supporter of Misty for some time and offered to do whatever he could to help them. Co-incidentally the late great, Joe Strummer of the Clash called me at home. He wanted RAR to organise a gig in Hyde Park to bring the punks together. I learned later that the Clash had had a falling out with the Sex Pistols over a tour of the USA.
We couldn't get Hyde Park so we asked Pete Townshend if he would sponsor two nights in July at the Rainbow Theatre in Finsbury Park for the Southall Kids Are Innocent gig. He could do one night and the Clash could do the other. My teenage mod hero was well up for it. We got Misty and The Enchanters, The Ruts, The Pop Group, Aswad and the Members to support and got the venue to take all the seats out. Pete provide the PA and the proceeds of the two nights went to the People Unite Centre.
The gigs were an amazing success but with a totally different sub-genre specific demographic. The Clash fans wore leather and Pete Townshend's wore denim. What was a real breakthrough was that we had got the ant-racist message to a totally new section of youth. This was a fact that unfortunately RAR's Punkoid faction would not take on board for the future.
Despite the emotionally charged atmosphere, my abiding memories of the two nights are: holding Joe Strummer's guitar at the side of the stage while he lay on the floor panting in recovery before an encore

and thanking Pete Townshend (the real mod-father) after the gig and him saying 'any time, mate'. In the run up to the show I had divided my time between working on the gig and attending the Blair Peach Inquest. I was running around with Misty trying to organise the gig with them, while trying to avoid the morning spliff building ritual in Pucky's (the singer in the band) sitting room. But we did beat the Clash in a five aside match near their rehearsal studios despite being kicked all over the shop by Strummer in his motor cycle boots. The rest of the time I was respectfully witnessing of the Blair Peach inquest with Jerry Fitzpatrick and mighty human rights solicitor, Gareth Pierce in support of the family.

Rock the Block

We were aware that although the British presence in Northern Ireland had been featured in *Temporary Hoarding*, we had not done much to support the youth resistance there. Jerry Fitzpatrick came up with the idea of doing a Rock the Block gig in Andersonstown and Ardoyne in Belfast, in the summer of 1980. Being fairly naive about the situation on the estates and terraced streets off the Falls Road, we were definitely up for the crack. We got the Au Pairs and Oxy and the Morons to come with us. Joe Austin, the Sinn Fein publicity officer, was the contact person at that end. For some reason I flew to Belfast and everyone else, including Wayne and Jerry, travelled with the bands and the PA by road and ferry. No Belfast based PA companies would get involved with the gigs so RAR stalwart Roger of Star Hire stepped forward. So we shipped the PA system from the Hertfordshire countryside into the urban warfare of West Belfast.

I think the reason I went ahead was that I was supposed to get things sorted out for when the rest of them arrived. I got a cab from the airport to drive me up to the top of the Falls Road and drop me off at the social club there where I was supposed to meet Joe. But the cabby would only drop me off in the street well away from the social club.

It was at that point, standing in the middle of the street alone with my English accent and the always present army helicopters overhead and Brit soldier pointing his rifle at me to check me out through the telescopic sights, that I realised that this might not end well. I stuck to the plan, such as it was, and wandered into the bar of the social club and asked the barman, as quietly as I could, if Joe Austin was about and explained that I was there for the Rock the Block gig. Needless to say Joe wasn't there and probably never knew of the arrangement. But fortunately they knew about the gigs and made me very welcome. Nevertheless I sat quietly in the corner of the bar sipping my Guinness waiting for everyone all to turn up.

The gigs attracted a mixture of punks, rockers and the mildly curious but faded against to the experiences that came after the gigs. On the first night John Ellis and I were to stay with a family in a terraced house just off the Falls road. The evening erupted into a scene from one of the many movies made about the "struggles". The kids, some of them very young, were down on the corner of the street waiting for the army vehicles to do their nightly patrol up the Falls Road. It was dark by then and the night lit up with the flashes and loud cracks from the rubber bullets fired at the kids by the army and petrol bombs lobbed back at their vehicles. All the mums in the street were leaning in their doorways proudly watching their kids take on the might of the British state. John and I were definitely with the mums. The next morning all the mums were in the street sweeping up the mess from the night before. John and I felt it only right that we should join in.

Later that day there was a demonstration on the estate up by the social centre and quite a large excited crowd was gathered. All of a sudden two guys with facemasks emerged from somewhere in the crowd with handguns and fired shots into the air. The crowd erupted with cheering and almost immediately the volunteers disappeared. From nowhere the army helicopters were overhead. We started to move down the Falls Road towards the city only to be met by a large number of army vehicles and riot control forces coming up the road to meet us. Three of us managed to get in a door way to get out of the way and I turned around to see a house brick land full square on the head of a solder in one of the armoured vehicles. We were about to be on the wrong end of a battering and only avoided it because the soldier got distracted by something else and moved away.

The next day were setting up for the gig in the edgy calm of a social centre in Ardoyne, a very beleaguered republican enclave in Belfast. The people were very friendly and welcoming. It felt like we were doing a gig in a youth club just down the road from where your Nan lives: cosy and a bit claustrophobic with the worst fish and chips in the world from out of a van. The kids kept asking us if we wanted to go round the corner to meet their sisters.

Needless to say everyone who made the trip came away from that short tour with the memories indelibly etched on their psyches. I had grown up on a council estate just like those in Andersonstown so the resonance was very powerful. We had witnessed the nightmare that follows the breakdown of social cohesion and the oppressive nature of the state when it can no longer govern by consent.

RAR's Greatest Hits

Because RAR was such a great success, we began looking for ways to culturally embed the campaign against racism in a way that was more than determined by the ebb and flow of electoral politics and funded by the sale of badges. We explored ideas for a regular club night in the London's west end, a record store, a record label – something to maintain an ongoing profile but that was financially viable as well. *Temporary Hoarding* was an essential part of that profile but it was not financially successful, even with national distribution through newsagents. Increasing the print run never led to increased circulation. Up to that point everything had been funded through the sale of badges and t-shirts to RAR groups, believe it or not.

The opportunity emerged to launch the RAR Records label when Red had a photo shoot with Richard Branson of Virgin. Branson declared himself a supporter so Red nailed him for a meeting with Simon Draper the head of the record label. While we were in reception waiting for the meeting I remember a young and spritely Boy George tripping by. The earliest sign that the music scene was beginning to move on. Basically everything we proposed the Draper, Branson said ok to. The proposal was that we would licence to Virgin a compilation of tracks from the bands that had supported the campaign. The resulting album would be released as the *RAR's Greatest Hits* album on the RAR Records label in all territories except Scandinavia. We had a deal with a sister label in Sweden who had a great grass roots distribution network throughout Scandinavia. What we didn't realise in the euphoria of this coup was that getting the contracts signed for the release of all these tracks was going to turn into a labour of love for the next 18 months. I have recently learned that when Red Wedge tried to put together the same thing some years later for their campaign, it just ground to halt because of the sheer bloody mindedness required.

Getting the quarter inch master tapes was a doddle compared to getting the signed releases from everyone who had a financial interest in the tracks. This included everyone from the band and their management to labels and producers etc. And that was not going anywhere near the publishing rights.

During the process of accumulating all of this paperwork our solicitor suggested that we consider our legal liabilities. RAR was an open source campaign driven by the grass roots dynamism of its groups around the country. It might be referred to today as part of the creative commons. No copyright and no ownership, that is to everyone but the Punkoid faction. However, legally the people who signed the cheques would be deemed a partnership and liable for any debts etc. Given that we were undertaking all the commitments around the licensing of the music for the album to Virgin, the solicitor suggested that we set up a not-for profit company limited by guarantee with no share capital and each director liable for £1 in the event of winding up. Almost all voluntary sector organisations and charities are set up this way. For this to work we had to formalise a membership who would then vote a board of directors annually. This was achieved with the agreement of what was effectively the RAR steering group and the RAR groups around the country.

So Who Shot Bambi?

The question should be, why at the height of its effectiveness and success did RAR fold as a national campaign? It was the Punkoid faction wot did it.

It was at this point the Punkoid faction, which had formed around *Temporary Hoarding* and were on the board, decided that they had now had enough of the grown up business of running a cultural anti-racist campaign. They'd had the debts of *TH* paid off by someone else's work. And they had secured their own payment out of the advance of royalties due to RAR, for the vapid apolitical album cover artwork that ripped off of American artist, Frank Stella. By this time I'd lost the will to live. But fortunately Red saved the promotion of the album by sorting out a stonking poster with *RAR's Greatest Hits* and a cop getting his helmet knocked off with a house brick. It caught the mood of the times. We got Terry the Pill, king of the fly posting mob, to put them up. We got a fantastic response. They were everywhere. Even Costello's manager rang me up and asked me how we managed to do it.

However, with the establishment of RAR limited and the fragmentation of the music scene, the Punkoid faction fretted that they could no longer use *Temporary Hoarding* as their calling card for their book and article deals, the sale of "their" campaign "photos" and that they had also lost the opportunity to pontificate about which authentic (punk) bands could play RAR gigs. Unfortunately they brought all this angst-ridden nihilism to a national meeting and tried to split the campaign by resigning from the board. They failed, but having sucked all the energy out of the room the campaign needed time to regroup. Thatcher had won the election, the NF had been obliterated and punks were morphing into new romantics. There was talk of another national Carnival but at the height of the campaigns' credibility the Punkoid faction had choked the life out of it. Representatives of the RAR groups left the meeting stunned. The Leeds group, clearly having had enough of all that grandstanding, promptly went away and set up the very successful Northern Carnival with The Specials as the headliners. RAR had died. Long live RAR.

I have been asked if the SWP ever interfered or tried to direct RAR. To my knowledge that only happened once when they thought that the proposed Carnival, mentioned above, would clash with a mobilisation of their own. I got a visit from two members of the central committee at the RAR office. Red and Jerry knew nothing about it. Ironically it was an acknowledgement of our ability to campaign at a level that would challenge the SWP ability to mobilise their supporters because they would be more interested in mobilising for a RAR event. Little did they know but RAR as a national campaign was imploding.

As I mentioned before, there were many ideas floated about to create an ongoing RAR presence; record store, club etc. but in the absence of a national campaign such ideas faded. However one idea that RAR inspired stuck and in '81 I got together with Jerry Fitzpatrick, Wilf Sullivan and others from Islington RAR. We set up an educational charity called Islington Music Workshop (IMW) that provided professional recording and rehearsal facilities for local bands. It is still going over thirty years later having expanded to offer music makers training in Music Production to HND level in hi-end recording facilities.

Over the last forty years many other projects and events have taken place inspired by, or under the banner of RAR. In 2008 Love Music Hate Racism (LMHR) celebrated the thirtieth anniversary of the first carnival with Jerry Dammers, The Good, the Bad and the Queen and many other bands to a crowd of 100k. Many adhoc gigs continue to be held around the country and overseas. The British embassy in Hungary sponsored a RAR day at the Sziget festival in 2009 with support from Roger, myself and LMHR. I for one occasionally get emails from the US from people asking if its ok to put on RAR gigs. It is a token of the amazing success of the original campaign that the RAR message continues to excite and be something those music fans, who are anti-racists, can campaign around.

Links

Nazis Are No Fun Video https://youtu.be/2k-67CeuBFI

RAR Twitter feed: @RAR_uk

www.imw.co.uk

● IMW inspired by RAR

Shaun Doherty

is a retired teacher of English who taught in inner city schools and colleges for 44 years. In 1978 he was instrumental in writing one of the first Anti-Racist policies at Holloway School in Islington, North London.

'Head Canes Racist Poison' was the somewhat lurid headline in the *Islington Gàzette* welcoming the establishment of an anti-racist teaching policy at Holloway school. The 'Head' in the headline was George Spinoza the head teacher of Holloway who had the courage of his convictions and made the policy public. The policy was initiated in response to very specific issues that related directly to schools, but must also be seen in the wider political contexts of the threat from the National Front and its overt embrace of openly racist policies that led to a proliferation of violent racist attacks.

The school initiative was one of the first of its kind and predated the equality opportunity initiatives of the Labour controlled Inner London Education Authority, which was part of Ken Livingstone's Greater London Council. The policy itself was characterised as being both interventionist and integrationist. Interventionist in it is determination to actively engage with anti-racist teaching practices and challenging racist attacks and was part of a resistance to the National Front's recruitment campaign targeting school students. It was integrationist in its commitment to ensuring that the policy permeated the whole of the school curriculum and went beyond a simply reactive response to an outside threat. Going public with the policy meant that we were drawing a line in the sand that other schools would be encouraged to follow.

The implementation of the policy included the involvement of the students and all the staff in its adoption; introducing a whole range of curriculum initiatives across all departments; inviting in outside speakers; affirming the spectrum of language and dialect backgrounds of all students and by addressing the 'hidden' curriculum to ensure that the whole ethos of the school reflected the principles of inclusion. The launch received widespread publicity and many other schools followed suit. The National Union of Teachers published the Holloway policy along with that of Quentin Kynaston school in Westminster and encouraged members to take similar initiatives.

Working alongside the Anti- Nazi League, Teachers Against the Nazis publicised these initiatives through conferences, demonstrations and the development of teaching materials. Similar initiatives were taken up in other unions and their overall impact made a major contribution to the eventual defeat of the Nation Front.

It is, however, important to recall the sacrifices that were made in this struggle. Ideological opposition came from 'liberal progressive' arguments that all voices, including those of the racists, should have a hearing in school and society. This attitude was characterised very aptly by Andy Green when he argued:

● Blair Peach

'Multiculturalism, then, initially the name of an educational philosophy espoused by progressive teachers who sought, in support of the struggles of black students and parents, to oppose racism in schools, is also the banner with which the state intervenes with its somewhat different and contradictory objectives'.[1]

The institutions of the state, particularly those of the police and judiciary, intervened in a more openly confrontational manner seeking to actively suppress militant confrontation against the fascists by protecting their marches and meetings. Southall April 1979 was one of the most tragic and brutal of these confrontations where my friend and comrade Blair Peach was killed by a blow from the truncheon of the Metropolitan Police's Special Patrol Group in April 1979 at an anti-Nazi mobilisation. He was one of the fellow activists with whom I had discussed our initiatives at Holloway and his anarchic sense of humour coupled with hard political sense was a major inspiration of all who came into contact with him. The staff and students at Holloway were devastated by his death and felt a great sense of anger and loss. His memory is enshrined in the continuing history of opposition to all forms of racism, inside and outside schools. His death at the hands of the police was a bitter testament to the conflicts between those of us who wanted to take the struggle against racism and fascism onto the streets and into the schools, colleges, workplaces and unions and the political establishment who sought to maintain their own control.

Looking back on this history more than thirty-five years later, it is instructive to note that the same fundamental battles are being fought albeit on a different terrain. Today the focus is on the defence of immigrants and refugees, victims of imperial wars and global instability, against state racism seeking to assert the 'integrity' of the nation. 'Refugees Are Welcome Here' is a sentiment and slogan that would have resonated with Blair Peach, himself an immigrant from New

● Thousands of black, white and Asian mourners joined a militant cortege for Blair in Southall, 13 June 1979. Photograph: John Sturrock.

Zealand. Today's racism has as its core Islamophobia in the wake of Middle Eastern wars and in Britain is enshrined in the government's 'Prevent' strategy aimed at demonising young Muslim students and constraining political debate in schools and colleges. In our determined resistance to this offensive we can draw from the reservoirs of experience of our earlier struggles and ensure that in doing so the memory of Blair Peach lives on.

1 Green, Andy 'In defence of anti-racist teaching: a reply to recent critiques of multicultural education', *NAME Journal* Spring 1982.

● TH#9

TEMPORARY HOARDING
RINSE OUT THE BLUE SCUM
MILITANT ENTERTAINMENT
JAH WARS GANG OF FOUR
RUTS & R AR NEWS/LETTERS

John Ellis

RAR Treasurer

After almost forty years a couple of events stand out vividly in my memory.

Most RAR gigs were organised by local RAR groups. However, Central RAR was heavily involved in arranging the musicians for the Carnivals and was solely responsible for The Militant Entertainment Tour in 1979. Some expenses of the Tour were paid out from the box office takings at each venue. However, there was usually a deficit. Unlike now, in the '70s band tours were not profitable and were done to promote an album. Bands performing for RAR did not receive fees but we did try to cover their expenses and then there was the PA, publicity, accommodation, travel and other expenses. As the tour progressed, debts increased on the promise of a big final event in London which would pay off everyone's expenses.

And we did – Militant Entertainment at Alexander Palace. I don't remember the music as I spent the evening locked in the box office with the RAR volunteers taking the ticket money, we took in nearly £25,000 in cash, no credit cards then. In today's money that would be almost £130,000. I left that night, the money in a briefcase, an escort and an advance guard checking the way ahead for trouble. I got home safely to a squat in Whitechapel where I lived with my partner and young son. I kept the briefcase in my bed for the rest of the night and didn't let it out of my sight until I got it to the bank on Monday morning.

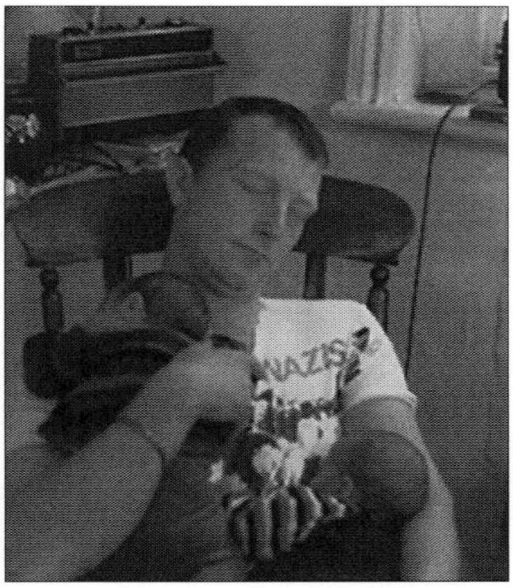

● John around June 1980, so a bit after the Ally Pally gig sleeping with his twins.

Another event which stands out in my memory was at the Rainbow Theatre in north London. Although the theatre provided the box office staff, once again I did not hear the bands as I was involved in organising the stewarding. As usual we were prepared for NF trouble and had organised stewards, many of whom were inner London teachers. However, when we got to the venue, we discovered the Rainbow management had their own bouncers. We quickly established that their idea of crowd management was to use their truncheons. We tried to persuade the management that we could handle any trouble. They wouldn't have it but they did agree to RAR stewards being in the front line and the bouncers would only get involved if they couldn't handle the situation. As expected skinheads turned up chanting NF slogans and our stewards went into action, they talked to them and discussed what was happening, RAR's ideas and politics. This not only succeeded in defusing the potential trouble but recruited some of them to RAR. It was awesome seeing the stewards in action.

Tim Evans

was an English teacher at Marshalswick Comprehensive, St Albans in 1978, where he later worked behind the scenes to help set up a school students' union. He joined the Anti Nazi League the same year. He now lives in Swansea where he remains active in the Socialist Workers Party and is a member of the poetry collective Poets on the Hill.

I missed the Victoria Park concert, but got down to the Brockwell Park one later that year. I had started working as a schoolteacher in St Albans in the early 1970s – my politics were sort of peacenik anarcho-Yippie: as a student in '68 I'd been at the Grosvenor Square anti-Vietnam war demos and had hitch-hiked around the US, including Berkeley, where I saw the national guard impose a curfew on the city. In the 1970s I'd been drawn to anti-fascist work, especially after the NF march at Lewisham was effectively smashed. I joined ANL in 1978, and we all went down in a coach in September to the Brockwell Park carnival. I remember walking for what seemed like miles and miles through south London and eventually arriving at the park where thousands were gathering. I don't think I'd been in such a huge crowd in my life, so what with the jostling and dancing the carnival itself was a bit of a blur... I remember Elvis Costello, Aswad and Stiff Little Fingers, but what stuck in my mind was Jimmy Pursey of Sham 69, some of whose fans were flirting with the NF and who, even though the band didn't play, came on stage himself to declare his support for RAR. I remember thinking what a courageous act it was. It was a great, exhausting, exhilarating day.

The next year, 1979, even if the NF had been knocked back, was more traumatic. The killing of Blair Peach by the SPG at Southall, and the election of Thatcher, convinced me to join the Socialist Workers Party, whose members seemed to be the best anti-racist activists around.

I still have photos of an ANL march in Watford in I think 1979. There were Asian guys with me who were in the martial arts club I was in at the time. They were both black belt second dans, and had the NF turned up would have given them a good hammering!

Jim Fagan

in the mid seventies was a student learning disability nurse, socialist activist and union rep. He is now retired, but continues to be politically active and campaigns to defend the NHS

I moved to Reading in 1976 to start nurse training. Reading at that time was a working class town with significant minorities of Afro-Caribbean and Asian workers.

The National Front was active in the town, targeting football fans. This was against a background of anti-immigrant and racist hatred, stirred up by papers like the *Daily Mail*.

There was resistance though, from those on the left who refused to let the racists divide us. The first political event I attended in Reading was with a delegation of socialists to a local Sikh Temple in solidarity in the wake of the racist murder of a young sikh in West London.

In August 1977 we supported the mobilisation that broke up the NF march in Lewisham. A moment when it became clear that we needed a united campaign to beat the Nazis.

At the meeting to launch Reading ANL Paul Holborow encouraged the setting up of groups such as teachers and civil servants against the Nazis. A school student asked what about school students, this led to the setting up of the first School Kids Against the Nazis group.

The first edition of SKAN was laid out by local school kids on our kitchen table. They also organised a RAR gig in a black youth club with a punk band and sound system. They received letters from across the country, one from a public school student who got detention for putting up anti-NF stickers, and from kids in Northern Ireland, even though the NF weren't openly organising there.

We saw no separation between organising political or cultural events. We filled seven coaches to the first Carnival in Victoria Park. The fascists tried to frighten us into silence, threatening socialist papers sellers, on one occasion trying to break up a public meeting, even making a bomb threat but it didn't work and the NF are history.

NEVER AGAIN!

AGAINST
AND
ROCK AGAINST RACISM

Colin Fancy

April 1978: In the middle of 70,000 young people who've come to rock against racism, me and two school friends join everyone around us singing, "Sing if you're glad to be gay..." If we dared utter these words at school we'd be beaten up – which is what happened to two lads caught kissing in the bushes. There's no sense of threat in this crowd today, singing along with Britain's first openly gay pop star Tom Robinson. We've marched five miles from Trafalgar Square waving Anti Nazi League lollipop placards to be part of this Carnival Against the Nazis and we will be leaving having expressed our solidarity with gay people. What an amazing day.

Leaving the area is not so much fun. As hundreds of coaches pull away from Victoria Park, handfuls of racists crawl out of pubs to heckle the thousands leaving. They are hardly brave to shout at departing vehicles, but the three of us have lost our gang of school friends so we slip past the racists searching for a bus home to south east London. Meanwhile skinheads in a pub in Deptford make one of the local punk bands play "Happy Birthday" for Adolf Hitler. The majority of Deptford voters put their cross against anti-immigrant Nazi parties in the 1976 local elections. People are divided.

May: Our Sixth Form is 98% white. Racism is not as bad as it was in lower years, but there's fear and ignorance about immigration.

Inspired by the carnival, me and some school friends agree to leaflet Eltham High Street against the NF. We meet outside the library (we are sixth formers) and an ANL man arrives on a motorbike with a pile of leaflets. As we hand them out some people are hostile, some welcome the leaflets and most don't react at all. One bloke sees the swastika on the leaflet say National Front is a Nazi Front and sees red. "I fought against the Nazis in the war," he spits. "We're Anti-Nazis," we say. "I don't care what kind of Nazis you are, bugger off!" When we manage to clear up the confusion, he tells us about chalking slogans on the streets in the 1930s against Mosley's Blackshirts and sticking posters on the backs of buses.

June: Despite being busy with exams, me and my mate Neal go to a gig at the Albany in Deptford. It's a Rock Against Racism (RAR) gig, raising money for local black kids arrested under the SUS stop and search laws, and we've come for punk band Alternative TV. Also on the bill is reggae act Misty in Roots, from Southall. Reggae is too slow for us but there's a toughness to Misty's music, "See them ah come, but we naa run". The Albany is a good venue and home to the local music scene which is growing under the jokey slogan Today the Albany, Tomorrow the World! July 1978 I finish my exams and, without any plans of college or career, sign on the dole. There's a real fear of unemployment amongst kids at school. The far right have been using this fact to blame immigrants and now Margaret Thatcher, new leader of the opposition, makes a speech about people feeling "swamped by an alien culture». Racism is moving right into the main stream. The Sex Pistols sing of No Future... I wonder what ours will be. The Albany is fire bombed on 14th July. The next morning a note is pushed through the door of the gutted building which reads, "GOT YOU". Within days the Albany, fly-posted all around Deptford, a poster showing the burnt out dance floor where we'd enjoyed the gig two weeks ago. 'Today the Albany,' the poster says above the image and below it, 'Tomorrow the World?' It's no longer a joke.

October: My family are always out at meetings – my Dad often goes to more than one each evening. There's no way I'd do that, but because of my love of music and hatred of racism I go to a RAR organising meeting in Lewisham – plus I'm hoping to get a gig for my punk band.
Sitting in a circle twenty people discuss bands, venues and PA hire companies. One of the punky kids has a clear plastic bag over his head for the first part of the meeting, everyone ignores him even as the bag steams up. Suddenly he tears a hole in the bag and speaks... "Some of the punks in Bromley where I live are Nazis like my cousin and some are anti-Nazi like me and my sister. You should put on a concert there". Despite some chuckles at the plastic bag, people agree to do the gig.

February 1979: I hear talk that Rock Against Racism is considered by other anti-fascists to be the soft end of the movement. Our motley crew are drawn together because of our love of music more than our ability to physically confront Nazis, but each month we make ourselves a potential target for the local fascists by putting on gigs in the very places the Nazis are gaining a foothold.
A good example is the gig we set up at in suburban Bromley's Labour Club for the Punk In The Plastic Bag. The night includes a couple of Bromley punk bands alongside a reggae sound system from Deptford and luckily draws a big enough crowd of black and white youth to make the Nazis keep their distance. The Nazis hate seeing the white and black kids dancing together and the night helps to break down barriers and create unity.

April: Back in 1977 when the NF marched through Lewisham the anti-fascists were divided. Some argued for "peaceful protest" while others called for physical confrontation with the Front's march. In what became known as the Battle of Lewisham, the local black youth joined the militant lefties and knocked the NF off the street. Since then blocking and stopping of the Front has been the accepted approach. Leicester is where the National Front had one of their best results in the previous election and are hoping to secure their place as the third party of British politics. They plan to march through the town centre with flags flying and drums beating. Anti-fascists have other ideas. Coaches from both sides pour into Leicester all morning. Thousands of our side take over the city centre and rain rocks down on the master race when the cops stupidly parade them past a building site. ('I got hit by a rock against racism', moans a copper when he later catches us fly-posting for RAR).

I am asleep the morning after the National Front election meeting in Southall when my Mum bursts into my bedroom – what is she doing? "They killed one of us", she says.

My Mum knew Blair Peach as a "nice gently spoken man" as they were both in the National Union of Teachers Rank and File group. She told me Blair taught ESN (Educationally Sub-Normal) kids and that National Front members had pulled him off his bike whilst cycling to and from the school in East London.

Going on anti-fascist marches and protests has always exhilarating and terrifying, adrenaline-fueled affairs – but from that day on they feel different again... It isn't a game.

The general election is the first time I have the right to vote. On the candidate notice outside the polling station NAZI SCUM is scrawled helpfully against the name of the National Front candidate. That makes me smile, especially as I recognise my brother's terrible handwriting. In the polling booth, as I pick up the pencil tied to a piece of string, I remember Paul Foot saying at the Rebel weekend – "They say they are trusting you to choose who runs the country, but they don't even trust you with the pencil".

All the campaigning, marches, gigs, leafleting and protests has had an effect and the National Front get a knock back which they never recover from. But Thatcher wins the election and you probably know how that turns out...

Did you hear the one about the skinhead and a bunch of Pakistanis? (aka Seething Wells and Alien Kulture, on the midnight march against the racists)

Alien Kulture and Seething Wells need to be remembered. Alien Kulture were the first (and only?) Asian punk band and very committed to RAR. One of the band, Zaf, worked in the RAR office. Seething Wells was an anti-racist skinhead who read poetry – a tough call.

There had been a number of racist attacks in Portsmouth so a gig was organised at the college in the centre of town. Alien Kulture asked my band, Dali's Car, and Seething Wells (later to be notorious NME journo Steven Wells). We all travelled down together in the band's van with Seething Wells telling terrible jokes. Alien Kulture had arranged RAR gigs that we'd played at and we'd organized Right To Work gigs against rising unemployment with them on the bill.

At the gig Seething Wells ranted about police dogs, Tetley Bitter-men and the *Sun* newspaper – some of his pet hates. Swells showed that to be a skinhead didn't mean you had to be a racist.

The very existence of Alien Kulture was a provocation to the racists and Nazis and all their gigs had an atmosphere, an edge... This was to be their final gig and they threw themselves into it. The band's intention from when they first started was to be The Asian Clash. Their songs had energy and impact and reflected their lives – 'Asian Youth', 'Airport Arrest' and their single which John Peel played a lot, 'Culture Crossover' – 'I don't wanna go to the mosque/I wanna go to the Nashville, I don't wanna read the Koran /I wanna read the *NME*'

In the great RAR tradition both bands and Seething Wells joined together for the encore of 'GarageLand' by The Clash. 'Back in the garage with my Bushell detector!' Seething Wells sang taking the piss out of a certain turncoat journalist.

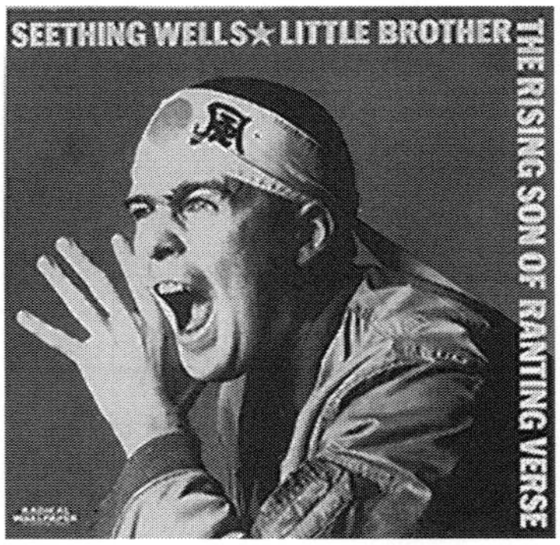

● Seething Wells/Little Brother EP: Photograph: Red Saunders, design: Roger Huddle for Radical Wallpaper

The gig ended with the audience and the bands going on a midnight march around the town centre in defiance of the racist attacks. "Black and White Unite – Kick the Nazis out!"

Then the band took us for a celebration curry. They told us to order, "Very hot tattie". But their giggles gave them away. Apparently we would be asking for a plate of shit. We were over the moon at the end when Alien Kulture said they were paying for the curry. However Seething Wells quipped, "Bollocks, I should have ordered a starter!"

That was Alien Kulture's final gig, the beginning of Seething Wells' lively career of writing and ranting. – tragically he died in 2009. And me? I'm still rocking against racism and for a revolution...

Colin (Revolting) Fancy

Kim Farnell

Birmingham RAR, 1978-1980

A long line of skinheads trailed down the street. And the Angelic Upstarts weren't coming. We huddled in the box office to discuss what to do. The consensus was that skinheads weren't renowned for their politeness if you took their money for something that wasn't going to happen, so someone had to tell them.

Annie, who had to strain to reach five foot, picked up a stray packet of chocolate biscuits. It was the best plan we could come up with. She went outside and offered one to the first skinhead in the queue. Then she told him. And so to the next. Some left, grumbling. Some paid to see the other bands – the Au Pairs were playing that night as well as UB40 – and caused minor havoc later.

Friday nights meant a gig at Digbeth Civic Hall. It later became a renowned music venue, but at that time it was a hole. But it was big, it was cheap and it was easy to get to. The council owners insisted a member of staff kept a close eye on us. They didn't explicitly say what they feared, but if we did it we'd lose the venue. The poor chap who'd drawn the short straw was bemused by our activities. He told us repeatedly that our days were numbered.

And then one evening he collapsed and had a fit. Of course we wouldn't tell anyone. We totally understood that he'd lose his job if they knew he was epileptic. And no, it really wasn't necessary to sing our praises, but if he felt like doing so…

So Friday nights were usually at the Civic Hall.

Saturday morning was when the political parties all lined up near the Bull Ring and sold papers, primarily to each other. This was the best chance of seeing politicos out in the wild. A lot of us combined our RAR involvement with activity in other groups. There was a wide selection. The Swerps (SWP) were the most numerous, but carried an air of grubbiness about them. The Migs (International Marxist Group) thought themselves a bit cleverer and a lot cooler. No-one could be bothered to give the WRP a nickname. And there were others, including the Communist Party. The uniting factor was that we all agreed the Sparty Party (Sparticist League) were dull as dishwater on a good day and we wouldn't be seeing them at any gigs.

Saturday night was usually taken up by seeing a band in a pub – sometimes a RAR gig, often not – and a party, generally be in Moseley, sometimes in Handsworth.

That meant Sunday afternoon meetings could be a blurred experience.

My school friend, Sheryl Garratt, who later became editor of *The Face*, had spotted an advert pleading for more people to join and suggested we went along. At seventeen, I didn't initially find the idea of being involved in any sort of committee thrilling, so I begged out of the first meeting. I was soon talked round.

Given that three of the Au Pairs – Lesley, Paul and Pete – and their manager, Martin Culverwell, were part of the group, they were often high on the list for a booking. That's a little understated. Martin was the power behind Birmingham RAR, partly due to his network of contacts. There were plenty of bands on the Birmingham scene who were more than happy to play for us, but sometimes we looked further. Mainly towards Leeds as Martin knew the Fast Products people.

Sometimes it was trickier booking the PA. We used Planet PA. It was everyone's first option, meaning you had to get in fast. There were other PAs for hire, but there was always a frisson of worry if Planet was unavailable.

Once we'd sorted a venue and the bands, we needed to get word out. Barry had a tie-in with a community centre in Saltley so we went there to design and screenprint posters. It seemed perfectly reasonable to quickly learn how to screenprint, produce newsletters on a duplicating machine and develop our own photos. It was a DIY time. However, we didn't make our own badges. They were easy to get hold of and everyone was covered in them. You could get a full account of people's views by staring at their chest.

Once we'd knocked together some posters (I became a dab hand at Letraset), it was time to go out with a bucket of paste and flypost. Mid-evening, we scurried through underpasses in the city centre sticking up posters as fast as possible. They stayed up long enough to get results. In fact, if you weren't sure what you'd like to do at the weekend, a quick stroll through the underpasses offered plenty of options.

RAR took over my life. Everyone did everything – I even mixed at a couple of gigs, although badly. I moved to Saltley which made it even easier to be part of the thriving music scene where everyone knew everyone and many threw politics into the mix. Socialists, anarchists. anti-racists, ant-sexists and other ists. Troops Out and Reclaim the Night.

But it was the music that really mattered. Always the music. Loud and earnest and sometimes rough and ready, sometimes polished. With words about something. With people who thought like you did.

Occasionally we ventured into London for meetings. After one of those trips our car flipped over on the motorway. We were fine, but a near-death experience is enough to make most people reconsider. Not long after that I moved to London to start college. After two years, it was over.

There were many defining moments. Like Ranking Roger jumping up to toast with the Beat. He was going to be in a band. He was going to do it all. Because you could. You could do anything. And he did. A lot of us did.

Victoria Park photograph: Red Saunders

● Below: Jerry, Mike Carver and Paul Holborow picket New Scotland Yard.

Jerry Fitzpatrick

was RAR/ANL Carnivals Organiser in Vicky Park and Brixton. Best summed up in Widgery's *Beating Time*, 'Jerry could organise everything from a riot to refreshments for 100,000'. Organiser of ANL's Lewisham demo that stopped the Nazi NF. Took RAR bands to Belfast during the hunger strikes to Rock the H Blocks. SWP Organiser and Trade Union Official. Returned to Ireland supporting the successful peace process outcome. Supporting Sinn Fein taking power in Ireland with a ballot box in one hand and a red rose in the other. Supports Jeremy and John McDonnell taking office in Britain.

An interview

Background

Jerry was 27 years old in 1977. He lived on Amhurst Road in Hackney and had been the central London organiser of the SWP since 1975. From 1977 he was employed variously as National Organiser and Carnivals Organiser for the Anti-Nazi League. There were three other people working for the ANL; Paul Holborow, Joan Rudder and Mike Barton.

● Jerry today

● Paul Holborow was a very cool political organiser as ANL National Secretary. He was very inspirational and politically courageous. He followed the party line but was prepared to be flexible. Paul didn't follow music like the RAR comrades, but he had the good sense to bring in others when required. He was a really good leader. He was the nuts and bolts of the Anti Nazi League.

Paul was proposed because he had organisational flair. I was proposed as a link with the comrades in RAR, who could spin off in creative and diverse directions. I'd worked for Equity in 1973/5, and had organised rank and file groups in the actors' and musicians' unions so I knew many of the personalities who were involved in cultural politics: Red (All Power to the Imagination) Saunders, Dave Widgery, Roland Muldoon

and Roger Huddle. Also I was a good street demo organiser.
You saw with RAR a coming together of fairly diverse individuals and several of them had a shared history in the SWP. They would meet in Red Saunders studio. Some of the discussion was un-coordinated but by spring 1977 the core themes were beginning to blossom. I remember the Carole Grimes gig in November 1976 and even then you could really see the potential.

Wood Green

I'd come from an Irish background. I was at Derry in 1969. I saw the physical resistance in the Bogside. We wanted to organise in the same way. We had a keen eye on confronting the NF. We bought flares from a boatyard. I thought they would add a sense of colour and cover and make an effective public spectacle. We sought a non-violent context. But we were willing to sharpen the demonstration, to confront the Nazis.

Lewisham

After Wood Green, I drew two lessons. First, we needed logistics, more supporters in the set area, more street planning, a better sense of what the police tactics would be. Second, there had to be an intense effort in organising among the local community, in this case, the black youth living in Brixton and Lewisham.
Six weeks before Lewisham, we had intelligence that the Nazis would be assembling at Clifton Rise. A group of us set up headquarters in a building opposite just off New Cross Road. We occupied a house and used it as an organising centre. Norma Humblebee, a local activist, was central to this organisation and Ted Parker.
We created an atmosphere, especially among black youth. People came in to collect leaflets and posters. You got a sense of people organising things themselves. There was one incident, a small trivial thing, really. About three weeks before the demo, the police were chasing a black youth, and he ran into our building. They grabbed him, and me too, accusing me of providing him with a false alibi. In court, we provided him with a solicitor. He didn't get off, but it was a light sentence. And in the days after I had a really strong sense that the barriers had come down. The word went round that we would support black youth against the police harassment.

Irish contribution

There were many Irish community members who provided us with logistics and support. There were other ways in which the Irish community contributed. There was an Irish hall next to our centre. We were allowed into there, and into the Irish pubs and dances, to raise money, to speak about the NF as the latest incarnation of British

imperialism and to appeal for support.
The day before the march, the police raided the centre. They were looking for megaphones, banners, the thing we would need for the demonstration. They found just two walkie-talkies. We were expecting raids, and had long cleared out.

Demonstration

In the negotiations leading up to the demonstration we tried hard to persuade the other groups, the Communists and the church people, not to organise a counter demonstration at the same time at a different venue, but to organise theirs in such a way that if people then wanted to stand with us – they could. In the event we succeeded because their demo finished in time for the bulk of them to join us at Clifton Rise. There needed to be a broadening of our appeal. If we were seen simply as boot-boys then we would fail. We had to convince the Communist Party, the Labour Party, the trade unions to join with us and broaden our support.
There was a buzz on the day, a networking. It wasn't communicated by posters or leaflets, but by people talking. This was black youth making a stand.
Lewisham was our Cable Street, we had in mind the slogan from 1936,"They shall not Pass". It was our generation's attempt to stop fascism. It was rugged, scrappy. It was a real success. The NF had been stopped, and their ability to march through black areas had been completely smashed.

The success of Lewisham

The organisation of Lewisham was done in meetings but key tactical decisions were taken outside structures. The 3-fold plan was (1) amass large numbers from early on at top of Clifton Rise, which stopped the police taking the NF through that route but out by Achilles St onto New Cross Road. (2) A determined SW contingent of our Builders Group, Irish activists, and Red Action with suitable material on a signal drove a wedge into the NF march immediately behind their front honour guard and split their ranks by shops on New Cross Road. (3) Holding onto the position of corner of New Cross and Lewisham Way and on the basis of the police regroup them, smaller mobile squads made their down Lewisham Way and side streets to Clock Tower to harass any NF that got through. The plan worked.

Brick Lane

Brick Lane was a serious example of how the NF were providing their supporters with a public focus, to organise racist attacks, and as a rallying point for their members. We responded. I remember waking up every Sunday morning, going down to Brick Lane. It was skirmishing followed by skirmishing. But the fact was, we were protesting against the Nazis and I know that gave confidence to the Bangladeshi youth. They became more cohesive. Self defence is no offence.

Rock Against Racism

The RAR folk were inspirational geniuses – the heroes – rock out Clapton/Bowie.

Who came up with the word Carnival? 'I think it was either Paul, Red or Roger. Red was moving towards the idea, with something bigger than the RAR gigs and the tours. They wanted something to bring together the cultural and political lefts, like the fetes organised by the Communist Party in France. But it was Paul who capped it.

We started planning the first Carnival in January 1977, at least three months beforehand. I sat down with Roger Huddle. I remember booking the event through the GLC. The form said that if you had more than ten thousand people you needed portaloos, and all that. So I booked a mini-festival, for ten thousand, not more. I knew we had no money. I wasn't expecting more than twenty thousand, tops. We made a deal to book the PA. Myself and Roger Huddle went to Covent Garden. Roger knew his sound systems and I knew how to hustle. We paid three thousand there and then, four thousand on the day. Paul drew the money out. I had to sew it into the lining of my leather jacket, so it wouldn't get pinched. There were scaffolders from Donegal who put up the stage. That went up the night before. We were expecting trouble. There were leaflets everywhere. But the night itself was stunningly quiet.

Red and Roger booked the bands. Tom Robinson and Steel Pulse. Tom Robinson (Glad to be Gay) got Xray Spex. Two weeks before the Carnival, we started trying to book the Clash. There was a meeting with the Clash band. Red, Roger, Syd Shelton and Kate Webb were absolutely brilliant. Mick Jones flicking ash into their hair, as manager Bernie Rhodes said 'Why should we bother?' Finally Joe Strummer spoke, and said, 'Fuck it, we'll show them, we'll fucking show them'. That was just 10 days beforehand. But it was the Clash that did it. The word went round the back streets of London. (No mobiles in that time). The Clash were huge. 'White Riot' and 'Guns of Brixton'. That contributed to the youth of London turning out – 80,000 people in Vicky Park.

Carnival Two in Brixton. The NF organised a demo in Brick Lane at the same time. I felt that the success of our ANL/RAR march depended on us going through Brixton. That was more important than any stunt the NF pulled. Even if we had sent more numbers to Brick Lane, it couldn't have been enough. The police always had it covered. The NF were contained. We were contained. We kept an eye on the big picture prize, on to the Carnival. John Dennis, who worked in the RAR office, was central to organising Carnival Two, particularly the bands and back stage with Red.

Southall

Compared to Lewisham, it was much more disparate. The ANL was trying to work with the IWA and with the local community. There was no centralised decision making. The police were much more determined, and willing to use violence. The police had much more control. We were broken up quickly. Blair Peach was killed.

1979

By April 1979, we'd won. We'd made a major impact. We'd mobilised way beyond anything the left had done in years. The NF was neutered, demoralised, in retreat. Our key organisers were in a state of physical exhaustion, it had been the most intense political period of our lives. Thatcher came into power and she was a more sophisticated and determined threat. The issues were different. The plates had moved. After Southall in 1979 and 1980 I was organising with John Dennis and John Ellis a RAR Tour to Belfast and Derry in support of the H Block prisoners who subsequently went on hunger strike for political status, so there were other priorities at that time.

Summary

The events of 1977 and 1978 in particular, Lewisham and the two Carnivals, they were a unique coming together of politics, music, rock and culture. A political co-ordinated burst of energy that made a real difference. Of course, I'd say that, I was one of the organisers. But it wasn't me or Paul or just the RAR comrades. There was Peter Hain, working in ways that were never acknowledged, winning us allies, breaking it away from the usual supporters. Peter was our most powerful advocate of "Unity in Action". Remember Stop the 70s Tour. There were the local activists across the country and people like Mike and Joan. How many leaflets did they send out, how many hours did they spend stuffing envelopes? There were plenty of individuals who did a huge amount, and it really was one of the most successful moments in the history of the political left.

Significance of 1977/8 – Lewisham and RAR Carnivals

It was a political action with passion and vision of its time and place. It was an insurrectionary and revolutionary moment post 1968 if you combine the mass Carnivals and the determined resistance to Nazi NF marches. The turbulence was sometimes visceral as well as intellectual and political inspiring and for that moment it demonstrated that the Left could organise mass action with the potential to change the world. I salute what was done as a tremendous success and prepare for the next opportunity'.

ps: We touched the sky

Paul Furness

The Leeds Club

Its hard to acquaint today's Leeds with the one I grew up in, when the only bling in town was the medallion around Jimmy Saville's scrawny neck I saw at work each day in Leeds General Infirmary. Everything else was "black bright" from over 200 years of industrial pollution and begging to be cleaned. Boar Lane, that glitzy quarter of a mile between the railway station and the Corn Exchange, was boarded up for over a decade awaiting the demolition which never came. Thatcher came instead and the mills and the foundries and the factories went. The police killed the Nigerian vagrant David Oluwale and the "Yorkshire Ripper" littered the city with the corpses of dead women. This was my world.

When I saw the letter in the *NME* it was like an overdue breath of fresh air – and I knew that something was going to happen. Then the same letter was in '*Sounds*', '*Melody Maker*' and '*Socialist Worker*' and, over the coming weeks and months, it was obvious there was something in the air. In Leeds, we put on the second ever Rock Against Racism gig when I got my mates in a pub rock band called Foxymaiden, who later changed their name to The Squares, to play a gig in something like a bungalow belonging to the hospital (years later I realised people thought I worked for a record company called Medical Records, as the phone number for my department was the contact number for Leeds RAR – after clinching a deal with Rough Trade to bring Stiff Little Fingers to town, I was barred from receiving calls!). And that was it – Lees RAR was up and running.

After "National RAR" brought Misty and The Ruts to a place behind the Hayfield – the pub the '*Sun*' called "the most dangerous in Britain" because it had a largely Caribbean clientele – we knew we wanted to do something a little more permanent. In 1978 I'd been over to Hull to see the Adverts and came back with the idea of starting a club night

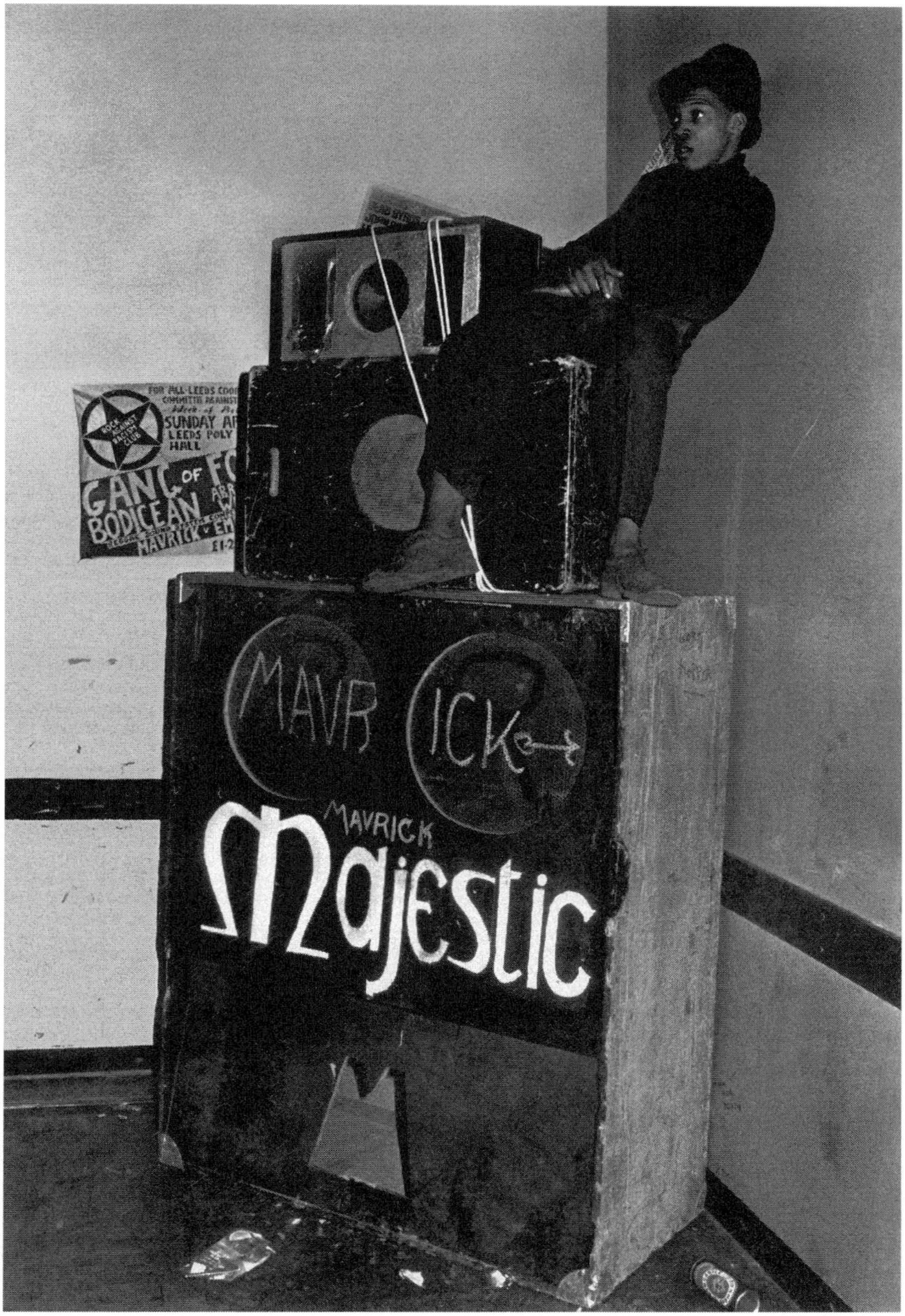

©Syd Shelton

in Leeds. I threw the idea around a few like minded souls (we were mostly working class kids from the estates who had just joined the SWP) and got a kind hearted woman in Leeds Polytechnic to let us use the students union common room (god knows why it was called that, as I can never remember any students going there – it was a cheap drinking den for Leeds people!). Then, in the great tradition of the Yorkshire working men's club circuit, we put "the committee" together and got to work. Every Friday night for the next 18 months, the Leeds RAR Club put on gigs and, for the last 6 months of its existence, we did so twice a week on Wednesday's too. I was 21 and working full time (then as now, working class kids only went to university to get pissed!) and remember my life then well – after work on Monday it was "the committee" meeting, Tuesday I'd book the gigs and help out with silk screening posters in comrades cellars, Wednesday's we had SWP meetings, Thursday we'd fly post, Friday we had the gig then went to Drags, the only late night gay bar in town, and Saturday we'd sell '*Socialist Worker*' or go on some demo and go to the pub and a gig again and did sod all on a Sunday except listen to my mother shouting at me as I refused to get off the sofa. Then it started all over again.
We went to Leeds market to buy yards of colourful cloth and got to work cutting and stitching anti-racist slogans on them, then pinned them up all around the room. You came into the club down a long, L shaped corridor which we plastered with RAR and Anti Nazi League posters – it felt like you were walking through a kaleidoscope! And we were unashamedly political – we had no bloody option coming from Leeds! – and geared our gigs around events and campaigns. On Saint Patrick's day, for example, we'd celebrate the Troops Out Movement, on International Women's Day (we took it for granted that lots of women should be involved in Leeds RAR – and the bands we put on) we'd highlight our little sister movement, Rock Against Sexism, before RAR women went on the Reclaim The Night demo's which started as a result of the serial killer, Peter Sutcliffe. When Gay Pride came around, we went to the market for tons of pink cloth and made "Gays Against Nazis" banners to hang on the walls of the club, which we also listed as a gay venue in '*Gay News*'. We had a stall for badges, papers and pamphlets, and had endless discussions with all sorts of people about everything you can think of – and we made announcements between bands about events such as the Free Nelson Mandela Campaign, the Anti-Apartheid Movement in South Africa and the Campaign for Nuclear Disarmament. From a small handful of activists, the Leeds RAR Club quickly established itself as one of just two live punk clubs in town – and our gigs were packed!
When my mate Hazel took me to see her boyfriend's band, I was at The Mekons first gig. This now legendary retirement home for Leeds musicians, along with their mates The Gang of Four, who soon became

our mates, were virtually the RAR House Band – I can't remember either band ever saying no when we asked them to play, and I suspect we only ever paid them in beer. The third local band who never said no was Delta 5 – a band Jon Langford insists originated in the Leeds RAR Club. Among the dozens of bands we brought to that small, corner stage in that room were Sheeny and the Goys (now in the Ukelele Orchestra of Great Britain), China Crisis, The Jerks, New Model Army, Butterflies (who became Girls At Our Best), Expelaires (they became Sisters of Mercy and manager of the Fat White family), Crisis, Au Pairs (they were never away!), The Cimerons, Angelic Upstarts, the Normal, Stiff little Fingers, 2.3 (our Sheffield pals) and, from nearby Bradford, the Ranting Poets Joolz Denby, Little Brother and the late, great, gregarious Swells – the journalist Stephen Wells. Because Leeds had no reggae bands at the time (Bodecian, who played for us, formed later), a sound system called Maverick Sounds gave us pre-release Jamaican Joy by Dennis Brown, Gregory Isaacs, Lee Perry and King Tubby, all courtesy of Sir Yanks record shack at the bottom of Roundhay Road – surely the garage of legend! Who can forget Sonny sitting on top of those massive speakers to stop them moving across the dance floor? When the Poly finally had enough of us, we took our club to Roots in Chapeltown, a former synagogue appropriately famous for its boys choir, which was now a West Indian club – this was where Joy Division played their one and only RAR gig and Ian Curtis slept on my sofa.

They were heady days indeed – and violent ones too. The National Front was very active locally, and it's no surprise that the short sharp shock called Rock Against Communism was founded here. We took them head on – at one time turning up to a gig and unplugging The Dentists, whose greatest hit 'White Power' was great for goose stepping to – and the only reason I wasn't in the Fenton the night they attacked it was because I couldn't get into town because of a bus strike. A right wing lesbian member of the Gay Liberation Front led a gang of hooded NF thugs into the pub and pointed out who to attack – one socialist teacher nearly lost his eye and was arrested for "affray"! The attack made the front page of the papers and caused widespread revulsion. My parents house had a KKK slogan painted outside (we know where you live, of course) and a Young Communist League, (Scritti Politti, yet another local band to play for us, were members) meeting was savagely attacked. I had to take off my badges and alter my bus routes into town to avoid where Nazis lived, but still managed to get beaten up by them. When I left home to live the punk lifestyle (it was party party time every night, and the neighbours got a petition up to get us evicted) bricks were put through my windows and racist graffiti spray painted inside after being burgled.
Such were the days. After 18 months, the music was changing – punk

gave way to two tone – and the National Front was in electoral melt down. It had been all but annihilated by the combined efforts of the Anti Nazi League, Rock Against Racism and the front page support of tabloids like the '*Daily Mirror*' and the '*News of the World*'. Even though racism was far from eradicated, the National Front soon vanished as a serious threat, so the Leeds club petered out and we called it a day in the winter of 1979. The next thing was for Rock Against Racism to come to an end too.

Appropriately, this also took place in Leeds when, at 11am on Saturday 4 July 1981, 25,000 people made their merry way through town to Potternewton Park (home to the Chapeltown Carnival, which is older than the one at Notting Hill, but nobody Down South seems to know this) to listen to Aswad, the Au Pairs, Joolz Denby, Misty and The Specials – Jerry Dammers remembers seeing the massed ranks of a few union jacks on a small fascist counter demonstration as his band drove into the city. The Northern Carnival Against Racism was the last of the big RAR/ANL carnivals and a fitting end to the movement.

35 years later, Ian Dyson went out of his way to find me on social media. I had no idea who he was until he told me "I caused you a lot of grief back then". He turned out to be Dickie, the lad who hung around with the Rock Against Communism lot who couldn't make up his mind about the NF or us. Every time he turned up at the RAR Club we had to argue over and over again about everything with him, and some of us got sick to death of trying. Ian was now convinced that the police, monarchy and government were one big conspiracy against the working class (that's one way of putting it, I suppose) and seemed to have spent most of his adult life working for a Chinese takeaway. "Nice people, the Chinese", he said to me. Proof enough to me that what we did, all those years ago, actually worked.

● *About the picture: Everyone knew them as Maverick Sounds. The lad anchoring the speaker – it was so bloody loud it used to walk across the floor when they played it – was called Skully Roots; he's now back to Jeff! The photo was taken in the Leeds RAR Club in 1979. We had no reggae bands in Leeds at that time but lots of sound systems, so we got Maverick to do the reggae part of the deal. When Bodacian, the first reggae band to form in Leeds, got together they did play for us.*

Rachel Gallagher

I remember as a teenager in the 1970s being aware of the threat from the National Front. Like all fascist parties they pretended to be respectable, playing on people's fears of unemployment, poverty etc. I even had an argument about them with a friend who had mixed race children, who thought that their ideas made sense. She had no idea what they actually stood for. The advent of the Anti Nazi League gave people like me confidence, and the arguments needed to fight against them.

This was also a time of great music, and Rock Against Racism was a massive part of my life then. A lot of the bands I listened to were involved in the fight against racism, by playing at the carnivals and gigs, and carrying the anti-racism message. Bands such as The Clash, Sham 69, Misty in Roots, Steel Pulse, the Tom Robinson Band, the Buzzcocks. The carnivals and gigs were a brilliant way to bring people together for a common cause, and the music was great too.

I am so proud to have been a part of this movement, and the knowledge that we really did stop the National Front (and future fascist parties) from gaining any kind of power in this country.

Events of recent times, however, have shown that we need to always be vigilant, especially when there is such a right-wing, anti-immigrant bias in most of the mainstream media. These days the fight against racism often goes hand-in-hand with support for refugees, who are constantly vilified in the media. I still go on anti-racist demos like the annual Stand Up to Racism ones, and others when they are called.

I have also been to events organised by Love Music Hate Racism, which is carrying on the legacy of Rock Against Racism. It is heartening to see that whenever fascist groups like Britain First organise one of their marches anti-fascists are always there to confront them, and to try to stop them marching.

Jacquie Garstin

A couple of weeks into my first job in 1967 I met Red Saunders. After a few years raising havoc in Rome, back in London I began working at Red's Studio in Great Windmill Street. There I met the rest of the Kartoon Klowns, and joined them. Jeff and I got together in 1974 and founded Sensible Music out of our house in Stoke Newington. I remember standing next to Red in front of the *Melody Maker*, open at the page of the printed letter that started things off. I remember soon after that a meeting in my kitchen in Stoke Newington, meeting David Widgery for the first time and discovering we had grown up yards apart in Barnet. The next meeting up at Red's Studio in Great Windmill Street needed a much bigger table for us all to sit around. I also remember yards of red silk lining fabric stretching across the studio floor as we cut out giant stick on fablon letters to make our first banners, I remember Robert Galvin being there too that day, its

40 years since I saw him and would love to know where/how he is now. Same goes for lots of people. There followed a much larger public meeting at North London Poly in Holloway Road, lots of new faces ready to come on board. That was shortly before the Brockwell Park event I think. A group of us stuffed thousands of pitta bread sandwiches in Nina's kitchen to sell to the crowds as part of a fundraising initiative to move RAR forward. We must have self funded the whole thing – I can't remember how that side of things worked. RAR soon grew from very small beginnings, those of us who had been together in the theatre group Kartoon Klowns being present at the birth and present in multiple capacities at the Round House gig. Performing to a full house as well as organising, setting up, carrying beer to the bands in the dressing room. I may have the order wrong here, but that was certainly a day to remember. At the beginning there was a local feel and a gig at Stoke Newington Town Hall stays with me, walking up the road with a camera to find some young kids hanging around and being keen to have their photo taken showing off their RAR stickers. (One of these photos is a *TH* front cover). There were all sorts of gigs, the big white hall of the Royal College of Art – Carol Grimes in a pub in Newham. Then meetings at Jo and Pete's to talk about the Victoria Park Event – I can see us there in the park that morning – a small group who didn't get to go to the march as we were decorating the stage and getting things set up and ready – I think the rest of that amazing day became a bit of a blurr.

Dav Gilchrist

I was in Glasgow in 1976 when I became active as a socialist. There was to be a Right to Work March against unemployment in London later that year and I got to know some of the people that would be going down to it. They were mostly unemployed punks. They wore kilts with safety pins and leather jackets. These guys would become well known on the punk scene in London and introduced the kilt and tartan bondage trousers to punk fashion!

In Scotland we collected for the Anti Nazi League which had recently been set up. Not long after that I moved to Luton and almost on my first day there I heard that the National Front were having an election meeting in a local school. I read that there would be a counter protest and I went along. After this protest there was a huge meeting and it was decided to set up a branch of the ANL in Luton.

We often organised buses from Luton to go to ANL demonstrations in London and around the country. We started to put on little local events to raise money and they became Rock Against Racism gigs.

We did RAR stalls at many big gigs in Bedfordshire and Hertfordshire. I remember one very tense night in Bedford Corn Exchange when there were so many Nazi skins in the hall if it had kicked off it would have been a massacre, or so it felt at the time.

I also remember getting arrested on an anti-NF protest outside Hemel Hempstead's Dacorum Centre one week and the following week leafleting inside the Selector gig at the same venue.

I went to the First Carnival, I had not really been to London often then and went to Finsbury Park instead of Victoria Park! I missed the demonstration and was in Vicky Park as it arrived. It was like a wonderful militant circus when it turned up. People dressed in all kind of outfits, punks, skinheads, dreads and everything under the sun, punk fashions had not hardened into uniforms yet. To be honest I was so exhilarated I don't remember much about the gig except for the audience changing places in big waves. When Steel Pulse were playing all the black kids rushed down the front and when it was a punk band the white kids. When The Clash came on the place kinda exploded. It was punk nirvana.

The second Carnival was the longest march I had ever been on! It also went through areas of London that I had never seen. I was experiencing the poverty that existed in London at that time first hand. Two things stand out. As we went down one street, someone had strung across the road from their windows a big banner that said 'Brixton Gays Against Racism' and a load of lesbians and gay men were waving from the windows in their party frocks. I had never seen anything like it! The other thing was in Brixton I spotted David Hinds from Steel Pulse on a corner watching the march. He was wearing an olive green flying suit and had his locks down – it was the coolest thing I had ever seen! He was a mighty lion welcoming us home.

Musical memories from the gig were Pete Townshend's arm whirling round as he thrashed his guitar and a fantastic set by Elvis Costello that peaked with one of my favourite songs at that time 'Red Shoes'. Just as he finished Concorde flew overhead. Shortly after I was almost knocked to the floor as someone gave me a mighty slap on the back. It was one of the punks from Glasgow. He told me that it was going to be announced from the stage shortly that people were needed to go down to Brick Lane as the National Front were there. We all jumped on the tube and went to Whitechapel. A few years later I was proud to be there when we drove the Nazis off that patch at the top of Brick lane for the final time.

It's hard to convey how open and intense racism was back then. The most important slogan from RAR was NF=No Fun. RAR won a whole generation of working class kids away from racism and to an active fighting stance against it and the fascists. RAR won the battle in the hearts and minds of young people and the ANL broke the Nazis on the street. Both were life changing and vital.

Darla-Jane Gilroy

What do I remember from the days of Rock Against Racism? A lot of things, but mainly a climate of inequality, discrimination and fear that has largely been forgotten but which was the norm for thousands of everyday people before what has become known as the multicultural society.

Racism permeated many aspects of popular culture and music was no exception. From the thrashing guitars and wailing songs of the most inexperienced punk performers to the mega stages of Wembley Stadium, where music icons had the audacity to enjoy a flirtation with fascism or openly endorsed racism.

RAR was necessary, important, a moment of significance.

One of my clearest memories is of a Sham 69 gig at the Rainbow in Finsbury Park, North London, where a bemused Jimmy Pursey helplessly nestled his head between his forearms whilst his following of hard core National Front skinheads invaded the stage and grabbed the mic from him to offer a sinister initiation. 'See you all up Iford tomorrow Sieg Heil! This referred to the National Front rally to be held there the next day and was the prelude to a waterfall of broken glass, splintering furniture and chairs raining down on the crowded most of whom had come for the fight whilst a handful of us had not.

I stood powerless to influenced the chaos around me 'Get out of here!" screamed the guy next to me as he produced a long metal cosh from his trousers and launched himself into the crowd like a deranged acrobat.

I took shelter behind a vinyl-covered blanket with a 14-year-old boy who had the foresight to close the substantial padlock threaded through the metal handles of the glass double doors that now separated us from our attackers.

We crouched in silence as we listened to the cracking of the door's safety glass and a mixture of football chants, groans and thudding of body blows.

My father used to say "Civilization can be lost" and in the moment when I peaked above the top of the blanket and saw a collage of contorted faces pressed into the glass doors, I understood exactly what he meant. Violence was their language, their means to be heard, expressions of hate, anger and a mindless desire to hunt and attack those who were different was their daily mantra.
I caught the eye of a young man of no more than 17, above his left eye was a deep gash, and a trail of blood had dried onto his cheek. For an instant I had the choice to withdraw and once more duck behind the blanket, but I chose not to be invisible, I would not look away. He banged on the doors with both fists mouthing God knows what, the glass continued to crack, fractures spreading across it's surface. Suddenly the picture before me became infused with dark blue and sliver, the faces looked older and cleaner, silence descended as literally everyone stopped fighting, too tired to carry on. The arrests began, a line of bloody youths were dragged from the building, arms twisted tightly behind their backs.
Earnest Hemingway said "There are many who do not know they are fascists but will find it out when the times comes". The time must never come.

● Ruth Gregory and Darla-Jane on cover of *Temporary Hoarding* #5

Paul Gilroy

It's absurd, but people do still try to deny that Rock Against Racism had profound and lasting effects on Britain's social life and political culture. The imprint has faded now and music has ceased to play the central role it occupied in the lives of young people. However, those changes mean that it is all the more important to grasp how RAR's successes happened as well as to explain the fact that a movement like RAR happened at all – making it seriously uncool to be racist, isolating rock and roll's Powel-lite dinosaurs and intervening to change the political direction of youth culture shifting it away from nationalism and xenophobia. In conjunction with punk, RAR marked a fundamental shift in cultural and political sensibilities that defined a whole generation.

Between '76 and '78 I was a student living in Brighton which was a significant centre of violent fascist activity at the time. I had been heartened by the original RAR letter in the music press and through my sister Darla, I became involved in a very minor way. I attended various gigs and ended up doing a small amount of writing in *Temporary Hoarding*. With her, Ric Fawcett and others I was part of the group that organized the big Brighton Poly gig, which became notorious because it was disrupted by feminists who took exception to a song that had been performed by The Fabulous Poodles, who had shared the billing that night with Misty in Roots. That debacle aside, I recall the nervous hours beforehand wondering whether all the flyposting and agitating had been sufficient to summon up a crowd big enough to cover our costs. I sat nervously behind the decks in the foyer area dropping Lovers' Rock tunes and hoping for the best. Two hours later, the place was full to the rafters as Misty lifted the crowd and made the night memorable for more positive reasons.

Around the same time, I got drawn into discussions about the desirability of putting out an edition of *Temporary Hoarding* written by black writers and aimed directly at the legions of black youth who remained on the edge of RAR's activities but occupied the front lines of conflict with the police in London and elsewhere. We gathered at a pub in Soho to talk this proposal through. My unreliable memory tells me that the collective was divided about the value of this particular strategy but that David Widgery was concerned by the absence of black involvement and was an eloquent advocate in support of the plan. The idea was a response to the problems that were arising as the antiracist struggle became increasingly polarized. There was a danger that the electoral chances of the newly branded "Nazis" would supply the principal focus rather than turning attention towards the institutionalized racism of the state – particularly with regard to criminal justice – this, after all, was the high point of the Sus law. That interesting proposal floundered because the organized black left was no more inclined than anyone else to appreciate the important lessons that could be learned from seeing how RAR had been able to bring culture and politics together in such an exhilarating manner. An explicitly anti-Nazi emphasis was required by the increasing visibility of the Anti Nazi League and that change moved popular anti-racism on to the mythic, nationalist terrain marked out by appeals to the spirit of the Blitz and the Churchillian memory of Britain's finest hour. In the meantime, the Nottingham Forest manager, Brian Clough, a notable catch for the league at a time when his team was riding high, could casually refer to Africans as "spear chuckers" and nobody dared to say anything.

RAR seemed to me to be a hinge that could connect the door of anti-racism to the larger frame of socialism. Its energy and creativity were infectious. They changed the Left's understanding of political style and altered the sense of what activism could achieve. RAR's approach disrupted the idiocy which saw culture as a kind of seduction or a sweetner that would enable later absorption of an authentic, bitter political medicine. If the message was lost on Labour, RAR's conspicuous success impacted strongly on the imaginative horizons of the revolutionary left. As a result, the resistance to pit closures was conducted in a different spirit.

RAR's slogan "Love Music Hate Racism" was important to me. It licensed the opportunity to make more of anti-racism than its critical, political oppositional aspects. Loving music and sharing the spaces where it could be encountered gave us a way to bring the world we wanted to see a bit closer, to find amid Britain's debris and decay, a way to love each other and life itself a bit more than our bleak circumstances would usually allow.

Debbie Golt

moved to Manchester in 1975 to join North West Spanner Theatre in doing *United We Stand*, a play about the Shrewsbury builders' strike in factory canteens and town squares. She got a post grad youth and community diploma and worked in crisis youth advice, pioneering girls' work. Debbie was a member of the SWP when she came to Manchester and really enjoyed giving her all to RAR and *Women's Voice*.

Now she broadcasts on Resonance FM and Threads Radio and trains people in radio skills as well as DJing. She is chair of Women in Music and very involved in campaigns like Save our NHS and Justice for Grenfell. She is part of the RAR Archive Project.

Rock Against Racism meant a lot to me personally as well as politically back then, and still does. Aside from its vital message per se, it made sense of my passionate involvement on the left to a wide circle of otherwise uncommitted friends and truly reached into my day to day community – and it inspired people of colour and white people to come on board all together: In the very necessarily defined community political context where some of the hardest social battles facing Black people took place, I learnt important lessons about self determination – that was heartening to me. It was at the heart of the matter involving local musicians that were already hot topics with young people and it was fun. RAR also gave me a very dear friend who was as full on with it as me and detached enough to keep it grounded, sadly Maggie Turner died in 2013 and this piece is for her as well. I began DJing regularly in public with RAR and I still play out now; I learned a lot of what I applied in the music biz about organising, marketing and promoting.

I also took the chance to write more widely, doing an iconic interview with John Cooper Clark in the Manchester edition of *Temporary Hoarding* and, amongst other articles, I did a strong piece talking with young Sound System guys about their scene and the safety especially of young girls lured by the idea of travelling far to hear a sound and getting stranded in the small hours with no easy way home. It led to

MANCHESTER

Contact RAR at 'The Squat' Devas Street off Oxfor

PULLING THE PLUG ON THE

ELECTRIC CIRCUS

ROCKING BURY INTO ACTION

FREE RADIO IN THE UK

RAR MANCHESTER

Left to Right

Ian Barnes (The Elite)
Berni Wilcox
Kevin Eden (The Elite)
Frank Manley (DJ)
Maggie Turner
John Kay (Poet)
Debbie Gold
Dick Witts (The Passage)
Paul Eastham
Glen Harding

This and other pics by Plain John Smith

Those not in Picture:

Steve Marland
Paul Cox
Jackie Manley
Vicky Pawson
Ken Wilson
Liz Turner

Manchester gigs coming up

Monday 10 April
Tower Club, Oldham
THE FALL

Saturday 15 April
St Johns College
Manchester
Band to be announced

Friday 28 April
Concorde Suite, Droyden
SOUL DISTINCTION

Saturday 29 April
SU Bar
Bispam Tech College
Blackpool
CHINA STREET

Monday 1 May
in conjunction with
Salford Trades Council
THE BUZZCOCKS
To be confirmed

Tuesday 2 May
Mecca Club, Blackburn
Bands to be announced

Saturday 6 May
Cavendish House,
Manchester Polytechnic
JAKIN STEVENS
FRANTIC ELEVATORS

ROCK AGAINST RACISM

VICTOR BROX BLUESMA

Interview by Richard Burrow

Rock Against Racism in Manchester. Text by Manchester RAR. Des

me organising a series of Sound System Battles with Manchester youth sounds vs leading Birmingham youths in our area, which were rammed. Maggie made all the difference to that working out as we collaborated with Baron and Kilowatt, the most responsible of the 3 Moss Side sounds taking part. I followed up their wish list and went to Handsworth, even climbing up to the 14th floor of a highrise, to discuss it with a lead contact – who luckily was in – and secured the participation of the Brum sounds! Due to council staff negligence leaving a cupboard unlocked

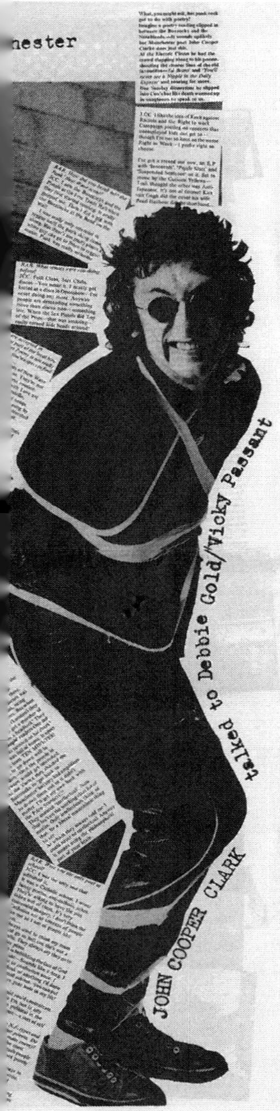

y Hoarding issue 5, February 1978.

in one of the venues, some equipment got stolen at one event, but eventually I won the court case demanding I pay for it and so lived to breathe another day.

I got involved in RAR through being in the SWP at the time, but I'm sure I would have found my way there anyway. I threw myself into it even taking flyers out to the blues and shebeens I loved to frequent as well as to my favourite reggae provider Duke Murray's shop, which I also wrote about. The Victoria Park Carnival and march was a big talking point and another member, Laurie, and I organised a coach full of very young participants. Some of them I am sure are in the wonderful Syd Shelton photo of exuberant boys in Victoria Park, I can just hear one of them saying 'See mi locks!'. I was concerned that some girls and boys seemed to be missing and went to look for them at the end but cannily they got to the coach on time and ironically I missed it and had to cadge a seat in another of the Manchester cavalcade. I still have my copy of the '6 one Penny' 7" Misty in Roots gave out from their float on the march and it's still one that gets rewind commands when I play it out with Sisters of Reggae in the here and now.

I wasn't so involved in the organisation of the Manchester Carnival Against the Nazis, as being so major and attracting so much interest it was more the central committee that took it on, tho I worked hard leafleting and many many friends came along. I was roped in as a backstage steward holding up the heaving fence as people tried to storm in. I was very happy to be able to find members of Moss Side's Xodus, who played there alongside Steel Pulse, The Buzzcocks and China Street – and who I used to know well – to contribute to the 40th anniversary film that was made last year.

I was made up to find that David Widgery had taken note of the valiant and successful effort Maggie and I made to save the Manchester leg of the National RAR tour in Spring '79 – which collapsed with big national names pulling out. In *Beating Time* he wrote 'two women pulled together a local bill and packed the poly on a Tuesday night producing one of the best gigs of the tour'. The poly was indeed mega-full and we sorted it in about 2 days. Maggie wasn't working and the Poly SU gave her an office and a phone. When it was all clear sailing,

Debbie today.

we sold 250 advance tickets and were expecting 650 people on the night, and suddenly had no gig so we sprang into action. Maggie got bold trying Jayne County and the Electric Chairs who would have stepped in but a key player was abroad and jokingly The 'Stones – but Mick 'had a cold' … We finalised with Exodus, Bad Stone and The Distractions – new wave Reggae, classic reggae and new wave punk and, in a stroke of genius, veteran Sound man President.

In a misunderstanding with the Poly management, we ended up with a steep security bill which we were outraged by but had no choice but to pay. Around the time of the gig there was a major trial of members of the 12 Tribes, who were violently arrested at a late night Christening celebration party. I had approached them a while before to see what support we could offer which they initially refused, but then we decided to offer the remaining proceeds to the ones who had been or were still imprisoned and that went down well.

Looking back one thing I would do differently would be to have looked harder for young women in bands, as nearly all the Manchester bands programmed, whether punk or reggae, were all male with rare exceptions like the manic Armed Forces. So it goes.

Maggie Turner [1945-2013], originally from Wythenshawe, was proud of being adopted and overcame tough times. Maggie was a strong member of RAR Manchester and saved the Militant Entertainment tour when national bands pulled out of the Manchester leg. She taught in Manchester and London having taken a degree and doing a Masters in Radio and TV creative writing as a mature student. Maggie's work when she died was Study Coach for Under and Post Graduate students at University of Manchester (2006-2013), supporting 'people who have been written off by the system but who have retained a shred of belief in themselves bringing themselves to university … and reinforcing that to help them make their dreams and ambitions a reality' with a stint in the Equalities division of the Council prior to that. Maggie also had a very popular alto ego as Marilyn Bracegirdle, a stand up character that allowed her to say whatever she wanted and get away with it. She always stood up for women and was passionate about challenging racism and achieving justice with a wicked reggae collection and the warmest heart.

Vivien Goldman

Writer on music and popular culture, RAR supporter. Did the Peter Tosh article for *Temporary Hoarding* 6

Every generation has its struggle. But not everybody is as lucky as we first wave UK punks were in the 1970s, to have a non-aligned, activist entity like Rock Against Racism as a channel for our energy and rage. Rock Against Racism belonged to everyone. As co-founder Red Saunders recalled, chuckling, if people from an untapped region would phone up asking for RAR activities in their area, the response would be – you ARE your local RAR activities, and a package of flyers and badges would duly be posted out.

The organization eschewing established leaders or bands was a genuinely popular uprising, without a top-down hierarchical structure. If you loved music and hated racism (the old RAR slogan, later much re-purposed,) you were an automatic life member.

Vivien with David Hinds, Victoria Park Carnival 1978. Photograph Caroline Coon.

There were meetings of the previously unpoliticised, cells held in living-rooms or squats or dank cellars in then shabby areas like Ladbroke Grove or King's Cross. The atmosphere crackled with the righteous sureness of a clear-cut cause; all was as black and white as a 2-Tone logo, the wave of racially-mixed ska bands that launched the 1980s. Apart from institutionalized and everyday racism, our number 1 enemy was the National Front, whose numbers were rising steeply. (They cottoned on to the idea of RAR, too, and soon had their own bands and shows. Luckily for our movement, in this instance the devil did not have all the best tunes.) The majority of marchers and concertgoers had probably directly experienced street, systemic or social conflict. At some point we all were fair game for the predators in our concrete jungle. Various Babylonian forces of evil included cops, obviously not all, but lots; likewise skinheads; the government; the National Front; the remaining Teddy Boys and rockers;

and then just plain horrible people, who didn't like the look of a free spirit. The more melanin-heavy you were, specially as a young male, the more aggro you were liable to get, (likewise innovatively dressed young females, race regardless). So a great cross-section of the population attended mass RAR gatherings like Victoria Park, which became known by their locations, like great battles. It was the first time that popular music had been harnessed so specifically and constructively for political engagement.

When do you have no more innocence to lose? Certainly, any illusions about one unquestioned rock god, Eric Clapton, shattered. Graffiti then used to say, "Clapton is God!" But even unbelievers were shocked by his drunken racist outburst onstage in Birmingham in 1976, worse still because of its hypocrisy; "Old Slowhand" (as he was called,) might never have got up to speed without Muddy Waters and B.B. King's artistry and lineage stretching back to Africa.

Gudrun Georges

At the time I was the Features Editor and writing a lot about reggae on the rock weekly, *Sounds*. It was glorious to be able to DO SOMETHING. In those comparatively freewheeling times, we could (very occasionally!) stay up all night in the office, laying out covers we wanted – like the one with mug shots of, among others, Carl Levy of the reggae band Cimarons, X Ray Spex's Poly Styrene and Thin Lizzy's Phil Lynott, all with the word DEPORTED stamped across them in red. Thus making an often unfamiliar link for the readers between the seemingly distant political process and the music they were into.

Identity is beyond skin deep. While Rock Against Racism was starting to take to the streets, I wrote a lot about reggae in *Sounds*. Part of the connection I felt with UK Reggae was the kinship of fellow first-generation-ers, despite our different circumstances. They were mostly kids of ambitious, economically-driven, immigrants from the former colonies. In contrast, four decades earlier, my lot had been fortunate to squeeze into the tight British quotas, on the run for their lives. As a child of immigrants, the arrival of Rock Against Racism was a huge relief. Before they met in London, both my parents had escaped Nazi Germany – we're Jewish — unlike most of my family. The failure of the safer world to believe what was happening helped kill them and shred my past.

But here we RAR-ers were, for whatever reason, all trying to reconcile our parents' cultures with our schoolmates'. Being a (dyed) blonde at the time, I got ambushed by many anti-Semitic conversations in my native London, because my "difference" wasn't as obvious. But in the sufferation stakes, I had it better than many of my harassed, unjustly imprisoned black fellow first-gennies. Words I had resisted from my father hit me: "Never forget, you are British, but you're not English." He didn't mean that I should not be loyal to the land of my birth, rather the reverse – that my country might not be loyal to me. Be vigilant, because you might have to fight to stay, or be ready to leave. Or worse. After all, it had happened to him and my mother (whose German family tree was recorded back to the 12th century,) and he was sensitive to the old demons stirring.

So, each for our own reasons, black, brown and white, WASP and kike, Rock Against Racism was OUR stand, and we were making change. Simply moving as part of such a motley throng, singing loudly together with our bards spinning our stories onstage, was empowering, elating. To quote Bowie's 'Starman' – You're not alone! For many of us, It was our first (a)political campaigning and our keen-ness bristled like a new broom, sweeping filth away to our beat. How aware were we that four decades before, near where Aswad, Steel Pulse, Elvis Costello, Misty in Roots and The Clash were jamming, the Battle of Cable Street had helped stop Mosley's Fascists? And now we were doing the same for Enoch Powell and his ilk. Finally, the world would wise up!

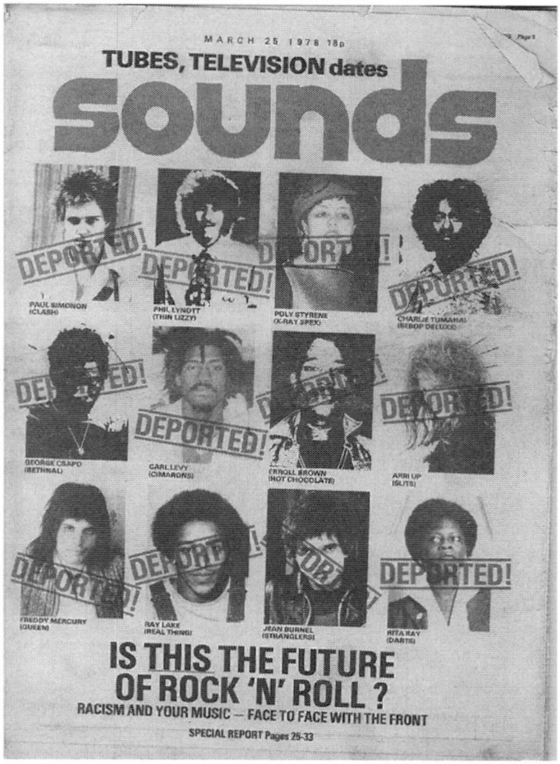

● Ground breaking *Sounds* front page imagined by RAR supporters on the paper.

Funnily enough, it didn't. Today's racist outcry in its even more virulent and entrenched form arises from the unprecedented floods of hapless people just like us. They're all displaced because greater swathes of the world than ever before have been decimated, made unlivable, in supposedly ideological wars that often did not have to be fought – and if they did, could have been much more cleverly handled. One loss of innocence is understanding that the struggle never does end. Don't feel discouraged! It's only another incentive to be how we would surely all like to be: fit, engaged and ever ready for anything. There is only one solution to the refugee crisis. End war and the rapacity that drives it. Everyone would have rather just stayed home. Is it part of a process? The way some multinationals manoeuvre to manipulate countries, pretty soon even being born in the developed world will be no guarantee of the right to live and work there. So we must keep resisting, as best we can, with whatever we've got. We'll definitely be needing the spirit of Rock Against Racism till enlightenment dawns and The Big Peace comes. Until then, Refugees-R-Us.

● TH#2

TEMPORARY HOARDING
No. 2
ROCK AGAINST RACISM
20p.
EXCLUSIVE interveiws with –
Johnny Rotton,
ASWAD,
Carol Grimes.
We want rebel music, street music. Music that breaks down people's fear of one another. Crisis music. Now music. Music that knows who the real enemy is.
Rock against racism.
LOVE MUSIC HATE RACISM

Nick Grant

was born and grew up in Selly Oak, Birmingham. After 5 years at art school he moved to London in autumn 1976. He taught in Ealing and Brent until retiring in 2014. Nick was active in the NUT and SWP during that time. He remains a revolutionary socialist, drums in the band Public Sector and has time to travel, get to West Brom matches, gigs – and take lots of photos!

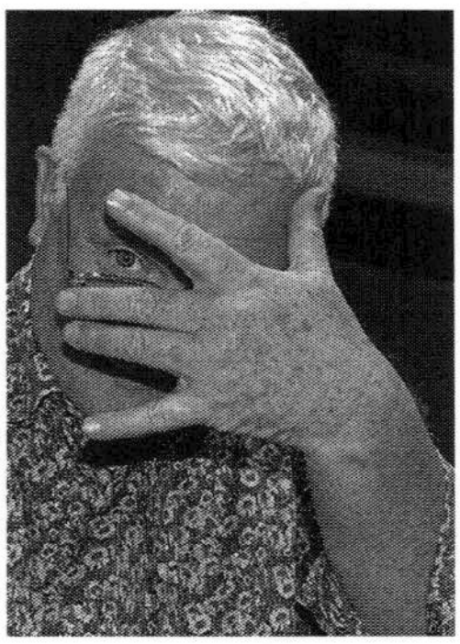

Ealing Kids Were Alright, apart that is from fuckin' Sean. Wonder – where he is now?

In January 1978 I was a fresh 26 year-old teacher in a Catholic high school in Acton, London W3.

Whilst the popular image of Ealing borough is leafy middle-class, all my students were working-class of Irish, Afro-Caribbean and east European heritage. Southall, on Ealing's western edge, later achieved notoriety as the site for racist and police attacks on its south Asian families.

A 1979 RAR gig in Finsbury Park

In the two previous years since I'd moved down from hometown Birmingham, I'd had a short-term job as publicity officer at the National Council for Civil Liberties, which taught me a lot.

I also became very active in the Anti Nazi League (ANL) and attended Socialist Workers Party (SWP) meetings.

There were ritualistic stand-offs involving dozens of us every Saturday morning in Ealing's main shopping centre between National Front (NF) paper sellers and us. Our members were regularly arrested and traffic blocked on the main Uxbridge Road.

But the Nazi threat was real. They were active in football grounds, housing estates, school playgrounds. They were coming third in some council bye-elections. I was soon to join the ranks of 'red teachers' named in the NF's youth paper *Bulldog*!

There were three ways that I wanted to bring my anti-racism into teaching.

The first was to get my National Union Teachers (NUT) branch to affiliate to the ANL. In those days over 100 members would attend monthly. But it was a shocking political lesson to be shouted at by the Communist Party (CP) branch secretary when I seconded a motion moved by a comrade. "You are exactly the kind of people who lost us the Spanish Civil War", he blubbered. In the vote their loyalists buried our proposal.

Ealing NUT was, in fact, I quickly discovered, part of the CP's power base within the union nationally. Us Trots were definitely not welcome! But within 12 months we had unseated them.

First we forced and won a vote of no confidence in their acceptance at a NUT Special Conference of a pay award. They resigned in a fit of pique expecting to win their seats back easily. Then we out-mobilised them and won all the key positions in the branch election. The CP locally never recovered from that.

The second initiative was to get Rock Against Racism (RAR) off the ground locally. It had taken off in other parts of London and the UK two years earlier.

The best local bands willing to perform were Southall-based reggae collective Misty in Roots and also The Enchanters. Hayes-based The Ruts and Acton's The Satellites were punk bands.

Fellow local NUT members Derek and Judith Merrill worked hardest on RAR gigs. But I helped with some. My most vivid memory is actually quite funny.

Many of our RAR gigs were held in the Student Union of what was then Ealing Tech – now West London Uni – in St. Mary's Road. Rock stars Pete Townshend, Ronnie Wood and Freddie Mercury had walked its corridors as art students in the past.

I turned up so early to help the first time that nobody else was around. I simply waited at the entrance table for the others.

But to my horror a bunch of skinheads strolled up to the building lead by a massive guy in customary attire – denims with braces, cherry-red Doc Martin boots and crew cut. I was shitting myself. I couldn't run. I couldn't hide.

They sidled up looking left and right. They wandered silently past me into the hall inspecting the stage, the amps, the lighting. They circled the room then came back towards me. Frozen to the spot my heart was going ten to the dozen.

But they started to leave. Apart from the giant. He spun round, produced a water pistol and squirted it at me. I shrieked a combined yelp of surprise, relief and hilarity. That gig was a huge success.

I had never personally experienced ethnic discrimination though my father's mild Irish nationalist views were grounded in his family history. But music was always a huge motivator of my own anti-racist convictions. To this day I believe that music has the power to amplify common, core human values across all social, sexual or ethnic boundaries.

As a mid-sixties teenager I was in awe not just of the Motown and Stax chart-toppers but also Ray Charles and Nina Simone, Cannonball Adderley and Charles Mingus, Muddy Waters and Little Richard. By the 70s superb black artists from Jamaica – Bob Marley of course – and Africa – like Fela Kuti and Miriam Makeba – captivated my attention. The USA Civil Rights Movement and African liberation struggles had long been a political inspiration also.

So I feel privileged to have helped RAR's daring success in bringing the dissident spirits of punk and reggae music – and many more genres – into a unified rejection of the No Future nihilism of UK neo-Nazi politics.

The third initiative was to help build a School Kids Against the Nazis (SKAN) local group. A lad at Ealing Green High School named Michael Pearce, I think, had started SKAN with a few of his mates…which is where Sean comes in.

Sean was part of a bunch of kids from the school I worked in to get involved with SKAN during 1978. He also came to local ANL meetings. I am pretty sure he came on the historic ANL march from Trafalgar Square to the Victoria Park carnival in April.

Imagine my fury then in summer 1979, following traumatic events in Southall on 23 April when police murdered my comrade Blair Peach and criminalized the whole community, that I should be invigilating a GCSE exam and find Sean working away – with a British Movement (BM) badge on his lapel! The BM were much smaller but even more violent than the Nazi National Front

Either Sean had just switched allegiance to this bunch of hardcore thugs – or had feigned interest in the ANL all along as a cold-hearted spy. He did live in south Ealing near a bunch of notorious NF goons, though many more were based in the Northolt and Greenford areas. Of course Sean was an exception.

Thousands of Ealing kids thrived on the positivity of RAR, savouring the joy of pogoing, booming bass bins, spliffs, pills, booze and much else, shared irrespective of colour; black and white truly united for the first time on UK streets and inside future homes.

There sadly are still bonehead racists and institutional racism around in 2016. Yet the social impact of RAR and the ANL made irreversibly significant political gains in west London and beyond that they could never reverse.

● Demonstration against NF paper sales in High Wycombe, 18 March 1978. Reported in *SKAN2*

● SKAN supporters join a protest at Finchley Girls School. Girls were suspended when they went to school in boys uniform. They were protesting against a book,'*Good Grooming for Girls*, in the library. Reported in *SKAN3*

● SKAN banner on school kids protest in Hackney, East London. Photograph: Jill Wallis

Roger Green

When SKAN was first launched in 1978, I was a full time organiser for the SWP in the Thames Valley area. As SKAN grew in popularity I worked full time for the Anti Nazi League. From 1985 to 2006 I taught physics at City and Islington College and was NUT rep.

The anti racist climate created by the Anti Nazi League (ANL) and Rock Against Racism (RAR) in1978 resulted in the proliferation of many grass roots anti-racist organisations, such as teachers against the Nazis, students against the Nazis engineers against the Nazis, to name but a few. The influence that these Anti Nazi League groups played in building a mass anti fascist movement (along with Rock Against Racism), cannot be overstated. They were crucial in mobilising mass demonstrations against NF marches in Lewisham, for example; building the ANL/RAR Carnivals, and isolating fascists in work places, schools and colleges making it almost impossible for them to spread their racist and fascist ideology. In many cases, but certainly not exclusively, it was socialists, including the Socialist Workers Party (SWP), who were the key activists in initiating and building these groups. Within weeks, however, these groups took on a life of their own, and rapidly outgrew the ranks of the activists who had been involved in the first meetings .

This was the case in one of the most successful Anti Nazi League groups – School Kids Against the Nazis (SKAN) launched in the spring of 1978. Within nine months it had produced 6 issues of the *SKAN* fanzine. At the onset, SWP members saw the importance of supporting school students who wanted to be involved in RAR and the ANL. They were involved in setting up the SKAN groups in Reading and Walthamstow. But very quickly both these groups took on a life of their own.

It was the school students themselves who were the driving force producing the six issues of *SKAN*, a rough and ready antiracist and antifascist fanzine. It was not long before SKAN groups sprang up all round the country, and were active in opposing the NF in schools and on the streets. In the first issue of *SKAN*, there were articles and letters that were fresh, militant and which showed a sophisticated understanding of fascism and the racist nature of capitalist society in general. The speed with which school students became politicised was breath taking. This is shown in the ever increasing socialist content of the SKAN fanzine as school students became increasingly involved in the National Union of School Students (NUSS) and Red Rebel, the Socialist Workers Party youth organisation.

There are many examples where school students were the key activists in building local anti-fascist activity. The first SKAN fanzine reflected the inspirational involvement of school kids in the fight against the NF. All the following quotes are from the six issues of *SKAN* all of which were written by school students:

> 'When the Nazis tried to march through the streets of Lewisham they were stropped by demonstrators, many from schools in the Lewisham area and beyond'.
>
> 'In desperation the NF are now trying to worm their way into schools. A paper called *Bulldog* (Bullshit) urges its readers to 'spread the racialist word'. .... School authorities have stood by and done nothing. Only school students have started to fight against the Nazi menace. All over the country, from Glasgow to Southampton, school students under the banner of SKAN have organised'.
>
> 'In October 1978 the National Front decided to try and hold a meeting in Reading's Civic Offices. The school students decided to produce a leaflet explaining what Nazi policies meant and urging school students to picket the meeting. Together with trade unionists and socialists they put pressure on the council to ban the meeting. In response to the NF trying to recruit in schools and set up a Young National Front, there are now 50 members of Reading Schools against the Nazis and not one National Front leaflet has appeared in Reading schools'.

The second issue of *SKAN* described how it was the school students that were the driving force in organising an anti-Nazi march in High Wycombe protesting about the parcel bomb attack on a local bus driver who had spoken the previous week at a RAR rally. The NF was clearly moving into terrorist violence. The bomb was sent to the bus depot by post. When the driver opened it in the works canteen, it exploded with a fifteen foot flame. Luckily the driver turned away at the last moment, so avoiding serious injury. It was no coincidence that the local chairman of the NF also worked in the depot. The response of SKAN and ANL/RAR supporters to this violence was summed up in the following third issue of *SKAN*,

'Neither Roger (bus driver), Rock Against Racism or the Anti Nazi League will be frightened off.'

SKAN reflected a growing involvement of Asian school students in the ANL, and the photograph of the High Wycombe march shows many Asian school students at the head of the march. An Asian school student also wrote a piece in *SKAN* calling on black and white unity to oppose the NF,
'The National Front are not going to be destroyed by the Asian Youth Movement alone, but by all of us, black and white, uniting and stopping the Nazi scum once and for all'

*SKAN*N also carried articles where school students had also fought racism internationally. In an article headed 'Soweto school students Fight Back', a school student interviewed Barney Mogatle, who was one of the leaders of the Soweto uprising who had moved to Britain. Barney's words reported in *SKAN* summed up the militant anti fascist politics that were growing in Britain's schools.
'People at school must think and decide for themselves. They should take an active part in politics and not leave it to their parents and so called leaders. Black and white should fight together against the National Front. It is on the streets that fascism grows, it is on the streets that it must be smashed. '
SKAN was not a dry political hackish paper written by socialists no longer at school; it was written by school students themselves, and reflected all their excitement and creativity in being active in the anti fascist movement. It was supported and nurtured by anti-fascist adults, but at its heart SKAN truly was driven by school students inspired by the activities of the ANL and RAR. From the very first issue of the fanzine, *SKAN* carried drawings, photos, letters and poems sent in by its supporters. The national SKAN encouraged school students to produce their own local SKAN fanzines. The Walthamstow *SKAN* front page had a photo of black and white school students picketing a local NF meeting.
This poem, written by a Waltham Forest school student, reflects a strong anti racism sentiment and political sophistication.

Don't listen to their dirty lies.
To find the truth like at the way Altab Ali died.
Hatred and violence are all they breed,
This kind of sickness, we just do not need
... Thatcher isn't alone in her racist ideas,
'Our' Labour Party's catching
on too, or so it appears.
"Get the blacks out and
England will be great again"
.... So please don't listen to the NF scum
Set up SKAN and have some fun.

Although the main thrust of *SKAN* throughout its six issues was the

fight against racism and fascism, particularly in schools, it also carried articles which reflected as mentioned above a growing politicisation among school students. For example, one page in the third issue of *SKAN* carried a headline 'Pupil Power', and reported a story about 'School students who were suspended because they'd rather revise than go to Sports Day'. The next day the school students contacted the NUSS, the Press, and called a picket of the school. 150 School students turned up. This forced the head to give in and reinstate the victims. Then there's the case of the girls in Finchley. They were suspended when they went to school in boys uniform. They were taking a stand against a book called *Good Grooming for Girls.* Following to pressure from the NUSS, including a protest by SKAN boys wearing girls dresses, the head backed down.
It was a reflection of the school students' confidence, determination and 'bottle' that students put their names and schools at the end of their articles. To my knowledge there was never any disciplinary action from school authorities, or bullying from pro NF sympathisers.

● SKAN picket army recruitment office.

Stories like this were an inspiration for other groups of school students to set up SKAN groups. As the Reading group said,
'There is nothing special about us – we are ordinary school students of different ages, with different likes and dislikes and different beliefs. But we are united by one aim – to wipe out the Nazi scum. 'Don't wait for the Nazis to appear in your school – form your SKAN group now. There are leaflets, badges and stickers for you and your mates'. In *SKANNING around* there were letters from Bristol, High Wycombe and London.

The number of groups and the sale of the *SKAN* fanzine grew at an extraordinary rate. Three thousand of the first *SKAN* issue were printed initially and then a further five thousand.
SKAN was receiving more than one hundred letters a week. In the second issue there were letters from Sheffield, Reading, Canterbury, Brighton, London and Surrey. A letter from Sheffield showed how quickly it was growing,
'Sheffield SKAN is now three months old and thriving. We started with a meeting in the local Poly 15 school students came. We now meet regularly every Thursday and cover 20 schools and colleges in the Sheffield and Rotherham area. We have distributed over 5,000 leaflets in schools and sold hundreds of badges and *SKAN*s. The badges seem to travel because we keep seeing kids from schools where we

don't know anyone wearing them. In some cases kids have recruited teachers into the Anti Nazi League. In one Sheffield school the Head banned the wearing of badges but a lot of kids wear them inside their lapels which made them even more popular'.

The example of *SKAN* puts the lie to those both on the right and the left that the RAR and the ANL were simply a Front for the Socialist Workers Party. The fanzines really were the words from the school students that were active against the NF.

The second issue of *SKAN* hit the schools a couple of weeks before the Victoria Park Demonstration. *SKAN* was now hitting the national press as one of the letters from a Surrey School student said

'Having read the article about School Students Against the Nazis in this week's *Observer,* I am writing to you to find out more about it. I feel very strongly about the NF. The only action I've taken against them is to scribble out NF signs on walls! But I don't think that is quite enough.'

● SKAN picket at North Tyneside Education Offices, against self-confessed Nazi teacher.

The credibility of SKAN was growing nationally, and this allowed a Reading school student to interview Tom Robinson who was headlining the Victoria Park Carnival. Tom proudly wore the SKAN badge and brilliantly answered the first question:

'What do you think about keeping politics out of our schools?'

'Tom gave me a quote – Hey man I'm not interested in politics, another guy replies 'No but politics is interested in you'.

The first *SKAN* contained eight pages and by the third issue it had grown to sixteen pages. Within months of its launch *SKAN* became a national school students organisation. Groups were formed in Merseyside, Doncaster, Sheffield, Luton, Manchester, St Albans, Walthamstow, Ealing, Hackney, Tyneside and Bonaventures Roman Catholic School Belfast. Many of these SKAN groups met regularly to organise local activities.

A report from the Tyneside SKAN showed the influence that school students were having on the ANL fight to stop the NF.

'We are busy organising and building throughout the North East and we are getting a great response. A SKAN picket at Northham High School against a self confessed Nazi teacher brought a huge response from kids in the area. Four hundred joined the picket, three kids were suspended but a SKAN picket on the Education Authority offices guaranteed their reinstatement'.

The school students organised around *SKAN* brought fun, creativity and activity to the anti-Nazi struggle. In issue five there were seven anti fascist poems all written by school students.

Sunday morning Trafalgar Square
Thousands here some already there
to march to Victoria Park is the aim
punks, hippies, black and whites
80,000 march for their rights

SKAN was really catching on and helped to organise imaginative antiracist activities like Rampage Against Racism for skate boarders. As was reported by *SKAN*

'The skate folk were up on the idea of the Rampage because we were bringing Rock Against Racism bands. And .... For your diary: None other than Mad Mark Baker, they guy who has 'Fight Nazis on his board (as well as being one of the most outrageous boarders around) has promised to do Rampage 2 at the Mad Dog Bowl. '

The growth of *SKAN* nationally and the strong line taken in opposing the Nazis on the streets drew the attention of the national press. The *Sun, Mirror* and *Sunday Times* all went on the attack: Smutty anti-police propaganda poison – disgusting.

One of the poems sent in by a school student that caused particular outrage was entitled 'Kill the Front'

It's a vicious circle
And it's making me grunt
I hate racism
I hate the Front
Don't beat up my mates.
You ain't no Gods.
Kill the Front
The fucking sods.

As for swearing – as SKAN said the only four letter word that worries us is NAZI.

The press also accused *SKAN* of not being written by school students. It was precisely the fact that it was written by school kids that gave it its unique, outrageous, rebellious style that was so appealing to school kids, and which led to such a rapid growth. It tapped into a rapidly growing rebelliousness and politicisation amongst working class youth. A letter published in the fifth issue of *SKAN* illustrates the politicisation and level of autonomy that *SKAN* had become.

'Me and my mates read the last one of your paper and thought it was really good. Before I read it I never thought about unemployment and all that being caused by not enough money being spent by politicians, only about there being too many people in the country. Anyway, now me an me mates have set up a *SKAN* group in our school and have collected some money from the younger kids pocket money and the older kids Saturday jobs to se set up our own fanzine. I wanted to tell people how easy it is do this for themselves- all it takes is a bit of time and energy and it's a great laugh – Honest' – Ron and Mark, NW London

Poems from the last issue of SKAN

My despairing soul sings
despair.
Keep away from the black midnight …
I am sad tonight
The vast sadness
Of a murdered Race…
It happened to the Jews is it to
happen again to the blacks
Take care to have means
Adequate for the job you
Undertake
Get the upper hand before it is too late '
Judy 17

'Poised; hanging on in trouble pain; causing vision to double;
parents worrying about their truth;
questions asking what to do.
Parents know no better than you
Tears washing away the lies;
Youth looking thru their own eyes
Parents trying not to let them see youth
Setting themselves finally free' Anon

'I wrote to Box No 151,
I did not stop to ask my mum
How we lay the Nazi Ghost,
They sent info by return post,
To bash the fash we must unite
All together Black and White
So I leafleted my school.
Though it was against some rule.
And now we're together all of us mates,
No Nazis come through our school gates'
John 14 S. London

Box No 151 was the first line of the address of the ANL

Reading through the back copies of *SKAN* almost 40 years after the events was the most uplifting experience. *SKAN* showed the creativity, energy, bravery, organisational ability and political awareness that can be unleashed once school students are given freedom and a political framework in which to act.

Take this report from a Walthamstow School Kid Skev in the last issue of *SKAN*.

'Another task of our group is to help other SKAN groups to start. For example we were asked by kids in Starcross School to help them start a SKAN group because of NF activity near the school. Ten of us went to the school and talked to those interested and the next week we came back with badges and leaflets and gave them out.

'The *Tonight* programme came down to talk to us for a programme they were doing on the ANL. Three of us spoke on the telly, Josie, Karen and me, Skev. They asked us questions about SKAN and our SKAN group and when, at the end, they asked what SKAN meant we told them. Fun, Freedom and Future'.

It is those positive attributes of youth that the present government through its narrow knowledge based curriculum and testing wishes to destroy . Thousands of school kids were involved and it would be wonderful to hear their stories. Many of those in *SKAN* went on to organise Red Rebel, which was the youth organisation of the Socialist Workers Party. By stopping the NF building a base in schools *SKAN* played a vibrant and important role within the ANL. And it was the ANL that played such a crucial part in the defeat of the NF on the streets and electorally in the 1979 General Election. A defeat which Martin Webster the leader of the NF at the time was a result of the ANL.

This is confirmed by the fact that in 1982 Peter Hain brought a libel case against Martin Webster, of the National Front. Hain described Webster's court defence:

'He was still extremely bitter and remarkably candid. The picture he gave, and he clearly believed it, was that prior to 1977, the NF were unstoppable and he was well on the way to becoming Prime Minister. Then suddenly the Anti Nazi League was everywhere and knocking the sheer hell out of them. He said that the sheer presence of the ANL had made it impossible to get NF members on to the streets, had dashed recruitment and cut away at their vote. It wasn't just the physical opposition to the marches, they had lost the propaganda war too'.

I would like to pay tribute to all those school students involved in *SKAN* as well as John Flaig, Paul Holborow. Roger Huddle and Red Saunders.

Roger Green, May 2016

Ruth Gregory

was a key London activist and designer in RAR, and *Temporary Hoarding* from 1977 to 1981. She collaborated with David Widgery in Save Bethnal Green Hospital Campaign and on his book *Beating Time* (1986). Set up a studio Hot Pink Heart/Red Wedge Graphics with Syd Shelton (1979). Joined by Andy Dark, to become Graphics International. Awards for illustration and design include: 25 years of *Time Out* competition (1993). Her work and collected archive from her RAR days formed half of the exhibition: A Riot of Our Own at Chelsea Space, 2008 and the East End Film Festival, 2010.

The point of life, is live, love if you can and pass it on.
– *Kate Tempest* 2016

When I reach back to those RAR days I experience a frisson of delight that by happenstance, I was there to participate in the defence and development of our home-grown roots culture. I was a bit old to be a punk and a bit young to be a hippie. I fell between two eras but at least I was in good company. I was – and still am – consoled, uplifted, soothed and instructed by rhythms and rhymes that have tracked along my way to the present. Roots music and poetry from Africa, America, Jamaica and Britain speak to me of the inherent justice of becoming one race, the human race. My assimilated white entitlement is challenged, as well as my response to assumed male entitlement. Aswad's 'Concrete Slaveship' released in 1976, begins with a soft drumming as if hanging back in a freedom found only in dreams. As a woman's voice calls once to the approaching day an insistent reggae beat wakens, wide-eyed to reality: the concrete walk-ways and underpasses of UK inner cities.

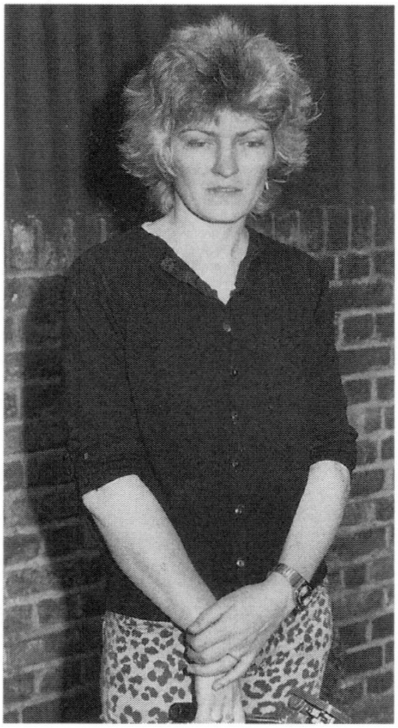
● Ruth 1978

I returned from Australia to join long unemployment queues in Brixton and rented a flat with Syd Shelton and his partner Jayne Harrison opposite the Prison! I felt a connection with those Caribbeans who had boarded H.M.G.B. Mothership in the 1950s and arrived into this new and often unwelcoming land. By the time I landed, they had long made the best of a bad situation and had irreversibly entangled our two cultures on a more positive level. They bought music derived from a long history of Caribbean resistance and it was celebratory and joyful. Britain still had deep-rooted working class communities in 1976, along with cheap rents and strong trade unions to protect workers' rights. My spare time (lots) was spent on becoming part of the fight-back and my spare pennies (few) on imported tunes from Jamaica and the new ting: militant British reggae. As instructed by Denis Bovell in his killer Dub album *Yuh Learn* I listened and I learned.

Back to brutality

On 4 June 1976, Gurdip Singh Chaggar was murdered in Southall by a gang of white racialists. He was 18 years old, his killers were never convicted. Chaggar's senseless murder marked a righteous upsurge by another group of young first generation Britons, who proceeded to shatter the commonly held perception that Asians were easy targets for racism.

When Right to Work Campaign announced a march on the Trade Union Cogress in 1977, I enthusiastically joined along with Jayne. As well as marching 60 odd miles to Brighton – ouch, many blisters later – to lobby the TUC, we met many colourful and noisy young punks along the way which made the journey easier. Thus before I bumped into RAR punk rock bumped into me. For me it was a case of just sprinkle water and watch me grow. I was a natural 'Warrior in Woolworths' (aka Poundland 2016).

'Some people say little girls should be seen and not heard but I say oh bondage up yours!' trilled Poly Styrene.

Punk women were not ashamed to be labeled 'difficult' 'shrill' or 'assertive'. Dissident and often deliberately discordant like scullery maids engaged in their own pots and pans revolution they took up instruments in the D.I.Y. fashion of their generation. Many were gender mixed bands but some all-female. Punk-feminist band the Slits used a reggae punk mix to ask 'Who invented the typical girl?' Helpfully laying the blame at 'another marketing ploy', punk women led the way in ripping up the rule book on sexuality, they were not objects but a new non-feminine-defined sexy. They exuded power, parodied bondage and slavery and wrote about taboo subjects like self-harm, self-gaze and stereotypes. 'There's a constant pain, behind her eyes. She needs to be tranquilised' sang the Au Pairs.

It seemed miraculous when Syd and I were offered jobs in the art room of the SWP print shop in Hackney. Even more so because it introduced us to RAR. Roger Huddle was already working there and the first issue of the RARzine, *TempoRARy Hoarding* had been designed by him and Andy Dark to great acclaim. On the cover in blown-up typewriter script was RAR's manifesto:

We want rebel music, street music. Music that breaks down people's fear of one another. Crisis music. Now music. Music that knows who the real enemy is. Love Music Hate Racism'.

TH's avant-garde style was set to wake-up the nation! Andy's photomontages; David Widgery's scorching treatise: 'What is Racism'; posters based on TRB's 'Winter of '79' and The Clash's 'White Riot' and what became a regular *TH* page, 'Guidelines for RAR Gig Organisers' – an essential tool-kit for the hundreds of small RAR groups who would put on thousands of gigs all over Britain.

Punk rock had just pushed up out of cracks in the concrete in English Harlem, like a cantankerous rose. 'Don't know what I want, but I know how to get it, I want to destroy the passerby. Cos I want to be anarchy' screamed Johnny Rotten in June 1977 bang in the middle of the Queen's Silver Jubilee week. It is 'the passerby' who sleepwalks through the reality of 'no future in England's dreaming' so I reckoned they deserved to have their peace destroyed if nothing else! Some areas of London were 'out of bounds' for a lone female or any man that did not fit and people turning a blind eye to racist remarks was an everyday occurrence. RAR, and the ANL, got people to stand up for anti-racism in those everyday situations. The racists were a minority, just as anti-foreigners are now in post Brexit UK. Some of the punk bands had NF followings, so one of the few rules RAR beamed out was to keep control of the stage otherwise fighting could – and did – break out on the dance floor. There was collective courage at play in RAR and Rock Against Sexism which made me a braver young woman.

The SWP print shop in Bethnal Green was always bustling and often pretty electric. Working there I met fellow conspirators in *TH* editorial collective: David Widgery, Lucy Whitman, Kate Webb, Red Saunders along with many willing hands, hearts and minds. We were afforded a long rope of effusive creativity by the many SWP/RAR supporters in typesetting, running the printing presses and in management. At first RAR didn't have an office only a P.O. box number (to protect us from the real threat of fire-bombing-fascists). Our London strategy meetings were held in Red's studio, but from little things big things grow, we needed a proper office fast and Kate was employed to run it. RAR operated in a collective, bottom-up fashion because the situation demanded it. For the punk and reggae bands, hierarchy smelled of oppression and we felt pretty much the same. We didn't always agree, which is why we were and still are many stories.

In Rasta terms, 'when the two 7's clashed' (1977) Babylon, i.e. England, was meant to disintegrate. Sadly the reverse happened two years later when Thatcher, not content with having snatched our school milk, began dismantling our health service, schools and trade unions so that today, how much freedom you have is dependent on your level of wealth. 'One step forward, two steps backward, down inna Babylon' sang Max Romeo back then and 'One step forward, don't step backward, step out of Babylon' he calls to us now. So like Ranking Roger we must 'Ignore the obvious' and continue to keep the faith.

By 1977 Red's vision of 'the greatest ever agitprop show-time of all-time' was on the road. Roger, Syd and I became the design hub in our RAR London agitprop factory, concocting graphics and handling print for *TH* and leaflets, posters, stickers, badges. Bob Humm of Deptford RAR, who worked in the camera room, became an essential part of our *TH* editorial – badges funded our operation and RAR sold millions of them – I designed one based on the rich mix of our cultural influences: the head of a tigress in rasta colours with the RAR star in her jaws: the surrealist Max Ernst's flying elephant metamorphosed into a charging rhino to lead RAR's Militant Entertainment Tour. Our design styles were quite different but I think that made *TH* sing and we had use of Syd's iconic photos to convey the power of the movement. Roger cemented Constructivist design as one our creative reference points. Art, film and poetry that poured from the Russian revolution in 1917 influenced the like all over the capitalist world, yet somehow retained its integrity. Our RAR star and the ANL arrow designed by David King echo the enduring militancy of Constructivism.

But wait… another design revolution was happening under our noses, Punk Rock's raw creative energy seemed to blow away the cobwebs from my ears and eyes. Everything I had learned as a designer had been torn up into little pieces and thrown into the air to land where it will. We stabbed and scratched at the images, pushed and probed the orthodox design rules. Driven by the back-beats in our heads, we ripped back the cellophane covering the bullshit to find a newborn truth within.

RAR published over 15 issues of *TH* and 10 of those between 1978-79. Each was built on core elements: letters and feedback from RAR groups around the country; instruction manuals on how to build your own PA system, or handle band management; interviews with RAR bands; the ubiquitous poster usually based on song lyrics, to stick on your bedroom wall and education/information about whatever else we deemed relevant at the time – 'No more Normals'; 'Up against the Berlin Wall'; 'How did Biko die'; 'Never mind the people, here's the bollocks'; 'Reclaiming the night'; 'Belfast no fun city'; '1 white, 2 black, 3 women with the blues'….

I think of the *TH*/RAR team as the Bash Street Kids of Beanotown gobbing at Little Lord Snooty and his gang of 'Eton Rifles'. Punk legitimised a level of audacity which had not existed before and creative talents showed up daily to be part of that. Lucy, who went on to start Rock Against Sexism, wasn't afraid to confront bands about misogynistic attitudes. She responded to a fashionable dalliance some punks had with the swastika by writing about the consequences of NoFun ideas. I decorated her article, 'Sex vs Fascism' with a photo of Hitler admiring an enormous phallus shaped bomb, which I slashed at so it looked like it had been sucked through an industrial fan. Such was the delightful – writer, activist, artist, production demarcation mix-up – that Lucy also wrote about the politics of shoes and designed it herself!

Women were a minority in both the London RAR and *TH* collectives, but it would be wrong to assume that men controlled the decision-making process. Dave describes me in his book '*Beating Time*' as someone 'who was to become editor and the force tranquille behind the graphic power of *Temporary Hoarding*', in reality he and I planned the issues because we were sweethearts at the time, but everyone was in control of what actually went down. Dave embodied an egalitarian spirit, hard for anyone to disagree with. His writing trawled through the remnants of the British empire to draw parallels with struggles distant in time and place. Winds of change from Africa, Bessie Smith and Billie Holiday, an 'India never yet quelled' were all given graphic life in that artroom.

Most of us had full time jobs so RAR stuff was fitted into snatched spaces: planning strategy, organising gigs and working all night sometimes on *TH*. We had very little rest, but I don't remember needing much, I think we hummed along on energy gained from making a real connection with playtime sorted as well. Because graphics, montages, photographs and illustrations had equal billing to words, we designers often got the balance so wrong that the words became illegible! We could only imagine the final result because we designed the pages on boards with each colour on a clear acetate overlay but in black and white. Each colour was printed separately as well so accurate registration was impossible. We got very good at second guessing these unpredictable colour-shifts to inject energy onto the printed page. These idiosyncrasies of the process inspired new typefaces such as dubbed typewriter and blurred headlines. Darla-Jane Gilroy and Rick Fawcett produced vibrant montages; Jo Wreford doctored an image of the Shah of Iran filched from the *Evening Standard* and still bearing the dateline November 26, 1978. U.S. soldiers pour menacingly out of his head while his dark glasses reflect snapshots of the Iranian elite's decadent lifestyle.

Back to brutality

On 4 May 1978, Altab Ali was brutally murdered in Whitechapel by three white teenage boys as he walked home from work. He was 25

● Illustration: Ruth Gregory *Temporary Hoarding* #8

years old. 7,000 people marched to Downing Street behind his coffin. Local elections run-up and the fascists were descending like a bunch of locusts to pick off the more easily led whites and scare the rest. The situation demanded an urban guerrilla response! The ANL hit the doorsteps and football terraces, we hit the music venues. British reggae was more militant than punk and as vibrant from the off. It too carried a restlessness from run down streets and estates in our cities and towns. Broadly speaking, there were black bands and there were white bands. The music industry operated the status quo, which routinely sent black bands to the back of the bus or ignored them completely. Two bands provided RAR with highly visible role models early on, Special AKA and UB40. Both were a mix of black and white musicians and that offered RAR a gift. A cavalry of two-tone music was a few years off but it seems to me now that it was instinctively heard a comin' over the hill.

Thirty-eight years ago we still dug for truth in old-school ways. Although, when you're trying to stage a RAR/ANL Carnival and some 100,000 participants decide to dance and whoop the full 7 miles from Trafalgar Square, so the folks controlling the stage in Victoria Park think no-one has turned up! I think a mobile or two would've come in handy. We had naturally borrowed the book on Carnival from the Caribbean Library in Notting Hill and followed the recipe therein:

THE SOUND – lively up yourself with militant reggae. Grate in a dash of bolshie punk. Sing if you're glad to be gay. Liberally spice with some home-grown bhangra. Mix in a thousand whistles. Mash-up as much as you can, then Pressure Drop.

THE STYLE – dress to kill boredom stone dead. Cover yourself with badges. Dance your hot-pink socks off.

THE MIX – jangle a RAR star or jiggle an ANL arrow. Gob at the Spitting Image giant Nazi heads. Jeer at the NF outside the Rat-hole Arms in Bethnal Green Road. Liberate the streets. At least for one day banish all fear of racist violence from the the East End of London.

COOK – until dusk, digest slowly with friends for the sheer joy of it!

We thought we were living in desperate times, like The Clash said 'the British Army are waiting out there and they weigh 16 hundred tons' but least they were not in our front gardens! Nothing could've prepare me for the frenetic rage of Belfast punk's Stiff Little Fingers, the first band to hit the stage in September 1978 RAR/ANL Carnival 2. But in true Irish spirit they offered a solution: 'Alternative Ulster, grab it and change it, it's yours, Alternative Ulster, ignore the bores and their laws. Alter your native land!'.

By the time the NF decided to wage war on Southall on 23 April 1979 the Asian Youth Movement was well organised. The demonstration was supported by local workplace strikes nearby; national trades unions and anti-racist groups including RAR and the ANL. Southall was full to bursting with determination to stop the NF meeting that day. 5,000 police were mobilized to defend them, including the much hated Special Patrol Group (SPG): they inflicted 30 serious skull and genital injuries and the death of Blair Peach. No police officers were ever charged for their actions.

Misty in Roots and The Ruts had formed the People Unite Collective and their building was used as an anti-fascist command headquarters. As a result it was smashed up by rioting police and Misty's singer Clarence Baker, badly injured. The Ruts wrote a song detailing the events:

'Hot heads came in uniform, Thunder and lightning in a violent form... Clarence Baker, No trouble maker, Said the truncheon came down, Knocked him to the ground, Said the blood on the streets that day'.

RAR quickly launched a 'Southall Kids are Innocent' benefit to raise money for the victims – performing at the Rainbow, London, were: Misty in Roots, The Ruts, The Clash, Pop Group, Pete Townshend, Aswad, The Members and The Enchanters.

Just listening to the on stage introduction delivered by 'Smokes' from Misty in Roots gets my ageing bones itching to dance caution to the wind. Their album *Wise and Foolish* seems to me to sum up that age – Wise enough to want to change the world for the better and Foolish enough not to be scared too easily back into a safe comfort zone.

In the wake of a militarized police response to public outcry over the death of unarmed Black teenager Michael Brown on 9 August, 2014, Ferguson, USA the LetUsBreathe Collective said:

'It is our duty to fight. It is our duty to win. We must love each other and protect each other. We have nothing to lose but our chains.'

This could have just as well come from the RAR/*Temporary Hoarding* Collective 1976-81 in Britain.

Carol Grimes

I was born in London. A long time ago when bombs were falling from the skies: there were no Bananas, and the radio was the music and the word. The years passed and then, in 1959 I fell in love with Ray Charles and Ella Fitzgerald. It was Margie Hendricks roaring out the chorus of 'Night Time is the Right Time' on a cafe juke box that ... 'made me wanna holler, made me wanna sing' and the voice of Ella on her hit of those times 'Every time we say goodbye'. These early musical memories gave me a life long love of the jazz and blues voice, both in melody and improvisa-tion.

● Benefit gig for the Local KIDS play hut in Powis Square

I started singing regularly in the streets of London, and the South Coast sea side towns, first as a Bottler for Paris Nat and then I sang for my supper, working with assorted guitar and harmonica players until I formed my first band; THE RACE. This blues and folk based outfit worked mainly in the London area with one or two visits to the continent to play at blues festivals. Now I am still singing-writing and per-forming..hopefully, until I pop me Clogs.

Black Echoes and London Jazz News interview contributed by Carol

Black Echoes
November 20 1976
ROCK AGAINST RACISM
Princess Alices, Forest Gate
Friday 12:11:76
Carol Grimes and the Boogie Band, once again delivered a rocking set to a delighted crowd who had turned up and put their money where others put their mouths. A tight hard-working seven piece band who enjoy a good blowing, funky evening, as much as the audience, they should be seen by more people, especially as they are fronted by one

of the best female blues/soul singers the country has yet produced. The repertoire was mostly songs from her album, recorded with the Memphis Horns, and she sounded good giving the Frederick Knight compositions a good shakedown. The band too, gave all, through some instrumental numbers with some funky jamming getting the audience stepping out as if it was really the JB's out front. Dave Brooks, playing sax like a reincarnated King Curtis, and Mick Weaver's keyboard work, received well deserved applause, falling back in counterpoint to Carol's powerful but sensitive vocals; the whole thing being driven effortlessly along by Terry Stannard's soulful 'percussion symphatique'. As often happens with this band, there were a couple of guest musicians up for a jam, and on this occasion it was notably Leroy Wiggins who helped Carol out by sharing the singing chores on a couple of numbers.

The event itself is worth noting as well. Instigated to set up a fund to combat racism (from whatever source), it is hoped to make it a regular event although not necessarily at the same venue (the have plans for the Acklam Hall and the Roundhouse). It is hoped also, to get the services of soul and reggae bands as well as rock musicians, and the success of the venture will eventually be measured by the ratio of black and white and vice versa in the audiences, one of the worthwhile grassroots objectives this could achieve. At this particular gig it was predominantly white, but that was due to the lack of advertising. I'm not sure of the role that politics takes but I'm sure that the Socialist Workers who got this thing on, will realise that racial harmony is far more important than any political party. The venture deserves support from anybody who cares, as the World is in the need of Love today. — *Fred Rath*

PREVIEW/ INTERVIEW:

Carol Grimes – The Singer's Tale, St James Studio

Carol Grimes was one of the very first performers to appear at St James Studio. In this new interview with Sebastian, she talked about the first outings of her new autobiographical project *The Singer's Tale* for which she will return to St James Studio with performances on Feb 9th and 26th 2015.

London Jazz News: What does the show consist of?

Carol Grimes: Songs, little beat poetry, it's a tale interlaced with songs, a lot of them written by Dorian Ford and myself. It's in two halves with an interval. Maggie Ford is directing. Neville Malcolm is on bass, Winston Clifford drums, Annie Whitehead trombone and Dorian Ford piano.

LJN: And the title?

CG: I nicked it from Chaucer – he never wrote a tale about a singer, but he travelled through south east London, knew it, trod the same paths I trod.

LJN: Where did the idea come from?

CG: I started writing a book and songs and poems in the 80s. And when some other people told me they wanted to write my life story, they sent me a draft script and I got cold feet about what they were doing. So I had the idea I would write my own.

LJN: And then?

CG: You have to leap forward to Deptford High St where I was living in 2005. Because I'd been born in Lewisham it felt like I had got back to where I'd started – and I started writing it again. I had a song at that time 'Blues for Louis' it was on the album *Mother,* it really worked, people tell me it's a beat poem.

Then I had a terrible accident; I was knocked over by two blindfolded dancers preparing for a show in Brighton. That accident held me back as a performer for a while, I couldn't even walk, so I picked up the book again. By that time I'd started working with Dorian and showed him the bits and the piece that ended up as the 20 min thing you saw at MAP in Kentish Town.

● Rock Against Racism gig at The Roundhouse Camden Town 1977. The drummers are Glen Lefevre and Mitch Mitchell from Jimi Hendrix Experience.

LJN: And both the book and the show have progressed quite a bit?

CG: I have got a book pretty much done sitting there waiting for me to do edits which I hope to get published. And so the idea is to tour the show taken from the book, and to sell the book while on tour....

LJN: Is there a theme running through the book?

CG: Why I am writing a book? It's not because I'm a celebrity (I'm not) but other people have had lives that are just as interesting. My story goes from my birth in 1944 to now. When I write about myself I feel as if I am the fly on the wall. So the story goes through the miners' strike, through the first few gigs of Rock Against Racism that were put on by Red Saunders, David Widgery and Roger Huddle. We did a pub in the East End, and the Roundhouse.

If you look at the history, all people talk about is Billy Bragg and Tom Robinson – and they lay claim to it, it became a much bigger thing. I got gradually left out. It is very easy to be written out of history. I did the first ever Glastonbury fair.

LJN: And mixed race bands, reflecting the society you live in, are an important feature of your life as a performer?

CG: I became aware that eighties two-tone bands claimed to be the

first to be mixed race. They weren't when I started there were bands like Graham Bond, and all the Windrush generation, and the exiles from South Africa. There were a lot of mixed race bands.
The bigger bands in the 80s were all four white men. So I wanted to redress the balance and give people a flavour of what it was really like, life in the sixties.
The changes that are still happening the venues that have been lost.
LJN: The show at St James Studio is going to bring lost of memories to life...
CG: It takes me back to London before the whole hippy thing. There were great bands. They reflected the city that I lived in – they weren't segregated bands. It wasn't long after the austerity fifties – the feeling something good was going to happen
LJN: Do you have some lyrics from the show that capture that feeling you describe?
CG:

Inside her room
Single bed
Sink and gas
She listened to the blues
Black vinyl, warm spinning
Her heart wanting the sound in her mouth

Nina Hammill

was born in Hackney in East London in 1961 and grew up in Bermondsey in south London. When Rock Against Racism was founded she was a 15 year old school student at Walworth School in Southwark. She is now aged 55 and lives in Crewe in Cheshire with her husband Steve and 15 year old son Bill. She works as an administrator in children's social care and she is still an active campaigner against racism, fascism and all forms of discrimination and oppression.

My experiences of Rock Against Racism

I grew up in Bermondsey in south London, just off the Old Kent Road. I remember people talking about racism from the police in the area, particularly towards black, Asian and Irish people. When we were kids, other kids or adults would sometimes say racist things to my black and Asian mates. I learned to challenge prejudice and bigotry. The National Front (NF) used to try and sell their paper in Bermondsey and down East Street, and also a fascist group called the British Movement (BM) gave out racist and fascist leaflets at Millwall football ground. I went to protests against the NF as a teenager. We would try to stop all their activities. The police always took the side of the far right and would attack us.
I got involved in Rock Against Racism (RAR) soon after it started in 1976 and also got involved in the Anti Nazi League (ANL) when it was founded in 1977. I found that RAR and the ANL worked well together in the fight against racism and fascism.
I grew up listening to lots of music, including jazz and reggae, and in 1976 I got into punk music.
In April 1978, when I was 16, I marched through East London with thousands of other anti-racists to the first RAR/ANL carnival in Victoria Park. On the march we passed a few very small pathetic groups of skinheads who seig-heiled and shouted insults at us. There was a big mix of people on the march and at the carnival. I felt so excited and

really felt the power we had by coming together. Lots of my favourite bands were playing, including X-Ray Spex, The Clash, Steel Pulse, Patrik Fitzgerald and Tom Robinson Band (TRB). The carnival was so good I felt very emotional. It wasn't just the music, also lots of the lyrics were political and straight to the point, and I felt part of something big. I went to other carnivals and gigs in many places, including Brixton, Leeds and Manchester. There were always coaches put on so ordinary people could afford to go, and the gigs were always affordable. One of the many important things RAR did was to bring together different musical styles, which broadened people's experiences, musically and culturally. The bands weren't well paid and didn't live celebrity lifestyles. They were the same as us, and we could identify with them as they could with us. RAR badges were easy to spot and were always bright and colourful. I was always proud to wear them.

● Some of Nina's collection.

I remember going to a RAR gig somewhere in central London in about 1978. It cost about 75p to get in, and Misty in Roots and Sham 69 were performing. A load of skinheads stormed into the gig and started seig-heiling and shouting racist chants. Sham 69 stopped playing and their lead singer, Jimmy Pursey, said the bands wouldn't play any more unless the fascists left. From what I remember, the fascists were massively outnumbered and they ended up leaving. It was a great gig and Misty in Roots and Sham 69 played together. It was a good example of beating back fascists.

There were lots of scary times as the fascists would stick in groups and pick on individuals, as they still do now, but I found that RAR and ANL opened up a network of people who would look out for each other and for others too, and provided some safety in numbers. People still got beat up and murdered because of the colour of their skin, or their nationality, as they do now, but I think we made a positive difference. For me RAR was about much more than just music, it taught me about unity, culture, politics and revolution, and how music is an important part of all those things, and showed me that if enough of us get together, we can stop racists and fascists from spreading their filth.

David Hinds

Steel Pulse

There is no doubt that the Rock Against Racism concert at Victoria Park, London, was a milestone in our career. Yet my memory of it has not been one of great detail, simply because things were happening at an alarming pace simultaneously, with the band's then recent signing to Island Records, the debut album recording and the immediate release of our very first single 'Ku Klux Klan'.

Looking back on it, that happening must have been down to divine intervention, because of the way we were introduced into the whole Rock Against Racism experience in the first place. Our stance against prejudice started in small pubs around Britain, attracting only a handful of people, then moved on to multitudes consisting of tens of thousands.

To the best of my knowledge we were the only reggae band to perform on that bleak day in 1978. From the line up, I remember The Clash, Generation X and the most memorable of them all, the Tom Robinson Band. History was in the making, as home grown black music was reaching a new and expanded dimension.

We were not totally aware at the time that it was the 'pro Enoch Powell' speech Eric Clapton had made two years prior in our very own back yard, Birmingham, that triggered all this. Not that it would have mattered in the least, 'cause although Clapton was a guitar player that I held in high regard during my college years, the Caribbean community were alienated from many a white music, especially rock, therefore, would not have taken on board who said what or who Clapton was, despite the fact that he had had a reggae hit covering a Bob Marley song, years previous to his speech.

My memories of the period and that RAR racism concert in particular, was that London was at a stand still, a human traffic jam... and for the right reasons. Posters and banners were everywhere, opposing the bogey men of Britain, The National Front. From then on, reggae and punk became married forever.

TH#3

TEMPORARY HOARDING
ROCK AGAINST RACISM
10p No 3
12 MONTHS UNDER HEAVY MANNERS
CARNIVAL ISSUE
PLUS: ELVIS, LEWISHAM.

Mike Hobart

was born in 1945 and grew up in north London. He started playing sax at 19 and did various manual and office jobs before going on the road with Johnny Johnson and the Bandwagon in 1971. He started a degree in sociology at City University in 1973 at the same time as he was playing with the glam rock band Junior High and the Rockets. While at City he joined the International Socialists. When RAR was launched he was starting an MA @ Essex University, playing in the cooperative funk band Limousine and helping raise his two children. Mike still plays, and has recently released an album under his own name.

I got involved with Rock Against Racism early on. I'd joined the International Socialists a few years previously, and was also playing saxophone in the funk band Limousine, a mixed race collective that had been going about a year. We were playing early Kool and the Gang, Commodores, Brecker Brothers stuff, which was popular in the clubs, but not many bands were doing it live.

From my memory, Limousine played a second RAR gig at the Princess Alice (Carol Grimes played the first ever RAR gig there), and played a couple more before the first big one at the Royal College of Art. There were lots of things going on, so precise details are hazy.

The RCA gig, though, stands out. It featured a triple bill of us, Carol Grimes and Matumbe. Each band did a set, and then we jammed together at the end. By then RAR was mushrooming, and the atmosphere of a movement on the move and scenting victory was fantastic. The great thing was the energy and optimism of the music and audience coming together. It was really transcendental, showed how music can be used as a focus and spiritual refresher.

Then we played the May Day 1977 gig at the Roundhouse, and I think there were other gigs in between. We were quite busy, and played other benefits as well as clubs/pubs etc.

I also got invited to an organising meeting, I think mainly of musicians, to see what bands needed, how to get in touch with people wanting to play etc. It was held in the old North London Polytechnic, in Holloway Road. A lot of the discussion was around forming an alternative agency, but it was finally agreed that this should come down the line. I remember the focus on fighting racism needed to be underlined. I didn't do any more on the organising side as I thought it would be too much of a conflict of interest with me hustling gigs for the band. Later I would help organise the ANL.

We played more gigs after the Roundhouse, always in the same format. Bands playing different types of music would play their sets and then jam together afterwards. By then, RAR had spread into the colleges and established rock venues, and loads of local community type gigs had sprang up.

Looking back, RAR's success was built on a strong centre focused on achieveing concrete ends, providing propaganda/ encouragement/help for anybody willing to have a go. With activity at the centre, all sorts of debates could go on without paralysing the movement. A similar, but not identical model, later lay behind the success of the ANL, and it worked brilliantly.

● Limousine at the Roundhouse May 1977

The early gigs, with Carol Grimes, Limousine and Matumbe, featured working musicians playing in established genres. Round this, scores of young bands got the confidence to pour their energy into RAR, and through this punk rock connection, bigger names got involved. It was a brilliant dialectic.

Now, RAR has got over-identified with punk. In fact, it was much better, with the older bands and experienced politicos, particularly from the SWP creating a basic structure which the younger bands grabbed hold of to power ahead. That the movement is at its creative best when the various sections work together is an old lesson, but needs re-enforcing.

The second thing to bear in mind is how divided Britain was, and still is. It really was two nations, and this was reflected in musical taste. We were essentially a club act with an eye on the circuit and a possible deal. When we started playing colleges, through RAR, many of our audiences had never heard of funk – I know this because people would ask us what we called it – let alone seen a band play it live, even though this was what many young workers danced to on a night out. It was hardly an undergound music, you could hear it at a local Mecca ballroom every Friday night, but played by DJ's rather than live bands. And that's without talking about race. RAR broke down these barriers with different types of bands jamming together and draping big banners round the venues listing different types of music and saying something like it's our music, keep it.

And it worked. But the understanding that that was what was necessary had to be there in the first place. And it had to be fought for and sustained, otherwise it could have gone horribly wrong.

At the Roundhouse, a section of the audience enthusiastically spat their appreciation of Limosine until the singer stopped the band dead and said something like "no white man spits on this black man". You could hear a pin drop. His quick unity speech cleared up any misunderstandings, the band snapped into gear and it ended up a brilliant gig with lots of the people dancing on stage and speaking to us afterwards.

Limousine's involvement ended when they weren't booked to play the second big carnival. The band felt used, and I felt stuck in the middle. It wasn't a major thing as Limousine continued to play for other left causes and got a toehold on a circuit that would soon disappear. RAR, meanwhile, hardly blinked, looked outwards and pulled tens of thousands into political activity. But I do think it was a minor mistake. The music Limousine played related to an audience which even the experienced left had difficulty reaching. One of our gigs in Hatfield, for example, pulled in dozens of apprentices who until then had been completely absent from political activity.

RAR was far and away the most successful political musical movement I have been involved with. At that time, playing funk always created good energy, it was a sort of movement in itself. But in the context of a RAR gig, this was magnified a hundredfold. And I know other musicians in other bands felt the same. What the musicians put into the music was taken up by the audience, magnified and given purpose instead of being siphoned off to make somebody else rich.

Finally, Red Saunders and Roger Huddle's joint letter to the *NME* revealed that the anti-racist mood in Britain once mobilized, was stronger that the racist filth pedaled by the Nazis and sections of the establishment. The organisation it gave birth to tapped into a reservoir of creativity and forged an anti-racist wedge. That is probably the most important lesson of all.

● Mike Holbart (tenor) Quintet 2016

May 6, 1978
MUSICAL EXPRESS
DYLAN CONCERTS
Full booking details
BO DIDDLEY
TELEVISION
Anti Nazi League
NAZI
PAGES 31,32,33

Paul Holborow

National Organiser, Anti Nazi League 1977-82

The Anti Nazi League link with RAR

11am, 30 April 1978 Trafalgar Square. I was standing on the plinth with my young son surrounded by huge and rather threatening piles of the distinctive yellow ANL lollipops. It was drizzling slightly and the Square was ominously empty. Suddenly huge crowds of mainly young people came from every direction and with in half an hour thousands had filled every available space. After a few speeches we moved off on a five-mile march to Victoria Park in East London where the first great ANL carnival of 80,000 people took place. The Anti Nazi League and Rock Against Racism had arrived at a crucial moment in British politics. The impact of this unique and hugely exciting development still reverberates today with the continued marginalisation of the Nazis in Britain. The contrast with many countries in Europe today with the growth of far right and neo Nazi parties right could not be greater. How did this come about?

The circumstances in 1978 were daunting. In May 1978 the National Front had polled 119,063 votes in the Greater London Council elections (5% compared with 0.5% in 1973) beating the Liberals into third place in 33 constituencies. An Essex University survey suggested that support for the NF would give it 25 MPs under proportional representation. This significant performance was the culmination of a ten year strategy by the NF to rebrand itself by attempting to shed its Nazi past and presenting itself as a respectable party entitled to a place in the mainstream of the British political spectrum. This approach had met with considerable success. In a by-election in 1973 for example, it polled 16.2 %. By 1976 in local elections in Blackburn the combined Nazi vote was 38%. In Leicester NF candidates won on average 18.5% of the vote. In a parliamentary by-election in 1976 in Deptford in south London the combined Nazi vote was 44% ahead of the successful labour candidate on 43%. This progress had been made possible by the actions of Labour in office who had caved into the demands of the International Monetary Fund. The result was huge cuts in the welfare, housing and health budgets; unemployment between 1974-7 nearly tripled to 1.6 million. In addition there were shameful campaigns in the media against unfortunate Asians who had been expelled first from Uganda and then Malawi, which the NF ruthlessly exploited.

But it was not just in elections that the NF made headway. In Leicester at Imperial Typewriters in 1973 for example, white workers first scabbed on their striking Asian colleagues and then went on strike in protest at their reinstatement. In the North London Divisional Post Office, the NF could raise enough money for deposits in eight parliamentary constituencies and a number of postal workers stood as NF candidates in local elections in 1979. The biggest NF branch in the country was to be found in the largest car factory (Longbridge, Birmingham) and it had members in both rail unions. In 1977 the NF felt confident enough to set up a youth wing with a paper *Bulldog* which encouraged its supporters

"to hold pickets outside schools with posters naming teachers considered to be left wing. It also suggested they should display photographs of the teachers concerned"

Several teachers were targeted in East London and elsewhere in this way. But perhaps the most disturbing measure of the advance the ideas of the NF was in the spring of 1977 when the police in Lewisham staged Operation 39 PNH. PNH stood for Police Nigger Hunt which led to early morning raids when young black men were rounded up and charged with conspiracy to rob. During their subsequent trial and defence campaign, they were constantly attacked and harassed by NF supporters and the police.

The NF however did not have it all their own way. As its influence grew in the 1970s, anti-fascists and the hard left, in which the SWP and its forerunner the International Socialists was the most active and influential, constantly attempted to prevent marches and meetings of the NF by physically breaking them up and preventing them from taking place. Both fascists and anti-fascists understood what was at stake in this no platform strategy. John Tyndall, the leader of the NF, learning from his mentor Adolf Hitler proclaimed.

"I believe our great marches, with drums and flags and banners have a hypnotic effect on the public and immense effect in solidifying the allegiance of our followers, so that their enthusiasm can be sustained."

This strategy was put the test at Lewisham in August 1978 when the NF tried to build on their previous activity and stage a highly provocative march through one of London's most multiracial boroughs with a large Afro Caribbean community. Around 10,000 protesters gathered at Clifton Rise, New Cross for which the SWP with other anti- racists had energetically organised in the preceding two or three weeks. The counter

demonstration was drawn from every section of the community – black and white, old and young, manual and white collar council workers, bus workers and taxi drivers, students and teachers and many more. Even now I vividly remember seeing the NF 'Honour Guard' with union jacks on spear – like poles swing into new Cross High Street preceded by a large detachment of mounted police. Our counter demonstration let fly a volley of missiles, broke through the police lines protecting the fascists and cut the march in two, leaving the 'master race' scuttling from shop doorway to shop doorway seeking cover. The police had no option but to quickly divert and disperse it. They then proceeded to violently attack our counter demonstration using riot shields on mainland Britain for the first time, resulting in 214 arrests. Unfortunately there were not just physical attacks from the police. The Labour Party in the person of its leading left wing figure, Michael Foot, denounced us as 'red fascists' and one trade union leader said there was 'little to choose between the SWP and the NF – both are political bootboys'!
But the battle of Lewisham was a famous victory and it was from this that the Anti -Nazi League emerged. It demonstrated conclusively that wide sections of the British population were horrified at the rise of the Nazis and were prepared to oppose them in whatever way seemed appropriate. What was required was the rapid creation of an organisation to stop them in their tracks by relentlessly exposing their Nazi origins and denying them a breakthrough into mainstream British politics. Drawing on the experience of Germany in the 1930's about which the Russian revolutionary Leon Trotsky produced some his most telling and brilliant writings, and the historic 'they shall not Pass' battle of Cable Street when Mosley's blackshirts were prevented from marching through the East End in 1936, the SWP threw itself into the task.

We approached key figures in the Labour Party who could see that the official line was entirely inadequate to meet the NF challenge. These included Peter Hain, who brought his experience from the highly successful campaign against the South African UK rugby tour based on direct action and had just joined the Labour Party from the young Liberals; Neil Kinnock, then a rebellious young left wing labour MP from the mining valleys of South Wales; the late and fondly remembered actor and activist Miriam Karlin, who was close to sections of the Jewish community; Ernie Roberts, the assistant General Secretary of one of the Britain's largest trade unions; and key representatives of the Indian Workers Association and Afro-Caribbean communities.
Having brought together this united front nationally, three months after the battle of Lewisham, the SWP worked hard to recreate a similar structure locally which was inclusive, active and imaginative. On this basis ANL branches mushroomed all over the country and provided the organisation to produce the huge Carnival Against Nazis at Victoria Park

in East London in April 1978. This was achieved in a number of ways. The appeal of the ANL encouraged anybody who wanted to oppose the NF to join and become involved – whether leafleting a street, setting up an ANL group, attending a meeting or putting up a few posters or taking out a membership card and donating money. The ANL was a single-issue campaign that emphasised what united people rather than their differences. So, for example, opposition to all immigration controls, which many on the hard left including the SWP rightly in my view advocated, was not a condition of ANL membership, which was a much broader organisation.

In addition the ANL had a straightforward message – the National Front is a Nazi Front – Don't vote Nazi. This immediately and directly challenged the NF's claim to respectability. It relentlessly exposed the direct links between the present leaders of the NF and their immediate Nazi past and Nazi affiliations. It delivered this message in fresh and eye-catching leaflets. All the ANL material – badges, leaflets, posters had a vigorous and dynamic look to them. This was the left reaching beyond the usual propaganda format combining an unambiguous message with new and striking design. This approach was realised through the brilliance of the first and youngest designer of the *Sunday Times* colour supplement, David King. It was David who designed the iconic RAR badge in 1976. This was followed a year later with a set of stunning ANL posters and leaflets which blew people away with the intensity of colour with the bright reds and deep browns and blacks. Their effect was even more striking through his bold use of photomontage which was strongly influenced by the anti-Nazi exponent of photomontage in the 1930's in Germany, John Heartfield. Wherever the NF attempted to organise – local and council elections, meetings, street stalls, a barrage of high quality propaganda met them. Nobody knows the exact number but the overall figure of leaflets and posters ran into many millions. The large cost of printing and materials was met by a huge flow of donations ranging from many working people and community activists and trade unionists a to a few wealthy businessmen.

This huge propaganda push was closely linked to activity. The ANL and RAR triggered a great wave of anti-Nazi activity in many towns and cities, on housing estates, in workplaces, on football terraces, in universities and colleges and a host of other places both predictable and less so. So for example, when a former Waffen SS Officer held a press conference in London to launch his memoirs, an intruder brandishing the poster Never Again rudely interrupted it – Stop the Nazi NF against a background of Auschwitz – behind him. This made the lead story for the *News at Ten* that night. The posters made early appearance when there was disruption in the High Court as a judge acquitted a Nazi councillor who following the murder of an ten year old Asian boy, had said 'One down, a million to go'. The ANL thought creatively and constantly sought to release the untapped energy and talents of many thousands of people. The result was that the ANL became an immensely popular movement very quickly. Its approach was summed up in the phrase – let 100 flowers bloom. In 1978 ANL groups were organised among school students, entertainers, footballers including the then notorious Chelsea and Leeds clubs, skateboarders, vegetarians, two Halifax night clubs to name but a few. This process was helped along by the public support of leading figures from the world of entertainment (comedian Dave Allen and Warren Mitchell) and football such as Brian Clough and Jackie Charlton.

But under the influence of socialists, the ANL also argued for special emphasis among organised workers not only because it was here that the NF had made some inroads but also it was the working class that had most to fear from fascism (as the experience in the thirties showed) and it was the force that could provide the most effective opposition to it. Groups of ANL supporters were formed in the Civil Servants Union (CPSA), among fire fighters, bus workers, and rail workers. Teachers in the NUT held a 1000-strong ANL rally and they then produced teaching packs exposing the present dangers of fascism. Mineworkers too held a conference to combat the growth of the NF and 60,000 miners in Yorkshire went to work on a designated day in May 1978 with the distinctive ANL yellow sticker on their pit helmets. Workers at the Longbridge car plant formed an ANL group, as did many others in factories, workplaces and offices up and down the country.

The catalyst for this explosion of self-activity had three aspects – the victory at Lewisham, the swift creation of the united front of Anti Nazi League and the great Anti Nazi League/RAR carnivals that were organised in the summer and early autumn of 1978. The first and decisive one took place in Victoria Park in London's East End – itself a daring choice of venue given the historic relative strength of the NF in the area. Dockers and Smithfield meat porters after all, had marched in support of Enoch Powell and against immigration a few years previously. The NF had an established sales pitch at the top of Brick Lane, the heart of the Bengali community, and there were several white only pubs in Hoxton, Bethnal Green and Newham. We were also told that young people would only turn up to the concert and not be interested in marching the five miles from Trafalgar Square. But there is always an element of the uncertain in politics – nobody could be sure that the carnival would come off. The excitement around the ANL and RAR gave us the confidence to break new ground. The result was spectacular and way beyond even our expectations. The sheer size, young composition and joyful vibrancy of the event – all against a sea of bright yellow ANL lollipops (designed by David King) took your breath away. The combination of the ANL and RAR had delivered a hammer blow against the Nazis on their own turf. The ANL offered the political framework and organisation to make such an event possible; RAR was vital to this process through their reputation established eighteen months previously with the publication of a letter in the *New Musical Express*. The letter denounced Eric Clapton, the blues guitarist, for expressing support for Enoch Powell, a Tory former cabinet member most associated with anti-immigrant racism through his infamous 'Rivers of Blood speech' in April 1968. RAR was born through the wide support that the statement received from young people, many attracted to the emerging trend of punk music, and through RAR to the anti-Nazi cause – by no means a foregone conclusion at the time. This fusion was clear for all to see when Jimmy Pursey of the punk band Sham 69 and Misty in Roots, a Rasta band from Southall, played together at the final set of a RAR gig in Camden. The opposition to the Nazis had taken a huge and qualitative leap forward – a magnificent and vitally necessary achievement by tens of thousands of ordinary people from across Britain. To this day socialists and activists are rightly proud of what they did to help make it happen. As Tariq Ali, the anti-Vietnam War campaigner and socialist wrote at the time "Hats off to the SWP".

But the success of the carnival achieved something as important. After nearly a decade of steady advance by the NF, anti-racists who often felt isolated in their workplace or where they lived, now felt immeasurably more confident to take on the racist arguments. Whereas previously the racist remarks had gone unchallenged, now individuals who found strong support from their colleagues at work and their neighbours took it up. As a consequence there was not only the rapid growth of ANL groups and branches described above but further carnivals were organised with RAR elsewhere in the country. Manchester for example saw around 35,000 marching and attending, Edinburgh (8,000) Southampton (5,000) Cardiff (2,000). In early autumn the final carnival that year took place in London – this time from Hyde Park to Brockwell Park in south London. The main speaker on that occasion was the serving Labour cabinet member Tony Benn.

But the acid test for the Anti Nazi League came with the General Election in 1979. Would the NF be able to carry out their stated aim of mounting a serious challenge and at least raise the prospect of gaining seats in the near future in parliament itself? This after all was their target following their success in the GLC elections two years earlier. Could the ANL rise to the challenge by delivering Don't Vote Nazi leaflets to millions of households exposing the NF's Nazi past as it had been created to do? The 1979 election results produced a resounding answer – they were disastrous for the NF. The NF fielded 303 candidates polling a total of 191,719 votes or 1.5% of the electorate where they stood. In the 1974 election they polled 1,265 per candidate; in 1979 that figure was halved to 633. Their share of the national vote rose from 0.4% in 1974 to 0.6% in 1979 – nowhere near the break through they had so confidently predicted only two years previously. Perhaps even more telling, in their alleged stronghold in East London, John Tyndall, leader of the NF and self-confessed admirer of Hitler, could not even match the NF's performance in the General Election of October 1974. Then the NF candidate polled 2,544 votes (9.3%). In 1979 Tyndall could only manage 1,978 votes (7.6%). The same pattern was repeated in neighbouring Bethnal Green and Bow, where their national organiser and most prominent figure, Martin Webster, also lost votes on their 1974 total – gaining 1,740 votes (6.1%) compared to 2,172 votes (7.6%) in 1974. Perhaps the definitive assessment of the success of the ANL was provided by Martin Webster himself when unsuccessfully defending a libel case brought against him by Peter Hain, one of the three original founder members of the ANL.

Peter recalls Webster told the court.

"He (Webster) was extremely bitter and remarkably candid. The picture he gave, and he clearly believed it, was that prior to 1977, the NF was unstoppable and he was well on the way to becoming Prime Minister. Then suddenly the ANL was everywhere and knocked hell out of them. It obviously still hurt. He said the sheer presence of the ANL had made it impossible to get NF members onto the streets, had dashed recruitment and cut away at their vote. It wasn't just the physical opposition to the marches; they had lost the propaganda war too".

Tom Robinson and Paul Holborow at press call for the Carnival.

A welcome consequence of this strategic defeat of the NF is that they split into several warring factions from which they took a decade to recover

At a more personal level, Darcus Howe, a leading black activist and writer, speaking at the memorial service for Dave Widgery, himself a founder of RAR, illustrated the impact of the Anti Nazi League. Darcus was the father of five children "four of which had grown up angry, forever fighting all around them". The fifth, he said had grown up "black and at ease". Darcus attributed her space to the Anti Nazi League in general and David Widgery in particular.

Perhaps, however, the most important legacy of the Anti Nazi League is to be found in a comparison between the present situation in France and Britain. Both countries have an unenviable history of vicious racism and discrimination. Both countries built their economic power on slavery and empire. Both countries are now in decline, facing a restless future of uncertainty and doubt. Why is it then that today France presents the appalling prospect of the fascist (albeit rebranded) Marine le Pen making a serious challenge for the French presidency next year having emerged as the largest party in the last Euro elections and done very well in this year's regional elections? Whereas in Britain the far Right have been confined to the margins and subsequent surges of the BNP, the successor to the NF, have been successfully beaten back? The answer is to be found in how fascism needs to be taken on. In France the response to the resistible rise of Marine Le Pen's father, Jean Marie in the mid 1980s was the promising formation of SOS Racisme. But it had a fatal flaw The dominant political influence was that of the ruling Socialist Party, which avoided the ANL strategy, which in the French context would have insisted on relentless exposure of the fascist origins and connections of the Front National combined with mass mobilisation to isolate and deny them entry into the mainstream of French politics. Instead SOS Racisme relied on winning public opinion, refused to directly challenge the FN wherever they appeared and did not seek to deny them a platform in mainstream politics. Unfortunately we are living the consequences today.

Later this year will see the fortieth anniversary of the foundation of RAR, followed next year by that of the ANL. We should undoubtedly celebrate what the ANL and RAR together jointly achieved then. However, the most important significance of what we achieved lies in what it can teach us for today. If the growing threat from the far right, which grows ever more menacing in far too many countries across Europe, is to be successfully countered and pushed back, we will need to draw again on the heady experience that we were lucky enough to live through in the UK in the late 1970s. It is unlikely too that the UK will be immune from similar developments and the need for a similar response will once again present itself.

This contribution draws heavily on an important article by Chanie Rosenberg in *International Socialism Journal* issue 39 for which many thanks.

Trudy Howson

Snapshots of an entertainer

I was born into a working class family in a mill town in the Ribble Valley in the north of England. By the time I was born, twelve of the thirteen mills in our town had closed down. Unemployment was the norm. Violence and brutality were commonplace. In this hotbed of frustration and bitterness, racism against the Pakistani community was rife. My grandfather "Wouldn't even keep black hens."

As a young isolated lesbian I understood the fear of being different and experienced how minority groups were ostracized and crushed.

I was one of the lucky ones. I was awarded a full bursary to study dancing/singing and acting in London. It paid not only for my fees but also my accommodation. I was the first person in my family to receive tertiary education.

I was seventeen when I arrived in London and, like so many of my generation, not so much re invented myself, but grew into the kind of person I wanted to be. In my case acquiring the skills and contacts that enabled me to work in the arts and entertainment industry for the whole of my professional life.

I voted Labour at my first election and have not (despite being troubled on occasion) voted anything else.

During the late 70's and through the 80's I sang and danced my way round London's commercial and alternative Theatre and Cabaret scene, interspersed with regular periods on the dole and touring with various theatre companies. I was active in a number of political campaigns, CND, Greenham, CHE, the Miners strike, regularly performing at fund raising events and rallies.

The reason I was attracted to Rock Against Racism was because it was a sound political philosophy mounted on music. I also felt I was able to make (small) amends for some of the things I had witnessed when I was living in Lancashire. I felt Rock Against Racism could make a difference to the way people thought and acted. Its events felt like a party, it made politics fun.

The groups I performed with during this period were: The Hackney Hot Taps. The Harmonettes. Sisterhood of Spit. The Guest Stars. The Doris Gay Sisters.

Now as the inaugural newly appointed LGBT Poet Laureate, a post I hold for three years (2016-19), I intend to continue to illuminate and dispel racism, homophobia and inequality through my poetry. The fight for Justice and Equality continues.

SCHWULE:

An interactive poem written for International Holocaust Day 2015. I'm wearing pink triangles inscribed with the (German & English) words used to describe homosexuals during the Gestapo Rule.

Remember those poor unfortunate men
Of every race, age and religion...the 175's.
Rounded up, incarcerated in concentration camps
Because they were Homosexual.

Respect those 20,000 men,
Who lost their friends, families and businesses,
Who were beaten, tortured and castrated.
Labelled with a pink triangle...the lowest of the low.

Resolve to never again return
To those dark days of terror and evil.
Fight injustice and inequality,
Encourage love, regardless of race or gender.

I can choose to remove these labels,
Live and love freely, be Glad to be Gay.
Those men were not so fortunate.
Remember, Respect and Honour them today.

Bob Humm

lived in Deptford for nineteen years from the early 1970s. After leaving Goldsmiths, and seeing the rise of the National Front, he became active in anti-racist politics. He was working at the SW Printshop when RAR was born and became involved in the production of *Temporary Hoarding*. He has now resumed his career as an artist and lives in Hastings.

Scary times – nazi parties get 44% of votes in Deptford by-election; police target black youth in New Cross and Lewisham; racist attacks on the streets (Nigerian student Terry Botu visciously beaten outside a Deptford pub); Prince Charles visits the Moonshot Club in New Cross. But there was RAR about to happen.

The Albany Empire, a radical theatre and music venue in Creek Road, Deptford, had a strong anti-racist tradition and lent some of its expertise and experience to RAR (notably through the late Kathy Crossan). And what nights they were – punk bands and reggae bands, African drummers and boogie bands, rock bands and sound systems. All music. The mix was black and white, and famous (slightly) and unknown local bands and musicians, everyone wanted to be there and everyone loved it. Badges sold out, each issue of *Temporary Hoarding* was eagerly awaited (I was working at the printshop and could report on the progress of the next copy). And some people just wanted to talk about music and politics and feel part of it.

The list of bands that played was impressive – Misty in Roots and The Ruts, Menace, Patrik Fitzgerald, Sledgehammer Sounds, Reggae Regular, the Cortinas – even Deptford's most famous son, Mark Perry, came along with his band Alternative TV, and we recorded an interview with him for *TH*.

On one memorable night, when the UK Subs were playing, the excitement was intense and Charlie Harper lost control of his microphone as the fans took over the show. Nothing got out of control, Charlie got his microphone back, the band got the stage back and the good time continued. At the end of the night when the lights went on they revealed that the floor had been decorated with spray paint.

Sadly in July 1978 the Albany was burnt down, a sign of just how important its work and that of RAR were that the racists saw it as such a threat. But it had played such an important part in the life of Deptford and all the people who went there, the music, the politics, the feeling of togetherness and knowing that things could change.

Jon Langford

artist, pop star and Welshman – left Leeds for Chicago, where The Mekons keep going. In April 2016 he performed at Berniepalooza!, a fundraising concert in support of Bernie Sanders presidential campaign during the Illinois Democratic Primaries.

I thought the RAR Club at Leeds Poly was the epitome of punk DIY make-your-own-entertainment. Friday nights with beer and loud music and wall to wall art students and commies. Met a lot of people for the first time in that room! We played early Mekons and Delta 5 shows there and I remember Mekon Delta 4 (The Mekons Gang of Four collaboration) and 100 Flowers Bloom with Mick Wixey our manager and Andy Sharpe doing strange improvised sets... Best band ever were Problemz featuring groovy Tom Lisle with their anthem of the times 'System Stinks!' The best period of gritty Northern political punk before we all signed to poxy London record labels".

— Jon Langford, Chicago, 12 April 2016.

The Mekons: Jon is second on right

Graham Larkbey

In the 1970s I was living in Swansea, where Nazis, the far Right and racism weren't really prominent issues at the time. With South Wales' strong Labour traditions, even the Tories didn't get a look in, let alone anyone more extreme, and the nearest black person was probably in Cardiff. The only occasions when any unpleasantness of that nature surfaced was if visiting football teams playing Swansea City fielded a black player, who would inevitably be subjected to barracking from the North Bank and the sort of casual racism (monkey chants, bananas, etc) that was commonplace and unremarkable everywhere back then. (A few years later, the Swans themselves acquired a black player, Steve Mardenborough. The home fans loved him; he was their black player.)

Nonetheless, there were people around Swansea who were aware of the wider issues and wanted to do something about them. My first memory in that direction is of handing out anti-Nazi leaflets to bemused shoppers in Swansea city centre with my friend Peter Dawson. Such was the lack of general awareness that at least one person initially thought we were handing out pro-Nazi propaganda – not that that seemed to concern them unduly.

It must have been shortly after this that our friend Nigel Ramsell told us that this organisation Rock Against Racism had been formed to fight racism and the Nazis through music, and were putting on this great reggae band called Misty (I don't think they'd yet acquired the 'in Roots' tag) at the old Swansea Grammar School (former alma mater of Dylan Thomas, and where his father had taught English). I went along with him; I'd never seen a live reggae band before, and I was knocked out. Naturally there were plenty of badges and leaflets around to explain RAR and spread the word.

By this time I had a band of my own (Sleever, bringing pub rock and even a dash of punk to an area largely still living in a heavy-rock/denim/endless guitar jamming timewarp), and people were starting to organise RAR gigs in the Swansea area. A primary focus of this activity was the city's small Virgin Records shop, presided over by everybody's heart-throb Wendy May (subsequently of the Boothill Foot-Tappers and regular DJ at the Town & Country Club in London) where the small coterie of local punks etc would gather to listen to records, form and dissolve bands and generally hang out. Wendy and others organised a RAR gig at a tiny former chapel (now an art gallery) down in the old docks area (then still undeveloped and derelict), around the corner from the legendary Circles (aka Pandora's or Dirty Dora's), gloriously scuzzy, carpet-sticky and the only venue in town which would touch visiting punk bands including Crass and Swansea's own Page Three/Four, led by subsequent Class War figurehead Ian Bone.

But I digress – Wendy & co asked Sleever if we would play at the RAR gig, supporting no-nonsense Carmarthen rockers The Inmates and a punky young singer-songwriter called Patrik Fitzgerald. He was a lovely guy, quite shy offstage, and hesitantly asked me if I'd tune his acoustic guitar for him as he wasn't very good at doing it. I duly obliged; as I recall, it had nylon strings and I was terrified of breaking one (something I was renowned for at the time). He went down very well with songs like 'Safety Pin Stuck In My Heart'; the relatively few local punks used to get a hard time around town from more traditional types so they could relate to his mix of vulnerability and defiance.

My memories of playing that night are that we weren't very good and suffered more than our usual ration of equipment problems, broken strings etc, but my mate Bob Cotterill remembers me unveiling the famous Frog Piano for one number. This was a child's plastic toy with eight keys, surmounted by eight frogs whose mouths opened as you pressed the keys. I still have it but the frogs were forced to retire some years ago. When this improbable device was produced, Bob was convinced I would get lynched by enraged punks, but they loved it. Additionally, our drummer John Harvey remembers me having to be dissuaded from a plan to equip myself with a tennis racquet and balls, to hit into the audience as a protest against the tennis player Buster Mottram, who was minorly famous at the time. Mottram was an odious little squirt who had declared his support for Enoch Powell and the National Front; he clearly remained a prize d*ckhead as in 2008 he was drummed out of UKIP for trying to broker a tie-up with the BNP. Bizarrely, he also formed a songwriting partnership with Kenny Lynch, who is black. Anyway, back to the gig – it was rounded off by the Inmates (not the more famous later band of that name) who rocked hard and were excellent. They certainly blew us offstage that night.

● Graham (in hat) fronting the Escape Committee, Leytonstone 2014

That about rounds off my own RAR memories; there may well have been other gigs around Swansea and I have a vague memory of one at the White Swan featuring the city's younger punk bands. By now Sleever had split (protractedly and messily) and I'd switched from playing in rock bands to writing about them for the weekly local paper, the *Herald of Wales*. The archives probably contain my reviews of other RAR gigs I've long since forgotten, but I lent all my cuttings to a guy called Paul Nicholas who was supposedly writing a book about the Swansea rock scene and I haven't seen them since.

Richard Lees / Hull RAR artist in residence

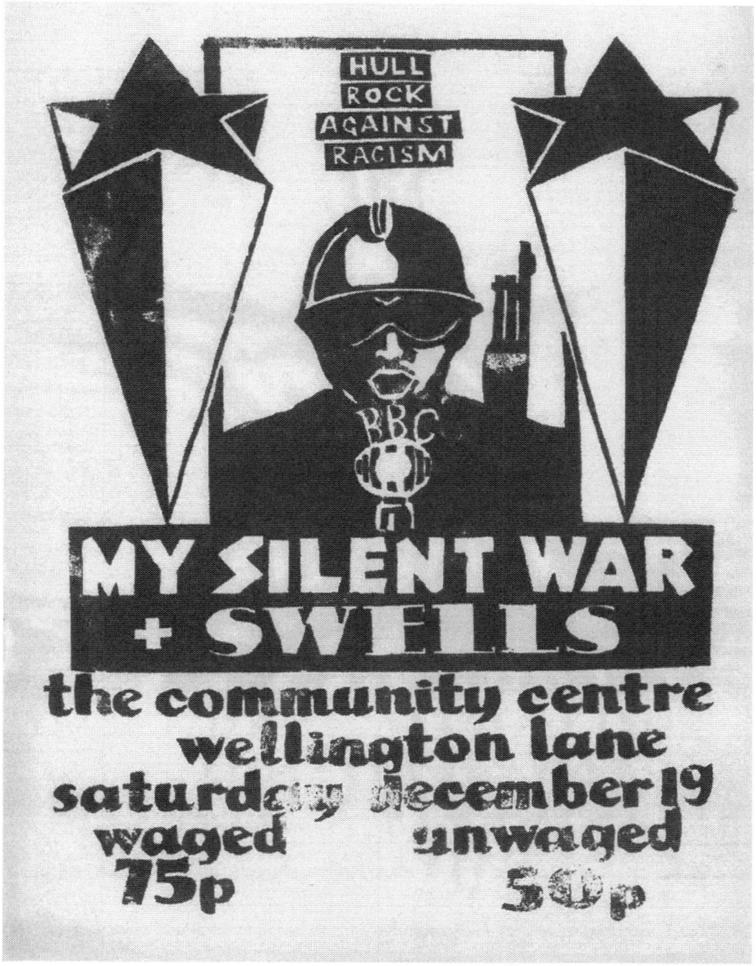

● Fresh from his Raw, Rough and Ranting tour with Attilla the Stockbroker, Seething (Steven) Wells gave us the best of his ranting verse, including Godzilla V the Tetley Bittermen and Cadillacs in Bradford. For the poster, I adapted a Paris 68 image which seemed to contradict/ironically comment on the name of the headline act, *My Silent War*.

● *Bushfire,* one of my favourite poster designs, was an adaptation of a woodcut by the German Expressionist printmaker, Karl Schmidt-Rottluff. The band itself, Hull's only reggae band, featuring Hull's only Rastafarian, Mark Douglas, on bass and vocals, went on to record with local label Vital Records. Bocks o' Phroggs were a popular and committed band from Bridlington who went on to play numerous political/benefit gigs, including Rock Against Thatcher at Hull College.

● A rare original design (more or less) for the Undesirable Aliens/ Abstracts gig. Our screenprint runs averaged 200 plus posters which we fly posted all over Hull, often in blocks of 4 -8 posters per site. Over the three years of my involvement, we created a powerful and prolonged anti racist street art presence in the city, just as important as the events they promoted.

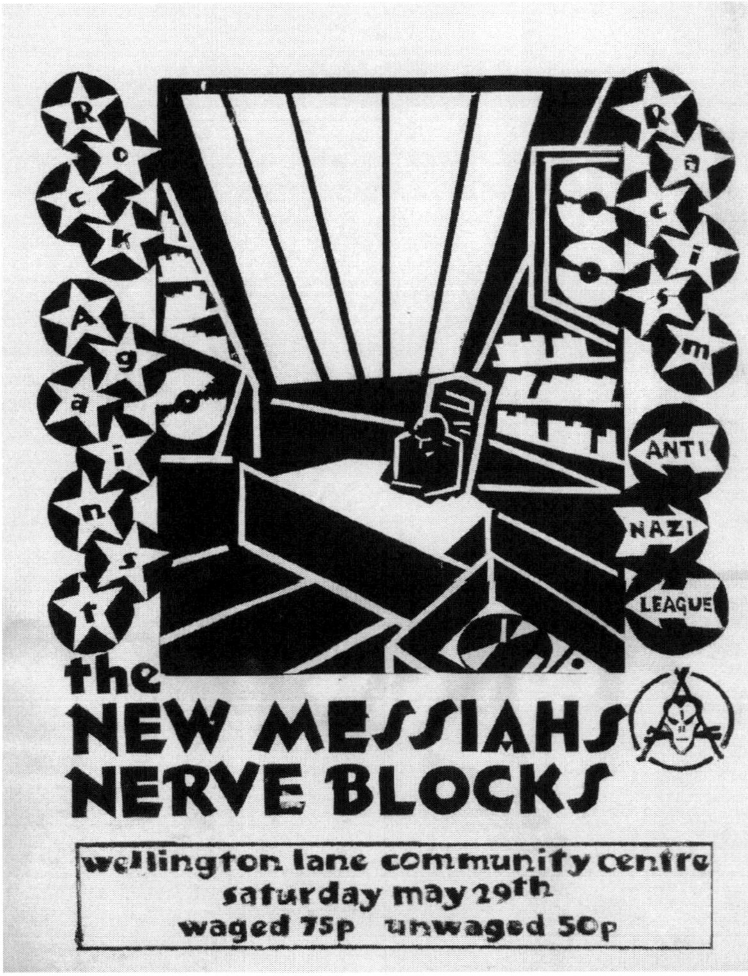

● The New Messiahs/Nerve Blocks gig was our last at the Community Centre on Welly Lane. Members of Hull RAR, myself included, were on the Centre management committee and helped organise other events, like Bank Holiday Carnivals and Thatcher-burning bonfire nights. As revolutionaries, we had followed the community activism path advocated by Sheila Rowbotham, among others, in *Beyond the Fragments*, with a great deal of success in radicalising and uniting a community to resist and defeat the National Front fascist threat.

Bob Light

Rock Against Racism memories

It really was the worst of times. 1976 was like living in a war zone. I lived in Plaistow in the East End borough of Newham, and I worked in the local Royal Docks and the National Front and their psycho- wing the British Movement had a small but very loud and very aggressive base there. They were never really a mass organisation (in a by-election in 1974 the NF polled nearly 12% in Newham) but the Nazis amped up white bigotry and created an atmosphere on the streets of violence and intimidation. This was a time when swivel-eyed strangers felt they had the right to engage you in conversation at a bus stop and launch into foul-mouthed fascist bullshit about "them". You always knew exactly what was meant and they simply assumed you would agree.

The Front were of course unwashable bullies so they were generally wary of the Afro-Caribbean community, because they had a tendency to fight back. But any Asian person on the street especially if they were female, alone or otherwise vulnerable was likely to be the target of abuse, even physical attack. It was here in Newham that the most pernicious verb in the English language "paki-bashing" came into currency; it was no accident that the first serious report on racism in Newham in 1978 was called *Blood on the Streets*.

I was also a member of the SWP (and still am) and to be a socialist and anti-racist during those times was also to be in harm's way every day. There were constant skirmishes with the NF fascists at work. They were still glorying in their success in pulling off the notorious Dockers' March for Enoch Powell in 1968 and I was especially unlucky that Nazi No 1 worked in my department of the Royal Docks. He was the usual ugly, fat and fortyish misfit, but this one had been in the army and he had a taste for putting it about. In the summer of 1976 a couple of black dockers were transferred from an isolated riverside wharf into our department, and the NF made a serious putsch to organise a white strike. As usual our union did absolutely nothing, and our shop stewards committee felt intimidated so they ducked the issue. For a while it looked like the NF might pull of another white coup and we only made the problem go away by some serious On the Waterfront 'persuasion'. Luckily for us it turned out that Big Nazi had been in the Mobile Bath Unit rather than the Paratroop Regiment.

Outside work the Nazis followed a low-intensity strategy of randomly attacking meetings and paper sales. And they also favoured screamed threats, the broken windows, the abusive notes (usually written in crayon) pushed through the door and the psychotic late night phone calls. They really did know where we lived.

A couple of days after my first daughter was born in August 1976 one of my old schoolmates, Pete Saunders, came round to see the baby. When he left to drive home he was tailed by a carload of fascists. Sadly for them Pete was an East End blowhard and he knew what to do – he led them into a cul-de-sac. Once they had got out of A&E and repaired the car windows the Nazis never tried that again. But it was scary stuff.

So we seemed to be in the firing line every minute of every day. More than anything else I recall being scared, being weary and having a gnawing feeling of being very close to the edge. I vividly remember a march through Newham organised by the Trades Council in early Summer 1976. It was originally a march against rising unemployment, but during the days leading up to the march, there had been yet-another racial attack so the march shape-shifted into a protest against racist violence. As we walked from Canning Town to a park in East Ham we were barracked and jeered and gobbed at by a snarling mob of white trash. Cersei's March of Shame had nothing on this (except maybe the nudity). At the end I felt proud to have taken part, but sullied and ashamed that the area I had grown up in was the scene of such a fascist goat fuck. And more than anything else I felt humiliated. It was a summer of fear and loathing alright.

But 1977 was to become the best of times.

That was the chase to the bottom that the Anti Nazi League and Rock Against Racism reversed. The launch of the ANL, with its incredible list of supporters, established a defensive line against the racial toxins that the NF and BM knuckle draggers spread. In 1976 it was oh-so-easy to be overwhelmed by the apparent relentlessness and savagery of the fascists. The ANL reminded us that we did not fight alone, that (to misquote Shelley) we are many and they are few.

But it was the founding of Rock Against Racism that turned defence into attack. It was RAR that electrified the anti-racist movement by inspiring and organising a new generation of anti-fascists who in the words of a later movement "loved music but hated racism". The fascists could get a couple of hundred thick-as-shit inadequates to gob at our local march. RAR could get hundreds of thousands of black and white women and men to march together for a world free of racism. RAR changed the order of the battle for the East End – and in a very real way it changed my life.

Apart from political alignments I had been long term friends with most of the signatories of the letter to the *NME* that launched RAR but my involvement was always on the margins. Ironically it was probably because of the experiences I wrote about above that those margins mainly involved security.

That's a very limited vantage point of course, but it was my perspective and I have three overarching memories of the heady days of RAR.

● The first was the very first RAR gig ever – held in the Princess Alice pub in Forest Gate. Compared to the achievements of the epic Carnivals, this was an almost absurdly small-scale initiative. I think it's fair to say that even the imaginations of Red and Roger had not yet grasped just what RAR could and would achieve.

But for those of us who lived in Newham (and I lived about a mile from the Alice) even a small-scale anti-racist events threw up the problem of security. The NF considered the East End as their "patch" and the BM held their weekly covens at a different pub a couple of hundred yards up the road. At least one of the local pubs was a no-go area for anyone with more than a millimetre of hair.

I can't recall the exact reason why the decision was made to have the first RAR gig in an unlikely (and fairly inaccessible) place like Forest Gate. Hackney, Camden even Central London would all have seemed more obvious choices. But looking back I would guess that it was Forest Gate precisely because the Nazis thought it was their own little Reich. We were taking the fight to the belly of the beasts.

I can recall going to book the pub though. The Alice was not one of the regular pubs we used for meetings – it was generally too big and a bit expensive. On top of that, one of the none-too-imaginative tactic, the Nazis regularly used was to frighten off a pub landlord either with a threatening phone call or a bomb threat. So we needed to forewarn the publican that the gig might be "warm" to give us some guarantee that it wouldn't be cancelled. In the event despite our fears, it turned out that the landlord was an Irish Republican who told us that as long as there was no fighting actually inside his two bars he didn't give a fuck about the Nazis. Which seemed fair enough.

We knew we could promise that because one big advantage the Alice had over other venues was that the function room was above the pub approached by a wide staircase with its own door to the street.

I cannot remember a thing about the publicity or anything else about the actual organisation of the gig itself. But I do remember only too well that we knew the gig would be in serious need of protection. Our

plan wasn't exactly D-Day – we knew that if the Bad Guys came we had to stop them on the stairs. If they got into the room, it would be bloody chaos, the police would be called and London's Finest would take the chance to beat up and arrest some Lefties, while letting their Fascist soulmates get away to their cars.
So on the night we had women and men placed on all four corners of the junction the Alice stood on to warn us if the Nazis hordes were coming, and we had a reception committee waiting for them at the top of the stairs. Just in case that proved inadequate, we had six pick axe handles in a cricket bag and several cans of pepper spray that I had bought at a motorway service station in France.
In the event the Nazis bottled it (Im pleased to say they usually did) but for me the evening developed a rhythm that would become all too familiar during the RAR days. You could summarise our evening under the headings Tension, Apprehension and Frustration. The Tension was driven by fear – fear that the Nazis would come streaming up the stairs, fear that I would get seriously hurt, fear that I would let my fear get the better of me. But as the minutes and hours passed that turned to Tension – we knew we had to keep our guard, we knew we had to keep everyone on their toes, we knew we couldn't afford to drink, we knew we couldn't relax, we knew we couldn't enjoy the gig. Then, as the gig inside was turning into a glorious celebration of anti-racist fun courtesy of Carol Grimes and her band came frustration. Frustration that we had not been able to enjoy the evening and even more frustration that we had not been able to give the Nazis the fucking good hiding they certainly would have got.

● My second memory is from the first RAR/ANL carnival in Victoria Park. Once again we were tasked with protection duty – this time protecting the sound system and mixing desk. The story was (and I've never known if this was true) that it was Pink Floyd's sound system that they had loaned to RAR. Whoever owned it, the system had to be set up and tested on the Friday before the Sunday concert, which meant it was vulnerable to sabotage. Our job was to protect the mixing desk through Friday night and then through Saturday night till the carnival was over. Our instructions from Paul Holborow the ANL secretary were simple: no-one was to get at the mixing desk or stage.

For some reason a decision was made that we should all dress smartly, presumably in case the police made enquiries. We also made the obvious decision that there was to be no alcohol until the Carnival arrived on Sunday afternoon. So I spent two days of my life drinking flasks of milky tea in an open air park dressed in a Burberry trench coat. On the Friday night we were in full Tension mode. We had a couple of cars parked nearby so we could snatch an hour or twos sleep (we also had the cricket bag with us). But on Friday it was all very strange, very chilly and very tense. A couple of times we imagined that gangs, Nazis were entering the park, but it was always groups of razzers looking to have a sly piss. About 9 or 10 on the Saturday the professional stage crew arrived and we went home to sleep.

We had to be back in the park in the early evening and during Night 2 the Apprehension stage kicked in. We were never anything close to relaxed, but we did feel that we had it. And that (with maybe some accrued tiredness) introduced boredom into the mix. Sometime in the early hours one strategic genius decided we might make an excursion to relieve the tedium. The leading NF gauleiter in Tower Hamlets (the borough Victoria Park is in) was called Maurice Styles and he had a carpet shop in nearby Roman Road. So that night to cut the Apprehension we drove to Roman Road and squirted superglue in all the locks in Styles Carpets. The joke was that we had added another point to the ANL catechism that NF meant "no fun, no freedom, no future, no front door".

You have to remember that this was 25 years before the first brick-like mobile phone so, as the Carnival began to assemble in their tens of thousands, we few were over-dressed and stuck six miles away on a mixing desk platform. About 11 we started to hear a buzz that big numbers were in the square but it was all very tentative. As we passed midday (when the march was due to leave) the word was that it was very big, then we were told it was massive, then we heard that the head of the march was nearing the park while the tail was still in the square. Then as the first marchers arrived in the park with those amazing giant walking puppets we knew that we were present at a political triumph. So – perhaps unwisely given the euphoria, the excess of clothing and the very warm day – we decided that a couple of long-delayed beers were called for,. That was fine till The Clash were due to play. Their manager Bernie Rhodes was famous as an obnoxious wanker even in the tosser-rich world of music management and just before The Clash hit the stage, Rhodes turned up at the mixing desk and demanded (with his customary "do you know who I am" arrogance) that we let him in. Sadly for Bernie, he was directing his superciliousness at Mickey Fenn, who did not respond well. Rhodes found himself slapped and thrown bodily back into the crowd. Just to make sure that Rhodes got the full message Mickey then proceeded to lift as many wheelchair fans as he could onto the mixing desk. Maybe the beer was a mistake.

● My final memory of RAR gigs was the Sham 69 RAR gig at Central London Poly. I googled this and discovered that it was in March 1978. I didn't remember that mainly because I have spent the 38 years since this night trying to erase all memories of that night. Brian Case wrote a fairly-famous review of the gig in the *NME*, but when I read it then and re-read it now I had the feeling that Brian was reporting from a parallel event. Jon Savage in his book *Englands Dreaming* says "the concert passed without any major trouble". I think Savage inhabits a parallel universe. What I remember was very different.

I remember that Sham 69 had always played catch-as-catch-can with RAR. On the one hand lead singer Jimmy Pursey seemed to be a genuine anti-racist, but on the other hand someone in or around the band knew that their hardcore fan base were core hard Nazis. Pursey went on stage at the first Carnival but not the band. So the Central London Poly RAR gig was a big deal. There was none of the Tension or Apprehension stuff on this night – we knew that Sham's Nazi fans would be there. What we didn't know was how to deal with them.
I remember that the gig was on a Friday night before the NF were due to hold a show-piece march in Ilford the next day. That marked a detectable hardening of the NF's fascism – Ilford had been chosen not because it was a black or Asian, but because it was a Jewish area. So before the gig began there was a meeting of ANL members to discuss stewarding the march. I think the plan was that these people would stay to steward the Sham gig – but that just didn't happen. They just went home.
I remember that as the NF and BM skinheads arrived (style tip: you could tell the difference by the colour of their laces and the number of eyeholes on the Doc Martin boots) there were no more than a handful of us. I remember being very very scared and wanting to just go home with all the other ANL people. Why me? Mary Larner, a RAR person on the door, searching everyone, the gig had to go on.
I remember that our job was to stop the Nazis creeping back stage, but that was made impossible because a couple of Sham guys kept waving various inbreeds through.
I remember that the mood backstage was fingernails-down-a-blackboard tense. There were gaggles of Nazis round the room trying (effortlessly) to look hard and threatening.
RAR held the gig together and at the end Sham and Misty united on the stage, jammed together.
I remember more than anything that the guys from Misty in Roots sat at a table in the middle of the room backstage playing dominoes. As the atmosphere got more and more intimidating, the Misty Rastas got louder and louder slapping down the doms and talking in the thickest Jamaican accent Southall-born men could muster. The NF and the BM Leader Group heroes didn't fancy any of that.
I still remember that game of doms as the single coolest thing I have ever seen in my life – before or since.

Liz Mackie

THE DARK MEMORY
Of an upstairs room at an East End pub gradually transformed by Carol Grimes and her band into a pounding soulful explosion of musical and political energy that had the crowd dancing all night.
The pride of Roger the catalyst, who organised it and was a friend of hers.

THE BRIGHT MEMORY
The amazing atomic fission of constantly interacting, splitting and re-forming visual and verbal energy that was Sid'nRuth'nWidgery, striking sparks off one another.
Generous and welcoming, drawing new energies in, forming new galaxies that split and re-formed in turn. Punks and Dreads and zine artists drawn into the nexus, releasing new forms and ideas and voices. Organisers and artists and fans and musicians bouncing off one another, reacting and creating in response to the dark, bigoted voices of racism and neo-Nazism, confronting and overpowering and transforming them in the overwhelming exuberance of ever bigger RaR events and an energy that spread and illuminated.
And what years was all of this?
You might remember better than me?

Hassan Mahamdallie

is a writer and playwright. He is Director of the Muslim Institute.

The 1970s in many ways seems like a world away – thankfully. I was born in 1961 at the old St George's Hospital, Hyde Park Corner, into a 'mixed race' family, which was then a fairly rare home set-up. In contrast, today, according to the latest census, five percent of the London population, over 400,000 people, are of mixed or dual heritage. My father, an Indian Muslim from Trinidad, had arrived six years earlier aboard the SS Colombie, a former World War Two troop carrier. His forebears had been indentured labourers, transported by

the British Empire from Calcutta to the Caribbean to work the sugar cane fields in the period following the abolition of slavery. He was the youngest of 14, and the only one of his siblings who was literate, and so was chosen to carry the family's hopes and be the one to strike out for 'the motherland'. My mother was 'white' working class, but like many 'white' Londoners, had foreign ancestors, in her case refugees caught in the crossfire of the 19th century Greek War of Independence who had fetched up in the Liverpool docks. My parents met, courted, got married and raised a mortgage on a house in Earlsfield, south west London, before moving to suburban Worcester Park, near Kingston Upon Thames, to raise their family.

My grandmother was an old-fashioned racist snob and opposed the union, provoking to my mum to turn her back on her family – she refused to speak to her mother for many years out of principle. My parents had twelve children in all, of which I am the second eldest. As a consequence, my father's wages were spread thin and money was always tight. The Mahamdallie family was looked down upon by many (though not all) of our 'respectable' neighbours for bringing the house prices down, being poor, for being 'too many' and for being an unruly mixed race brood. In those days for white women to marry 'a coloured' and produce 'half-caste' kids was widely seen as an unforgivable crossing of the race-line, with the offspring regarded as cursed and pitied for 'not being neither one nor the other'. A survey at the time showed that 91 percent of white Londoners polled disapproved of mixed marriages between 'whites and coloureds'. My mother was spat on in the street. Fortunately, she was a resilient woman, and taught her kids by example. My father was more passive and ultimately embittered; one of the Windrush generation who was conditioned over time, through the sapping experience of everyday racist slights and years of thwarted ambition, to keep his head down and provide for his family as best he could. He did attempt to hold onto his faith – I was taught Qur'an by the Pakistani Khan family up the road, and one of my earliest memories is going with him to the picturesque Shah Jahan mosque in Woking, Surrey.

So growing up we had to cope with, or resist if were able to, a certain level of racism on the streets and at school. But this uneasy, but not unhappy, existence was twisted into something darker in the late 1960s with the rise of Enoch Powell to the level of a national political figure and the revival of Britain's fascists in the wake of his race baiting speeches. I have a clear memory of the impact of Powell on my young consciousness. He was a threatening nightmare presence, whose incendiary speeches entered our house via the black and white telly. His glowering features and ponderous old-fashioned delivery invaded our living room and my imagination, sending shivers down my spine and eroding my self-worth. After all, weren't we kids just the same as the 'charming wide-eyed grinning piccaninis' that had so terrified the unnamed white pensioner cited by Powell in Birmingham during his April 1968 'Rivers of Blood' speech? We could be a noisy lot at times, just like the uncivilized West Indian neighbours in Garrett Lane, Earlsfield (where we had first lived!) whose incessant clamour had driven 'a widow with two young children' out of her family home – another example raised by Powell in a speech to the Rotary Clubs of London in November of that same year.

It must have been of some comfort to my parents to see Powell sacked from the Tory shadow cabinet by leader Edward Heath the day after the Rivers of Blood speech. Heath, repulsed by Powell's calculated hate-mongering, never let him back into the Tory fold. However, by January 1969, Heath was playing catch-up. In a speech in Walsall Heath demanding the Labour government 'tighten the grip' on immigration, so as to stop 'abuses of the present law – false identities, false ages, false claims to relationship, phony fiancés'. (That one also struck uncomfortably close to home – given the possibility that my father had originally entered Britain on someone else's passport, thereby falsifying his age so as to avoid national service). And who was sitting behind Heath that day? Enoch Powell, captured by a press photographer with a cadaverous grin stretched across his face. Heath's misery was compounded at the end of his speech by the audience member who asked "May I say how delighted we are that Mr Heath appears to have adopted many of the views of Enoch Powell?" (To be scrupulously fair to Heath, he could perhaps claim more honour than the Labour prime minister Harold Wilson, who had pre-empted Powell's Rivers of Blood speech by over a month; rushing through racist legislation against British passport-holding East African Asians in February 1968).

Paul Foot's superb and timely 1969 book *The Rise of Enoch Powell* peeled back the layers to reveal the venomous opportunist lurking behind the 'Mr Chips' schoolmaster image. In 1998, when Powell finally kicked the bucket, Foot, horrified by the respectful tones emanating across the parliamentary political spectrum, cut to the chase when he wrote: "the most important thing by far about Enoch Powell was that he was a racist pig of the most despicable variety".

Since Powell's death there has been a sustained effort by the Tory right and those around UKIP to rehabilitate the scoundrel so that they can be as violently racist as he actually was, and deny it at the same time. Like him, they have shifted from their victim's race to their 'different' culture. They have somewhat succeeded, given that Nigel Farage can brazenly stand in front of giant posters remarkably similar to 1930s Nazi anti-semitic propaganda, and deny even a scintilla of racist intent. But as Paul Foot wrote in his book on Powell: "The tiger of racialism, once unleashed, knows no master. It devours its liberators and its prey with equal ferocity".

At the time of Powell's ascendency (before the fall) all I knew was he wanted us, and families like us, out, and that we didn't belong in Britain, but I couldn't comprehend what we had done to deserve it. The racist storm he whipped up thus became another, if unpleasant, aspect of life. I didn't really think anything could be done about it. It just was. Powellism quickly manifested itself on the streets in gangs of fascist-inspired skinheads. (It would be a long time, years after the skinhead movement was brought to an end, before I managed to de-learn the deeply imbedded instinct to cross over the road when faced with a group of white men with short haircuts coming towards me.) One morning sometime in the '70s we awoke to find 'NF' painted in two-foot high letters on our garage door. We were an obvious target; given we were one of the few immigrant families in the neighbourhood. My dad silently painted it over, but it left an ugly stain that served as an enduring visual reminder to us kids that someone, somewhere, hated us enough to mark us out in the dead of night.

Although I was not politically aware, as a young teenager I did know that there were parts of London I shouldn't go. Hoxton was top of the list – somehow I heard that Hoxton Market on a Saturday was a no-go area, that it was run by a family headed by a NF monster named Derek Day (and his equally vile son Derek junior), and that if you were stupid enough to go there you frankly deserved to get your head punched in.

The rise of the National Front coincided with the punk rock explosion. My taste in music shifted from David Bowie and Stevie Wonder to The Clash, The Damned, The Adverts and The Vibrators. I laughed my head off when patriarchal belligerent drunk TV presenter Reg Grundy got trashed by The Pistols and their foulmouthed Bromley crew on the live *Today* show in December 1976, instantly ending his career. I took to walking up and down the Kings Road on a Saturday afternoon with other punks and going to gigs at the suffocatingly hot Marquee club in Soho, where, along with the punk and pub-rock bands, I first saw Linton Kwesi Johnson perform – his low, melodious tones perfectly complimented by a backing dub band fronted by the amazing musician/ producer Dennis Bovell. The parallel rise of punk and the 70s British live reggae scene, and the way the two genres were completely entwined, musically, socially, politically, and in terms of a shared audience, has yet to be given its proper significance in the struggles of the time. For example, I regarded Junior Murvin's 12" single 'Police and Thieves' as being perhaps the tune of 1977. Punk/Reggae – different roots, same outlook.

On Sunday nights I would go with my schoolmate Simon to The Greyhound pub on Park Lane, Croydon, which billed itself as Surrey's Premier New Wave Venue. It was an unpleasant dump, but it was the place to be if you were from south London and into punk. It reeked of stale beer, cigarettes and body odour even at the start of the night. There would be two or three bands on the bill, and between the sets the floor and chandeliers would vibrate with the heavy bass of a reggae sound-system. Every punk, new wave and pub-rock band around at the time, except the Sex Pistols and The Clash, squeezed onto the tiny stage at the Greyhound at some point to be spat on by the pogoing crowd. At the Greyhound I saw many bands including The Jam, the Buzzcocks, The Adverts, Generation X, The Damned, The Stranglers and Penetration, and a long list of other bands now largely forgotten. It was probably inevitable that punk, which began an inchoate youth revolt against a suffocating, no-hope, grey society and its conservative norms, would become a space the fascists would seek to dominate. Through 1977 and '78 there was always the possibility at gigs of violence from NF skins lurking in the shadows. There were bands that attracted an NF following whether they liked it or not – obviously Sham 69, The Cockney Rejects, and later on, the Ska groups. I vividly recall going to see The Selector at a north London pub venue called The Nashville in Kensington, west London, only to find myself in a room completely packed with drunken NF and British Movement skinheads, who, en mass chanted seig-heil and gave the fascist salute the instant the multi-racial two-tone band hit the stage. I quickly retired to the back of the pub. Pauline Black, the band's lead singer didn't have that option open to her, and did her best to face down the audience who simultaneously (and bizarrely as it seemed to me) loved her music and hated the colour of her skin. I also remember a Specials gig at the Electric Ballroom in Camden during which a fight broke out between NF and Red Skins, and watching in amazement as vocalist Neville Staples took the opportunity of an instrumental break in a song (quite possibly the band's cover of The Maytals' 'Monkey Man') to leap off the stage and land some righteous punches before clambering back in time to sing the next verse.

The worst skinhead violence I witnessed was in 1978 at a Sham 69 gig in Kingston's Coronation Halls. As soon as the band came on stage a huge contingent of NF skins erupted into violence. I remember looking towards the stage at singer Jimmy Pursey, who was pleading and weeping, attempted in vain to get the fighting to stop. The entire hall seemed to be one mass brawl, which soon spilled out into Kingston town centre. The final image I have in my mind is of Pursey leaping off the stage and running through the hall and out the (broken) front doors. The gig had lasted maybe ten minutes.

The best live band as far as I was concerned was The Clash, and the one closest to my emerging political outlook. I was luckily enough to see them a few times – at the Lyceum in The Strand, the Harlesden Roxy (supported by The Slits) and The Rainbow in Finsbury Park. When in early 1978 I heard that The Clash were headlining the ANL/RAR carnival in Victoria Park, Hackney, I was hundred percent determined to be there, even though I regarded East London as 'a bit dodgy'. On the morning of the carnival I marched with my mate Simon from Trafalgar Square to Victoria Park. I can still picture us marching past the old fascist haunt, the Bladebone pub on Bethnal Green Road where we shouted at a load of boozy demoralised Nazis standing outside. (It's now a Chinese takeaway). I wasn't at all used to seeing Nazis stripped of their menace – it gave me a good feeling and put a spring in my step. By the time we got to Victoria Park we had made our way to the head of the march, and were in time to see Poly Styrene and her band X Ray Spex open the gig with their anthem 'O Bondage Up Yours'. Later on we all had a sing along to Tom Robinson's hit single 'Glad to be Gay'. I remember Jimmy Pursey coming on stage, which was a surprise, although I couldn't hear what he was saying. By this time the park was overflowing, with people hanging from trees to try and get a decent view of the stage. The day was full of highlights, including the theatrical moment when a group appeared on stage draped and masked in white KKK outfits...Then out of the stunned silence rang the unmistakable ding, ding, ding of a cowbell that led-in Birmingham reggae band Steel Pulse's superb song of resistance 'Ku Klux Klan' – the cue for the group to whip off their pointy hoods, releasing their dreadlocks and launch into the tune, to the roar of the crowd.

Towards the end of the day a team of helpers started going round with buckets collecting for the ANL/RAR and selling the punk fanzine *Temporary Hoarding*. I looked beside, around and behind me at the sea of mostly white faces, and something clicked. I realised for the first time that there were lots of white people who hated racism and were prepared to fight it. Maybe Powell and NF skins weren't an inevitable part of life and could be fought and perhaps driven back or even overcome? It sounds naïve now as I recount it, but some kind of negative psychological burden was lifted that day in Vicky Park. It was an utter, complete revelation and changed my life forever.

Looking back, I can see that although the ANL/RAR was necessarily a defensive movement, it did positively change the course of British history, in ways its organisers and participants cannot have imagined at the time. The campaign was both the promise of, and roadmap towards, a radically different future – the opposite of the one Powell and the NF had in mind for us.

The unifying vision that drove the ANL/RAR has been made real in the grassroots, multifaceted multiculturalism from below that has steadily advanced in recent years, despite the efforts of hostile forces to and stunt its development and even reverse it. Anti-fascist activity, from the end of World War Two to recent times, adds up to a significant and decisive force in clearing the way for a rebirth of London (in particular) from the backward-looking and dangerously divided conurbation I recall growing up, into the free-flowing (if horrendously expensive) multicultural citadel its present inhabitants happily take for granted. For me, it means that whatever challenges we presently face, the 1970s still feels a world away.

Walking through Hoxton these days, I do yearn to somehow inform its trendy denizens about the sacrifice of those who fought to liberate the East End from fascist menace. But maybe for once, I should just be thankful that sometimes ignorance really is bliss.

Gered Mankowitz

Photographer

The gang at #41 Gt Windmill Street – a feeling of doing something, being part of something, believing in something.

I had been working as a photographer in the music business since 1963, and by the mid-sixties was working extensively with the Rolling Stones, with whom I toured America in 1965 and observed the segregation that still existed in many of the Southern states. I also worked with Jimi Hendrix in 1967 and heard from him about the infamous "Chitlin" circuit, where he had paid his dues with Little Richard, the Isley Brothers and Curtis Knight.

I had known Red Saunders since the mid-60s and had shared studios with him for most of that time, so, by 1977 I was both very close to him and well acquainted with the gang of friends, co-workers and followers who would gather at the studio towards the end of most days. From this extraordinary group of people the embryonic RAR was formed.

There had to be a response to the ghastly ramblings of the drunken Eric – who shot the sheriff, right?

Music had been such a major part of all our lives and most of it had originated with black American artists – soul, R&B, blues, Stax, Chess & Motown had all been part of the fabric to our existence and the potential of this amazing culture being sullied by some drunken musician ranting from the stage was unacceptable. Creative energy! Creative communication!! Creative unification!

Something had to be done to counter the rise of the NF, which was increasingly menacing our streets and in particular the youth. Music was the force that united so many of us that it seemed particularly important to try and utilise that energy to fight the creeping fascism that was steadily infiltrating society, taking advantage of the disillusioned and deprived who had endured years of recession and failing government.
I was on the fringe of the early discussions about how to respond, a small cog in what was fast becoming a movement, and before too long it seemed that everything was moving fast...

RAR seemed to embody everything that we had felt about music over the previous decade.
I tried to contribute what I could and took on a few tasks like lighting the concert at the Roundhouse on 1 May 1 1977 – the atmosphere around the venue was terrific with great crowds of supporters gathering outside and almost filling Chalk Farm road to the point that the traffic was backing up – what a fantastic night...
ASWAD arrived with an entire village of people, none of whom were very friendly, but they sounded and looked wonderful. I think they cooked their own food backstage...
I tried to light the gig as best I could, bathing the stage in the colours of Rasta – it didn't really matter though, the band and the entire show were wonderful anyway.

My daughter Jessica, aged just 17 months, grooving to the sounds in Vicky Park...
In April 1978 I helped organise equipment for the carnival, calling contacts and encouraging them to support us – I don't think it was difficult as the movement had become such a force that people seemed very happy to help!
It was a special time – being part of something so positive!

● Aswad

Derek & Judith Merrill

In the days of RAR we were teachers in Southall and Hanwell. At school we developed special interests in cultural diversity, anti-racism and community links. This extended beyond school to work with Southall community groups and musicians (Misty in Roots, The Ruts and The Enchanters) and from that to RAR events in West London, particularly Southall.

Over thirty years ago we moved to Ipswich and took with us the same principles to our continued work in education. Firm friends in Southall remain and through one have developed frequent links and friendships on the island of Grenada. We are now retired, enjoy our garden and still love music; Derek presents a weekly internet jazz show: www.cosmicjazz.co.uk

Roots Controllers in the Ghetto of the City

Sure and steadfast as a rock I shall stand but we nah run
See them ah come, see them ah come, but we nah run

These lyrics from 'See Them Ah Come', the first 12" inch single released by the Southall reggae band Misty in Roots in 1979 on their own People Unite label, are a poignant testament to the events in Southall, a place where in the words of another MIR tune Ghetto of the City:

Dreams are just an illusion
Pavements are not gold
Hatred, hatred and oppression
Down in the ghetto
Down, down, down in the ghetto of the city

Misty in Roots encapsulated, through their words and actions, how the communities had to struggle, stay strong and stand proud in order to make their voices heard. At the time there were a growing number of pioneering community groups active in West London, Southall in particular, who were working to combat racism, fight for justice and empower their communities. RAR locally operated alongside these groups, especially Southall musicians such as Misty in Roots, The Ruts and The Enchanters. These bands played a key role and ultimately contributed not only to RAR in West London but also made highly significant contributions to RAR nationally. Misty in Roots always delivered powerful and emotionally-charged music and played more RAR gigs than any other band. The Ruts gave high-energy show-stopping performances with their Southall crew in tow. The Southall punky-reggae party toured the land mashing up all the venues they visited; the name of the MIR record label was appropriate – People Unite!

How did the Southall/RAR connection come about? The story began at an Ealing meeting of the National Union of Teachers (NUT) in 1977. For once, the usually dreary meeting had a useful outcome. Martin Gerald told Derek Merrill (both young teachers) that he was planning a RAR gig at Ealing College. Derek responded that there was a girl in one of his classes in Southall whose brothers were in a reggae band and he would try to get them along. They came and that band was Misty in Roots. Misty had supported and learnt from Jamaican artist Nicky Thomas and played in roots clubs but the Ealing RAR gig introduced them to a wider audience. After inspirational sets at two Ealing College gigs reports were passed on from Ealing to the central RAR group that Misty in Roots were a top live reggae band.

At the end of 1977 central RAR organised their second night at the Royal College of Art and the reggae band Merger had to pull out. Red Saunders phoned Ealing RAR to see if Misty were available. They were; they came and with irresistible, uplifting roots reggae booked themselves into many future RAR gigs. Also on the bill that night was the punk band 999, who came with a crew of frenetic white youths from Southall, one of whom was heard still volubly proclaiming 'Southall' in April 2016 at an MIR night in Brighton.

Ealing RAR made a conscious decision to use local home grown bands and sound systems and there were plenty of quality bands who shared the RAR ethos and wanted to play. The RAR nights at Ealing College, the first on 23 July 1977 and the second on 15 October 1977, were sold out. The non-stop energy of the bands and the crowd reverberated throughout the Student Union Hall as never before. Besides Misty, there were performances by young musicians, many of whom were still at school. From Ealing came the new wave bands: The Decorators, Frumentry, Soho Rats and The Prisoners. From Southall came the first-ever public performance of the reggae band Black Enchanters.

Recent recollections of The Enchanters evoke the spirit of the times. Drummer Styx remembers RAR coming to the youth club they frequented to give them a booking for a week later. This required rehearsals every night to get them "fired up". That was not all they had

● MIR shown in performance with Pucky (Walford Tyson) lead singer and writer for the band who still leads the band today.

● Southall Carnival 22 July 1978. The Ruts were one of the local bands that performed that day and, as ever, put on a dynamic performance. Band members were Paul Fox (Foxy) on lead guitar, Malcolm Owen on vocals, John Jennings (aka Segs) on bass and Dave Ruffy on drums.

● Protest on a cold 7 November night 1978, against the Park ban outside Ealing Town Hall with RAR & 'Tories Are No Fun' placards.

to think about. There was the important question of what clothes to wear. Permission had to be sought from singer Bollo's dad for him to come along for such a late show. Schemes had to be devised for other members to climb back through hostel windows or to evade detection by parents when returning home after curfew.
Once a successful format had been created gigs were rolled out across the borough and if it was hard for an audience to come along then RAR went to them. For example, a gig was held for young people in a Southall school to make it accessible for Asian girls. Southall became the main hub and Southall Community Centre a key venue. It was here on 9 December 1977 that a RAR night featured Misty, XTC, The Decorators, Black Enchanters and The Ruts who appeared as a significant addition to the bill. Their lead guitarist Foxy and lead singer Malcolm Owen were from the area and the band were friends with Misty. They were later to release their first single In a Rut on Misty's People Unite label. That night they provided a raucous, non-stop performance which was the first of many for RAR, as word of their exploits, like those of Misty, went out from West London to wider RAR and then to other places nationwide. Malcolm Owen told the *New Musical Express (NME)* later "The spirit of the thing was great. So we obviously got into the thing of doing more RAR gigs "cos they seemed to be working. We had a really good audience"; (quoted in *Love In Vain: the Story of The Ruts & Ruts DC* by Roland Link). Drummer Ruffy looking back commented that as a teenager he realised that nearly all his favourite music was black music and that although they grew up poor and moved among potentially bad influences "music gave me a clear vision of what I wanted to do. It was obvious to me from an early age that racism has no logical argument and is there purely as a tool of oppression. When we were asked to participate in RAR shows there was no hesitation and it was a personal not a political choice to show my allegiance to the music which had saved me".

Around this time Misty, People Unite and friends established an Educational and Creative Arts Centre and occupied a large Georgian building; Number 6 Park View Road, Southall. As well as providing opportunities for young musicians, there were classes and workshops to re-address education with black history lessons, adult literacy classes, the growing of crops and cooking Ital foods. It became an inspirational centre.
Other local organisations championing minority ethnic groups also took a prominent lead in the community as the younger generation of black and Asian youths became increasingly frustrated and determined to make their voices heard (for example: Southall Black Sisters, Southall Youth Movement and the National Association of Asian Youth, while the local black bookshop Bogle L'Ouverture published the work of young

local writers). Southall was and still is a unique place. It is a borough with complex histories. Following direct labour recruitment from the late 1950s of Caribbean and Punjabi workers by local businesses, these workers were now the elders whose children were more forthright in challenging the racism they experienced regularly both from individuals and institutions. The racist murder of Gurdip Singh Chagger in 1976 led to mass anti-racist demonstrations in the streets. Southall Rights was established to speak out and fight for the legal and human rights of the communities.

● Inside 6 Park View Road, where, in March 1979, the police raided (not for the first time), arrested people, including band members of Misty in Roots, and mashed up the studio and the expensive equipment inside. Ealing Council not long after demolished the building as a way of trying to bring an end to People's Unite.

Plans were devised to hold a Southall Carnival Against Racism on 22 July 1978 that were supported by a wide spectrum of groups and organisations who attended weekly planning meetings. Besides RAR, these included People's Unite, Southall Youth Movement, Southall Black Sisters, Anti Nazi League, Southall Rights, Sikh Students Federation, Scope Southall, Ealing Community Relations Council, National Association of Asian Youth, Indian Workers Association, and others. With this wide base of support and knowledge, it became possible to host a free carnival for all ages which showcased the diverse local talent. West London RAR drew upon the experience and knowledge of local and national RAR events. The Carnival was provided for the community by the community to which everyone contributed whatever skill or resource they had; someone had access to a generator, another to scaffolding to build the stage. The strength and determination of the locality overcame the many obstacles that the organisers faced. When Ealing Borough Council on the very morning of the Carnival hand delivered to the home of RAR organisers, a previously unseen seven-page document in small print detailing all the conditions and terms which had to be signed and agree, ahead of the Carnival, everyone rallied round to make things happen. This document included the requirement to have a number of fire extinguishers – if not it would be a serious breach of contract. This was quickly resolved by a local fire extinguisher salesroom. After closing the shop, they simply emptied it of fire extinguishers and brought them all down to the Carnival for the afternoon.

● The Carnival itself was an eclectic mix of talent which was rolled out throughout the afternoon. There was a spectacular performance of traditional bhangra from the Great Indian Dancers; Karla Sona and Karla Preet provided contemporary bhangra sounds. Malcolm Owen from The Ruts electrified the event and even climbed the scaffold poles. Misty played a magnificent set and brought guests such as The Enchanters and Bongo Danny. The audience was a huge mix of peoples. Asian women turned up with their children and picnicked on the grass. There were punks playing cards with elderly Asian men. Steve Novy, a puppeteer, amused all the children. The mood was not just inclusive it was a coming together, and sharing. It felt great and we all thought this was just the beginning of even better things. The Local Tory Council, however, had other ideas. Despite RAR protests outside the Town Hall, (using the slogan 'Tories are no Fun'), the General Services Committee of the Council quickly banned all music in parks (except the Police Band!).

Tensions increased between the local community, especially the black community, and the police. People Unite had their property 'searched' by 13 plainclothes policemen in March 1979, resulting in serious damage to the property and the equipment inside. The local community responded with a picket on the police station, against police harassment later that month. On 23 April the National Front held a meeting in Southall Town Hall. Despite thousands of people protesting, the Council let the meeting go ahead and huge numbers of police, including the Special Patrol Group (SPG), were drafted into Southall, with horses, shields etc. The local Community turned out in their thousands and sat in the streets. The scene turned nasty when the police charged into the crowd. That day Blair Peach was killed, and many people badly injured, including Misty's manager Clarence Baker who suffered a fractured skull and blood clot on the brain. Number 6, which hosted a First Aid Centre, was raided and trashed by the police with thousands of pounds of Misty's musical equipment ruined. Amongst the injured was a first aid worker who was hit on the head by a police truncheon and hospitalised. 342 people were arrested, including innocent members of Misty; their keyboard player never played with the band again after being sent down for 6 months for 'assaults' he never committed. Whilst all this violence ensued, around fifty National Front members held their meeting in the Town Hall. It was a day Southall will never forget and one that changed many lives. A tune of The Ruts, 'Jah Wars', graphically described the events. "What you experience, you write about" explained the band's bassist Segs in *Love in Vain*.

© Syd Shelton

● Vince & Smell

RAR along with other local groups set about supporting all those who had been arrested and injured. Weekly gigs featuring Misty, The Ruts and The Enchanters were organised upstairs at the Dominion Cinema in the heart of Southall, with a small entry charge for the Defence Fund. There was even TV coverage. Misty and national RAR drew upon old associates to support these local initiatives with two huge concerts at the Rainbow in July 1979. Alongside the local bands, Aswad, The Members, Tom Robinson, Pete Townsend, The Clash and The Pop Group came out to perform for free under the banner 'Southall Kids Are Innocent' and to stand alongside the many who had been victims that day.

The links between Southall bands and RAR had created a two-way platform. The bands made a massive contribution to RAR locally, nationally and internationally. RAR provided wider exposure for the bands. Together they delivered powerful messages to audiences of young people both black and white. As Puck, the lead singer of Misty told *Black Echoes* in 1978, "RAR is good because man could show it isn't just white man better than black man or so, you know, is all one".

Looking back in 2016 members of The Enchanters, who went on to be involved in many other music projects, described RAR as "part of an era, a golden age, a people's vibe". "RAR", said drummer Styx, "gave us the opportunity to express ourselves. It was black and white together, it was a unity, it was a coming together. Everyone performed and did what they had to do and then at the end jammed together". Segs from The Ruts also recalled recently "For us, RAR was not a political statement more a natural extension of our lives. We all had black and Asian friends and indeed friends from the many diverse cultures that make up our world. There is no argument for judging people on the basis of their race, creed or colour.... The RAR movement and People Unite helped to pass this on, in a non-violent way. It has to be said also that there were some great bands involved and those gigs were extremely good fun"!

The music continues to this day. Misty in Roots are still playing and are as strong, if not stronger, than ever. Kaziwayi, a founder member of The Enchanters, has long been their lead guitarist. Malcolm and Foxy from The Ruts have sadly died but Segs and drummer Dave Ruffy still perform as dynamically as ever and tour and record as two-thirds of Ruts DC. Kurt Leacock of The Enchanters, and at one time Misty, has just released his latest single and The Enchanters, bass man Chester is in a funk and soul band.

The memories remain. In 2015 when sitting in an Indian restaurant near Southall with Puck, an Asian man visiting the restaurant, with his young family, came across to Puck and excitedly exclaimed "You are from Misty in Roots, me and my dad used to go to those great gigs at Southall Community Centre".

Northgate High School Y7 & 9 pupils; words/ phrases to describe RAR

On 29 June 2016 Derek & Judith Merrill ran a workshop about RAR in Northgate High School ,Ipswich as part of a wider project studying human rights called 'Sharing Stories, Shaping Futures" and 'Branching Out For A Better Future', for which the school won the Dora Love prize from Essex University – a prize awarded to a school making a significant contribution to the study of human rights,

During the RAR workshop the pupils went on an investigative trail of evidence from photos, information, books, artefacts and videos about RAR in small groups of two Year 7 pupils accompanied by a Year 9 pupil. After studying this evidence they were asked to come up with up to five words/phrases to sum up what RAR was about. Below is a list of words/phrases they came up with.

Power of music
Unite
Community
Fairness
Powerful
Equality
Purposeful
Come together against discrimination
Protest
Encouragement
Make a stand
Political

After that the pupils placed questions on post-its and stuck each question beside the appropriate piece of evidence. We then provided some answers to their questions.

Derek & Judith Merrill July 2016

RAR

Z Bends from Durham, Z men from Hull, X certs from Cambridge, X Ray Specs from London, Xero from ? XS Discharge from Paisley, Wanton Destruction from Liverpool, Warsaw (Joy Division) from Manchester, Wendy Tunes from Leicester, Wilful Damage from Manchester, Worst from Manchester, Verbals from Hull, Vice Squad from Doncaster, Voice from Hull, V.I.P.s from London, Vacants from Hull, Valves from Edinburgh, Vapours from Guildford, UB40 from Birmingham, UK Subs from London, Urban Disturbance from Reading, Urban enemies from Paisley, Users from Cambridge, Tom Robinson Band from London, Tour de Force from London, Transisters from Milton Keynes, Trwynll Coch from Swansea, Table and Tennis Club Ladder from Stevenage, Tar Babies from Hull, Thompson Twins from Clapham, Those Helicopters from Maidstone, Timber Flesh from Hull, Stunt Kites from Sheffield, Syndicate from Stevenage, Sadstone from Leicester, Sandy Beach and the Deckhands from Kent, Scars from Edinburgh, Scritty Politti from Leeds, Section 25 from Blackpool, Seething Wells from Bradford, Shaking Stevens and the Sunsets from Wales, Sham 69 from Hersham, Sheeny and the Goys from Leeds, Shocking Stocking from Ireland, Shy Tots from Doncaster, Sincere Americans from Leicester, Siren from Bow, Slip Hazard from Nottingham, Sneex from Paisley, Soft Centres from Cardiff, Soviet Tractors from Prestwick, Spartacus from London, Specials from Coventry, Spectres from London, Spiked Coffee from Stirling, Splodge from London, Squares from Leeds, Standard Issue from Leicester, States from London, Statix from Leeds, Steel Locks from Birmingham, Steel Pulse from Birmingham, Stepping Out from London, Stiff Little Fingers from Belfast, Still Earth from Doncaster, Stop Outs from Liverpool, Straights from Leeds, Strand from Andover, RAF from Edinburgh, Raincoats from London, Reach from Norfolk, Reality from Brighton, Red Express from Cambridge, Red Night from London, Reds from London, Restricted from Sheffield, Restricted Hours from Stevenage, Revelation Rockers from Coventry, Roots from London, Rudi and the Rationals from Birmingham, Ruts from Southall, Proles from Tyneside, Painkillers from ? Parrots from Brighton, Passage from Manchester, Passions from Shepherd Bush, Patrick Fitzgerald from East London, Paul Jones from London, Performing Ferrets from Maidstone, Pete Townsend from London, Pilgrim from London, Pirhanas from Brighton, Plague from Brighton, Pop Group from Bristol, Prams from Rotherham, Press from Nottingham, Prince Titian Sounds from Islington, Private Vices from West London, Oxy and the Morons from Hackney, Odessa from Birmingham, One Takes from Ayr, Only Ones from south London, Neat from Belfast, Negatives from Bradford, Negus Esquire Sound system from Acton, Normal Day from Bedford, Now from Peterborough, Numbers from Ayr, The Mekons from Leeds, Members from Staines, Mental Block from Hull, Mentol Errors from Paisley, Merritone Sound system from Acton/Southall, MetroPack from Edinburgh, Militant Frank from Manchester, Milk from High Wycombe, Misty in Roots from Southall, Mo-dettes from London, Mod Cons from Paisley, Mods from Dewsbury, Monos from Edinburgh, Mosiah from Birmingham, My Willie from ? Magnets from ? Mark Perry from Depford, Matrus from Birmingham, Matt Vinyl and the Decorators from Edinburgh, Matumbi from Hackney, Medium Medium from Nottingham, Limosine from London, Lastarza from London, Leyton Buzzards from Leyton, Leopards from

London, Little Brother from Bradford, Live Wire from London, Living Dead No.5 from Redditch, London Underground from London, Lost Property from London, Keons from Paisley, Kick Starts from ? Jam from Woking, Jerks from Edinburgh, Jerks from Leeds, Jimmy Colon from Edinburgh, John Cooper Clark from Manchester, John Martyn (and friends) from London, John The Postman from Manchester, Juke Box Express from Swansea, Jump Gravity from ? Iganda from Birmingham, Infested from Canterbury, Injection from Southall, Interference from Lancaster, Invaders from Bradford, Investigators from London, Harpies from London, High Flying Clive from Brighton, Hostage from Mull of Kyntyre, Human Zoo from Hull, I'm So Hollow from Sheffield, Graham Parker and the Rumour from London, Groundation from Leicester, Guilt Edge from Stevenage, Gang of Four from Leeds, Generation X from London, Glaxo Babies from Bristol, F104 from Manchester, Fabulous Poodles from Greenwich, Faction from Leeds, Fakes from Stirling, Fall from Manchester, Fan Club from Brighton, Fans from ? Far Cry from London, Fast Relief from Birmingham, Favourites from Nottingham, Feed The Enemy from Ayr, Fegs from Paisley, Flat Out from Cumbernauld, Flying Mallet from Essex, Fool from Oldham? Frantic Elevators from Liverpool, Freeze from Edinburgh, Freeze from Lithgow, Ed Banger and the Nosebleeds from Manchester, Eclipse from Birmingham, Eddie and the Hotrods from Canvey Island, Elite from Slough, Elvis Costello and The Attractions from London, Enchanters from? Everreadies from Birmingham, Ex Rippers from ? Excerts from? Exits from Swansea, Exodus from Manchester, Duncans from Reading, Dangerous Girls from Manchester, Dansette from London, Dead Byrds from Paisley, Deaf Aids from Sheffield, Defiant pose from Paisley, Deleted from Edinburgh, Delta 5 from Leeds, Desperate Bicycles from Dalston, Devils Dykes from Brighton, Disease from ? Distractions from Manchester, Docile dogs from Ayr, Doctor Bird from Southall, Downbeat from Stevenage, Dry Rib from London, Carol Grimes from London, Charge from Camden, China Street from Manchester, Cimmarons from Hackney, Clash from London, Condemned from Newcastle, Cool Ghoul from London, Cool notes from south London, Cowboys from Leicester, Crass from Epping, Criminal Class from Coventry, Crisis from London, Cryshark from Hackney, Crystals from Manchester, Culture from ? Bad Stone from Manchester, Barry Forde Band from London, Beat from Birmingham, Beggar from Leyton, Belt and Braces from Camden, Black Enchanters from Southall, Black Jade from London, Black Slate from London, Bongo Danny from Acton, Boyfriends from Bristol, Breakfast from London, Bush Fire from Hull, Butterflies from Leeds, Buzzcocks from Manchester, Abrasive Wheels from Leeds, Accents from Brighton, Adam and The Ants from London, Administrators from London, Adverts from London, Again and Again from London, Agony Column from Leeds, Akrylyk Vytymz from Hull, Alien Kulture from Greenwich, Alsatians from London, Alternative British Army from Brighton, Amba from London, Amba Strutts from Bristol, Amhric from Birmingham, Androids from Manchester, Androids of Mu from Notting Hill, Angelic Upstarts from Newcastle, Animation from Hull, Another Pretty Face from Edinburgh, Arbs from Manchester, Armed Forces from Manchester, Art Failures from Leyton, Artery from Sheffield, Astronauts from Stevenage, Attila the stockbroker from Harlow, Au Pairs from Birmingham, Auto Pilot from Cambridge, 2.3 from Sheffield, 999 from London.

Wayne Minter

Full-time RAR Organiser 1978-81

WHORAR?[1]

On previous two pages a draft list[2] I put together for this piece of some of the bands who played Rock Against Racism gigs from 1976 – 1980[3].

During that period I was lucky to be part of the RAR movement ; putting on gigs, going on demos, helping with the fanzine, events and publicity. For the last two years I worked, with Katy and John, as one of the three full-time, paid national organisers for RAR. Mostly we worked out of a shoebox office over the socialist bookshop in grimy Finsbury Park, north London.

Before that we were fire-bombed out of our first office in Cable Street, East London, then squatted for some weeks in a corner of the Belt and Braces/Cast/Kartoon Clowns radical Theatre company office in the Clerkenwell workshops. After we moved we, uncharitably, kept the RAR mailbox there as a precautionary filter for the weekly hatemail and other possible postal nasties.

Katy ran the office, enthused and communicated.

John plotted and planned, schemed and networked.

I drove the van (ex- GPO, 1950's Morris Minor, distressed yellow), sorted the mail and badges, and worked with local RAR supporters and bands all over the UK – on RAR gigs and tours.

The larger London RAR organizing crew was a gang of strange bedfellows from the radical left, art school/punk/media diaspora of 70's London. In the early days we'd meet in Red's photo studio above a strip club in Soho. What we had in common was being overactive, over-political, over-creative, over-stimulated and grievously miffed with the status quo. We conceived, conspired organized and delivered terrific

1 Rock Against Racism

2 There will be bands I've missed or got wrong. Do send corrections to Redwords and I'll update it.

3 This is just UK bands. It does not include those in Belgium, Germany, Holland, Ireland, Norway, Sweden, Tasmania, USA and all the other countries RAR took off in.

and barmy ideas, propaganda and products in hothouse sessions. We had our spectacular and regular beefs.
To me it was a joyful time.
In the office we three were sustained and fueled by fervent anti-racism, steaming styrofoam tea, class warfare, donner kebabs, obsession with the *NME*[4], and Kit-Kats.
We were united by the daily, dazed disbelief of actually being paid to do this brilliant work.

RAR'S PACKAGED HISTORY
Local, grass-roots political organized activism is hard to get a handle on historically, just because of its very localism, scale and diversity. The most visible forms from the '70's would be those, like e.g. ELWAR, 'People Unite', Brixton Black Women's Group, that bothered to give themselves a name and a platform [5]. Or, those who, like the miners and later the Greenham women, caused enough trouble confronting the state to make the national papers or TV. Also, the very success of the ANL as a united front against racism tended to absorb and further homogenise these groups in the eyes of today's commentators. Most just got on with it locally and remain largely invisible to the gaze of history.
Today's academics and sociologists are happy to expound at length on the 'roles' of significant individuals and the organized left parties in RAR, for which abundant sources and references exist.
However, they generally offer little to explain the rapid spread of RAR ideas and activities across the UK at grass roots level outside the well worn 'isms'; "collective activism", "radical populism", etc. which serve to both describe and conceal.
Similarly when the music of RAR is discussed today, in media discourses, exhibitions, anniversaries and celebrations, only a handful of the RAR bands from my list above will merit a mention.
Most contemporary discussion of RAR and anti-racism in pop music in the late '70's and early '80's unsurprisingly references a tiny subsection of name bands, usually: The Clash, Elvis Costello, Steel Pulse, The Specials, sometimes Sham 69.
I would not disparage these 'big' name bands; They did their bit (and, in some cases, quite a bit more) but they are nowhere near the whole (or most important part) of the story.
The gold RAR star award for the most gigs played for the cause in those crucial years must go to the 'Leyton Buzzards' probably followed by 'The Barry Forde band' and/or 'The Pirhanas'.
I suspect that if we took their stories and those of their symbiotic

4 *New Musical Express*. Popular Musical weekly newspaper.
5 eg: ELWAR, Southall YM, People Unite, Indian Youth Fed, Trades Councils, Womens' movement campaign and protest groups; Brixton Black Women's Group, Southall Black Sisters, community and neighborhood action and development projects, Defence Committees, cyclists and anarchists, etc.

followers, and added them to the hundreds of others from the above band list, we would get closer to an understanding of RAR's rapid birth, growth and decline as a national (and international) social and political force. WhoRAR?

EXTRAPOLATORS FROM ALL OVER

© Syd Shelton

© Syd Shelton

● Barry Forde & Leyton Buzzards 1979. Below: Lewisham August 1977

To indulge in some dodgy but satisfying statistical extrapolation:

There are 273 UK bands on my list. There would be an average of three or four people in each band. Giving us over 1,000 RAR people.

Each RAR person would have a social diaspora of boyfriends, girlfriends, mates, siblings, ex's ... etc. Lets say around 20 each. That gives us a potential of around 20,000 RAR people.

Lets say each band does an average of 6 RAR gigs and picks up a dozen or so supporters. That would give us around 240,000 potential RAR people based all over the UK from Acton to Ayr, Belfast to Bristol, and so on...

THE PEOPLE

These would be the ones who daily inspired Kate, John and me in our little office in Finsbury Park as we tried to service them with RAR badges, stickers and posters, information and bands for RAR gigs.

These were the people ... from the cities, towns, villages across the UK (which, in the '70's were steeped in boredom, cuts, unemployment, repression, boredom, political and musical frustration, sexism, isolation, police violence, and boredom)... who embraced punk, reggae and anti-racism and formed the local RAR groups as activists.

Who hired/ blagged or occupied their local church halls and put on their own RAR gigs, (often in direct opposition to their parents, local councils, neighbours and teachers).

Who bussed in their thousands to the RAR Carnivals in Edinburgh, Leeds, London, Manchester.
And to the national demos; eg ANL[6], Rock Against Sexism, Troops Out and Right To Work (often along with their parents, local councilors, neighbours and teachers).
Who put me up on their bedroom floors and in their squats when I was driving a mini round the UK scouting locations for the RAR Militant Entertainment tours.
Who, after those tour gigs, opened their chippies, curry houses and homes in the middle of the night to feed and succor the exhausted RAR crew and bands.
Who ordered, read and spread the radical *Temporary Hoarding* fanzine, and who wrote passionately to the *NME* and *Melody Maker* letters pages.

Photograph: Red Saunders

They it was who confronted, and usually defeated, racism, sexism and the National Front locally and directly in gigs, local government institutions and trades unions, in high streets, local markets, shopping centers and newspapers, in council estates and football grounds.
These people were RAR. Sadly, we shall not see their like again.
Wayne Minter (aka: Ed Rest)

6 Anti Nazi League – mass organization launched in 1977 to oppose the rise of the Nazi National Front in the United Kingdom.

Sharon Moore / artist

There were a lot of free concerts on around that time (late '70s early '80s). Usually they were playing for a good cause such as RAR or Anti Nazi League. I have a memory from one of the RAR concerts; outside in a park. My daughter was about 4 and she bent down to stroke a little dog next to her. A tall black man bent down and they struck up a conversation. I remember thinking how lovely that my little girl had no idea of racism. How it is a thing we learn, to our detriment. We lived in Tunbridge Wells where the amount of black people could be counted on one hand- with fingers to spare. It was a great day out. Many different people from all walks of life getting together with one aim; to support everyone whoever and whatever they look like while listening to brilliant music.
So much hope. So much energy!

Steve O'Donahue / singer songwriter

Outside our local football grounds and down the market place
Selling bullshit they called Bulldog stood the so called master race
Pathetic little patriots keeping fascism alive
That the grandad's had defeated back in 1945

It was somewhere in the midlands
When old slow hand took the stage
He was spouting racist rubbish in a crazy drunken rage
And from that very moment a movement quickly grew

Who shot the sheriff Eric Cos it sure as hell weren't you?

A simple yellow button badge
Was pinned to my lapel
With an arrow flying true and strait
And the letters ANL

There were Nazis on the High Street and a fightback couldn't wait
o a gig was booked and organised at a pub in Forest Gate
There were Dockers on the door that night we lived in scary times
And we rocked against the racists and we danced to Carol Grimes

Nelson on his lofty perch then waved us all goodbye
We must have been an awesome sight even with his one good eye
We were punks and we were rasta's we were strait and we were gay
And it felt like everyone was there in Vicky park that day

A simple yellow button badge
Was pinned to my lapel
With an arrow flying true and strait
And the letters ANL

Prav Parmar

1978: February, working with ANL and Asian Youth Organisation against NF meeting in Bolton Town Hall; April, filling coaches for first carnival in London; summer on strike against victimisation by Bulmer & Lamb; September on Right to Work march to TUC in Brighton; then back in Bolton to run weekly RAR disco. 2020: keeping sane in an insane world

Enoch Powell's big mouth... that's where all the skinheads started. People started cutting their hair short, Ben Shermans. Then the kids who were with you in junior school suddenly change. All scruffy haired, then suddenly everybody's got a skinhead, Ben Shermans and Doc Martins or big bovver boots or they used to wear steel toecaps. The skinheads were always going Paki-bashing, always looking for things.

School wise, secondary school, there was racism even by the teachers because they picked all the white kids to play football, in the teams. They used to just say 'Here's a ball, you lot, all you Pakis, go and play in that corner.' Even catching a bus, they used to say 'Oh, there's a smell round here.' You daren't catch the bus and you walked three miles home and they used to groz on your back, spit on your back, things like that. So you didn't want to catch the bus. And it wasn't just me. All Indians, Islamics, everybody who looked different to them.

Prav, centre, on Right to Work March to Brighton 1978. Photograph John Sturrock.

I finished school in 1971, I was 15. By that time we were six children in the family. My dad was working nights, my mum was working days. Straight after leaving Friday, on Monday I was in a job at a fit age of 15.

In a paint factory, trainee tinter, mixing paint for people like BP, Post Office: Post Office red, BP green, things like that. It was smelly. I don't know how my lungs and everything are still functioning. I don't think there was health and safety in those days. I remember going inside a one thousand gallon tank and scraping it out. Sometimes I was nearly fainting, collapsing. And not just I did it, a load of English folks did it, everybody did it. If it was your round to scrape the tank and so it be. It was a non-union place and it was a family-owned small paint factory. It was only 4 pound a week. My dad thought 'How many years are you going to train before you get 6 pounds, 7 pounds, 8 pounds?' And then he took me to the textile mill where I was earning 18 pounds a week, the Bridgewater mill in Swinton, a large mill. They bussed in all workers from Bolton surrounding to work there because the English people wouldn't work there. The only English people were the ladies in the day shift. Nights, afternoon, evening, there were all Asian people and they were all bussed in from Bolton, Farnworth where the Asian communities were. ... I was a winder [for] two years. I was working mornings, six to ten or two to till ten. If nobody turned up, I did 16 hours shift but wanted the money and we worked weekends as well.... We had to give our pay packet to my mum and she would give us a pound a week to spend or something like that..... We used to go around collecting heavy metal, selling it, lead, copper, doing things like that to get extra money, get new clothes, things like that because we never had money.

For politics there was only the trade union which was a textile union and we voted Labour and that was it, there was nothing else. The only time we saw politics was at the time – what was it? Edward Heath, when it was the three day week. I remember being switched off so there were no power. If the power came on, we had to go to work – between 8 and 12. I think the power was switched off at 12. That's the only time I knew real politics. I went to the union meeting and tried to get a shop steward position. The conveners and shop stewards were all white when 90 percent of the workforce was Asian or foreign from the Far East or East Africa. It was surprising just trying to become a shop steward or a union representative and my union wouldn't allow me to be a representative despite having the vote of the whole of my floor. It was sad... After leaving Bridgewater mill, then I went into working night shift with my dad and everybody else [at] Eagle Mill. And that's the period I try and get into being a shop steward – I had no chance. 1975 I went into British Rail which was union organised, in the foundry. Same story again, all the Asians, Jamaicans, Pakistanis worked on the night shift.

And that's where I got involved in politics. Dave Gibbons and Paul Kennedy. They used to be outside on the picket line, whatever the issue was, they was there. I was helping them all the time, selling papers now and then and that's when the fascists started. It was the National Front who started coming selling papers in Bolton. And that's when we, all Asians, we used to all meet up. The meeting place was Bolton Town Hall steps. Not just for us, mods, rockers, everybody. And they started coming, recruiting all these people and we drove them out one day. So they came back with more people. We collected more people and drove them out again. And this happened about five or six times and it became slowly, slowly more violent and more violent. And what happened was it was only the Asians who got arrested. It was funny. Every time an incident happened, they come selling, giving abuse to Asians, foreign people, calling us Pakis and all sorts and we were the ones getting arrested. Well, everybody in the town heard about it. They all came out. We were demonstrating outside the police station to let the people go. The fascists went to the council and the council was more right wing than what we thought. I thought they would be Labour councillors; it was a Labour-run council. They would be in sympathy with us since the Asian people ran all the mills, worked hard, gave their dedication all these years and you let these people outside town to preach racism into this town. It was terrible, shocking.

Rock Against Racism really related to us because after kicking out the fascists, Asian people couldn't go to many bars or pubs. They wouldn't let us in. So I used to hire a little pub rooms upstairs and all us friends, we liked music so we collected PA systems, picked up records and from that, then we latched ourselves to Rock Against Racism. Then they started coming and we started selling. Every time I did a do, like Indian Valentines do or Indian Independence Day, it was a Rock Against Racism do and that just snowballed. Then London and everybody were doing big...It shifted because the interest became bigger, minute by minute. I had to move rooms in Bolton to accommodate. At the end, because no people like the Tory club or the Labour Club would give me their big room, so I ended up having, I think it was the Polish club. And I remember then we had to book big bands because our Asian bands, we didn't have the equipment. We had just little triangles to play with and a little keyboard. I remember getting Exodus. Exodus came over, a few other bands. Then we also got the Bolton Institute of Technology, we started involving the union there and we used to get their big hall. I remember when we used to get African bands in. You can't stop, can't print enough tickets. I had to send girls out selling tickets. Always Town Hall steps. They used to meet here or they went to the library because the Asians didn't go to pubs. They went to the Octagon theatre, used to all meet there so you went there or the library because mums and dads wouldn't let girls and boys meet in them days, if you remember. So they used to meet somewhere silent, the museum or the aquarium or the library. Or the Octagon theatre, so they all used to go selling tickets there and when the Anti Nazi League started doing these big,

Anti Nazi League

big concerts. We couldn't afford to get the coaches. If we got two or three coaches, they were sold out. At that time we didn't have a vast amount of money, every penny counted. You made your butties on the coach and drank water at the service stations. But the atmosphere down there was colossal, fantastic. I think we had five coaches [to the London carnival] from Bolton, two from the socialists, one from us and two from the trade unions and other people went by train, their own cars, making their own way. When we came back we want to do something. We have to do something. And the best thing was all the skinheads were coming on board. Mods and rockers were coming on board and were totally different. They were chasing you before, calling you also. Now and especially all these new bands, new wave bands

were coming through. Then I got one club, free of charge from Mr & Mrs Sherrington, Labour supporters, give me this club and I used to run all the New Wave music discos, two nights a week, packed out. They used to come from all over Bolton.

From outside Strangeways prison, straight up Deansgate and right through to Alexandra Park, the Manchester carnival were fantastic, the atmosphere and everything. They had so many police, thousands of police, nothing to do. They were sitting there, all on the floor, helmets off, sunny day and everybody is enjoying it. There's all these reds. They're trouble makers and everybody were there with prams, kids. Coloured people, everybody. Mix fantastic. They were all wearing the badges, these people who were racist before, they were wearing the badges now. It was funny.

Opposite: in Alexandra Park. Above Steel Pulse on stage. Photographs John Sturrock.

1977 was the year of discontent, unemployment was going up and up and youngsters were all just roaming round the street. They had no mission in life. The people who came with me on the 1978 march to the TUC in Brighton. I was out of work after the Bulmer and Lumb strike, I were blacklisted. It was impossible, I couldn't get a job anywhere. [We had] the UB40 badge. That represented your dole card. And we all wore them because we used to like the music. [And the] hi-viz jackets. Everybody got all famous people to sign [them]. I remember all the youngsters who I took, I think it was about 50 from Bolton. We had a coach load going down. Yeah. They were still wearing them two or three years later down the street and they'd nothing to do politically. They're still wearing it. If they went to like a New Wave do, like a punk do, a punk rock do, they had their hi-viz, 'Hiya, Prav, you all right?' 'Still can't get rid of it?' 'No, it's stuck on my back.' They still had it on. So all the punk rockers still had [them] 'Oh, I'm not selling my hi-viz, it's mine.' It was all the buttons were ripped, they'd got a lot of holes in it but they're still wearing it. Then when Maggie came in she made sure unemployment went up and just shut everything down. It didn't matter, any community, the coal miners was the worst. Their community was all destroyed. It was sad. Wiped them all out, all in Wales, all in Yorkshire. And the shipyards, everything moved. Instead of investing, putting new investment in to move the country forward. No, they didn't do that. They wanted the private sector to invest, so they can make the profit. And the more you had unemployed, the better. Less money to pay their wages. As I see it, other people will say different, you know, economics. People will say different things. 'We broke the back of the unions and everything.' You didn't. You broke the back of the community and the country and the nurses who did it with love and affection. You've lost it. It's sad. Now people just work to have a pay packet and come home. No feeling for that job or for the community. There is no communities now. It's sad. I could go out and shout and everybody wouldn't be there. There is no communities because everybody's trying to make a day to day living.

I thought in the late 70s revolution was taking place from the young people to make a change in the country but, as you know, Tories came in power, sold off all the family silver i.e. the electric, gas, water, the right wing press went on overdrive and we have gone backward. Prosperity has taken place at cost to the planet. Today, young kids who are fighting climate change remind me of me when I was fighting racism and fascism and political injustice in society. I hope in my time that the revolution does come from these young children to make a difference not just for the people but for the planet and everybody.

Sam Pattinson

is a BAFTA nominated Producer of projection and screen content for the live event, touring, fashion and theatre industries. He grew up in Camberwell and went to Peckham Manor school 1979 – 84. He graduated from Fine Art Sculpture at Central Saint Martins in 1992. Over the next decade, he wrote for several publications including *Dazed and Confused*, worked with photographer Dennis Morris, on his Sex Pistols retrospective *Destroy* book and exhibition at the Proud Galleries – its first photographic exhibition. He produced the self-funded documentry *AIPS* directed by Adam Smith in 2000, shown on Channel 4 in 2001, and was producer at the seminal Vegetable Vision.
Sam started the music video production company Treatment in 2001, working on videos for Death in Vegas, Manu Chau and Stereo MCs. He began producing visual content and design for major rock shows. His extensive portfolio covers acts such as U2, Ed Sheeran, The Rolling Stones, Jay Z, Lady Gaga, Red Hot Chili Peppers, You Me Bum Bum Train, Rhianna, ACDC, Sigur Rós, New Order, Adele, George Michael, Motörhead Pet Shop Boys, Kasabian, Deadmaus, Black Sabbath, Elton John, Nitin Sawhney and A Tribe called Quest. His work in fashion includes Louis Vuitton catwalk shows 2014/2015 and installations for their exhibitions Series 2 and 3. He lives in south London with his partner and two sons.

Through my elder brother and a friend Mathew I got into punk when I was young. It was 1978 and I was 10 years old.
We were real Saturday punks, bin liners on the weekend and all that. We loved the Pistols and The Damned, but I really liked Stiff Little Fingers; *Inflammable Material* was such a great album, even though I remember being confused about 'White Noise' at the time.
We were aware of the National Front, British Movement and the whole skinhead thing, it was unavoidable in London then. Growing up in Camberwell, our world was multicultural so it was natural to reject racism. We'd heard about Rock Against Racism and we understood the need for it, even then.

My Mum taught us about prejudice and the harm it can do. She was liberal generally and encouraged us to get out and about. So we used to go to the Kings Road on a Saturday morning, bin liners and all. She let me and Mathew go to a Damned gig at the Electric Ballroom 1979. We were kids but we could pretty well go to whatever we wanted to.
Mathew told me that there was going to be a RAR gig at Brockwell Park, which was just down the road from where we lived, and that SLF were playing. I think I actually went on my own, but to be honest I just cant remember. I do remember being quite overwhelmed by the crowd and settled quite far back having bottled getting to the front. The crowds were pretty lively and I later learnt that that was just the norm, there was a lot of violence then. So it kicked off at the front and the crowd swayed and jerked about. I was far enough back not get caught up in it. They were crushing beer cans and throwing them back into the crowd. The crushed cans had sharp edges and one hit a woman near me; it cut here forehead open. I had seen plenty of fights with other kids but I was shocked by that as it was the first time I had seen someone hurt like that. Rumour had it was the British Movement but I'm not sure. I don't remember much about the band except the sound wasn't very good. I think I was too scared to take much in.

● Carnival2: Brockwell Park 1978

Punk was strange in that most of the bands were anti-racist and left wing, but the scene was really white and there were plenty of racists in it. It wasn't just those fucking skinheads and Nazis that were dishing out the kickings. I really believe that RAR made people aware of the problem and gave us a platform to fight from. I'm sure it informed a generation and had a bigger impact on the far right than its given credit for.

Mark Perryman

Straight out of Tadworth, Surrey

I can still remember it as if it was yesterday. Me, Jeremy Turner, Ashley Stark, Deborah Tween at the bus stop in the Surrey commuter belt village of Tadworth. It was early, we had a bus to catch, then the Northern Line from its southernmost tip, Morden, before a couple of changes to Bethnal Green. When we got there, me with A-Z in hand, we picked our way through unfamiliar surroundings to what we realised was the wrong end of Victoria Park. A boating lake? Surely this wasn't the place for a Carnival. But then we saw it, a huge, if rather ramshackle stage, with people pouring into the area in front of it from every direction. We'd arrived.

No we hadn't gone on the march. I was in the Upper Sixth at the local Comprehensive, De Burgh, the others from the year below me. We were a bunch of teenage committed musos. Every week we devoured the *New Musical Express,* which with a rather brilliant mix of the political and the cultural had been carrying news of the growth of Rock Against Racism, known to everyone as 'RAR' alongside breathlessly enthusiastic reporting of the emergence of punk. The two of course weren't un-related. Meantime scarcely never out of the news was the National Front, NF, kicking their way into the headlines. Every march a violent confrontation between them and the recently formed Anti Nazi League, ANL. This was horrible, these were Nazis, isn't that what our parents and grandparents fought to defeat?

The others were there more or less for the music and the urban adventure. All four of us tempted though to make the trip for the musical line-up of our dreams, and what's more it was free. But we were nervous too, as we had picked our way through Hackney to the park we were convinced we'd be set upon by Nazi thugs round every corner. Nervous? Scared rigid in my case. So going on the march was a bit beyond the scale of our commitment and what was marching for any way? Of course when I saw that huge, joyful, powerfully surging crowd arrive all the way from Trafalgar Square with enormous paper maché heads of NF leaders John Tyndall, Martin Webster and their co-thinker on racial superiority Adolf Hitler at the front, I immediately regretted not joining in, and I'm not sure my political credibility has ever recovered since either.

Waiting for the music to start, we wandered round the stalls. Most didn't interest us, socialist this, revolutionary that, communist the other. It was the dayglo RAR stickers I was after and anything with that brilliant ANL arrow on too please, comrade, as I soon learned to say. Somewhere along the line I was pestered by a particularly determined member of the Revolutionary Communist Party into buying a scarcely readable pamphlet on why Labour was an imperialist party. I think I've still got it, the single tract that came closest to putting me off the Left for life; sorry, comrades, was the first one I ever shelled out for. Every other word an ism or an ist, nobody any good except the followers of the one true faith, the certainty in being right unquestionable, those who were wrong risible. Blimey, was this what I was getting into, I thought we were just here to stand up to the latter-day Nazis my dad's best friend, Alan, who's name I was given for my middle name, lost his life fighting in the Battle of Britain.

And the music. There was this bloke up on stage in a boiler suit who seemed to be running proceedings yet he was totally unlike any figure of authority I'd ever come across before. He was a livewire of infectious enthusiasm; he made us all, whether on stage or in the crowd, hardened politico or slightly wayward sixth-formers from Surrey feel like we belonged. Polly Styrene belting up 'Oh Bondage, Up Yours!' helped too. I'm not sure I even knew what bondage was back then but that saxophone riff and a young woman screaming the words into the microphone was more than enough for the crowd to erupt. I'd never seen anything like it, a seething mass of intermingled bodies throwing themselves into the air seemingly without a care in the world. Except we did care. These bands were the voices of our moment, TRB, The Clash, Steel Pulse, Patrik Fitzgerald. They wrote songs about what we cared about, against the NF, or the kind of place we felt Britain and the world could be but without all those isms and ists.

What made this day so special, for me at any rate, was that it was fun. There was even a RAR badge that turned NF into No Fun. They, the Nazis, were against the multicultural Britain we were becoming and behind that miserable mask of the hateful was something even worse, Nazism. In the late 1970s there remained a generation, like my parents, framed by the war, the Second World War. It hadn't quite become the stuff of make believe nostalgia and ritualised ceremony to mark a past of all our yesterdays instead it was part of our families,

present today. And so when the ANL successfully stuck the word Nazi, deservedly so, on the racist NF, we had won and their lot lost.
But then of course we learned that you didn't have to be a Nazi to be a racist. Wrap it up in the so-called respectability of warning against our culture being 'swamped', describing our nation's borders as reaching 'breaking point' or predicting a community will be a 'tinderbox' because of immigration and its no longer Nazi, just plain nasty, and wrong. Stopping all of that, and more, takes politics, having an argument, collective action which must involve those who otherwise might not think of themselves as 'political', not part of existing campaigns, a politics that is popular. It is a lesson too much of the Left never fails to forget. We revel in the cult of the activist, we privilege the most committed, the dedicated. But a politics restricted to these hardened souls will never amount to a mass movement. Of course most political campaigning is boring and we have to be prepared to accept defeats, more than our fair share. And it takes guts too. After Victoria Park, I used to pester the ANL office for supplies of their leaflets. Up and down the roads of my Surrey village Banstead I'd go popping the leaflets though letterboxes, the stickers up on every bus stop. Quite what the locals thought goodness only knows. Either the place was about to be invaded by Nazi thugs or their rampaging opponents, possibly both. Still it made my eighteen year old self feel like I was doing something. I'd been inspired. It was the fun, the community, the identity of Victoria Park that did this. I'd become politically active, as I soon learned to describe myself. And the rest for me isn't history.

● Steel Pulse singing Klu Klux Klan in Victoria Park, 1978

Balwinder Rana

came to this country from India in 1963. In 1969 he became the founding president of the Indian Youth Federation of Gravesend, the first Asian youth organisation in this country. From 1974 onwards, after joining the SWP, he became active against the National Front, becoming full-time national Asian organiser after the Anti Nazi League was launched in 1977. He was the chief steward in Southall in 1979 where the police killed Blair Peach at the massive anti-NF protest. He was also the convenor for strike support groups, in West London, supporting the four year long strike by Hillingdon Hospital workers, and then the Gate Gourmet strikers. More recently he launched the Sikhs Against the EDL organisation and helped to divert support away from the EDL amongst some Sikh youth.

My Memories of RAR Carnival, 1978

I came to this country in 1963, from India, at the age of sixteen and proceeded to spend about five years working in the factories. At that time there were often notices outside the factories saying 'No blacks, No Irish' and inside the factories racist jokes and remarks like 'send them home' were quite common. There also seemed to be a complete divide between the white and black workers and white workers seemed to agree with and support each other most of the time.

But, by 1968 I had started full-time education at a local college and with the student radicalism of that period including all those protests against the Vietnam war, things began to change and I began to feel much safer. Thus I started to think that, after all, not all white people were the same! However, about the same time, with that infamous 'Rivers of Blood' speech by Enoch Powell which had led to the Dockers marching in his support and especially a wave of racist attacks by the 'skinheads' upon Asian and black people, things still did not seem quite right. In response to those attacks in Gravesend (Kent), where I lived at the time, we set up the very first Asian youth organisation in this country, called the Indian Youth Federation and I was elected its first president.

Then in 1974 the fascist National Front began to march in the streets and began to gain considerable support. Although their marches in their thousands, with all those Union Jacks and marching bands and 'sieg heiling' skinheads looking quite intimidating, but we were glad to see that there was also tremendous opposition to the fascists from white anti-racists. That opposition, at the time, was mainly led by the International Socialists, later known as the Socialist Workers Party. Thus, during that year, I joined the SWP and by 1977 became its National Asian Organiser. Soon after, the Anti Nazi League was launched, which, almost immediately, mushroomed into almost every sphere of life pushing back the racist advance. Together with the rising militancy amongst the Asian and black youth, it created a period of solidarity which gave tremendous courage and hope to the Asian and black people, who had been facing the sharp edge of the racist advance.

Above: Police in Southall harrasing demonstration 1978. Photograph: John Sturrock

In 1978 when preparations were being made for the Rock Against Racism carnival, I went to Southall and talked to the local youth and community leaders. The Indian Workers Association promised to book a number of coaches to the carnival and I also got in touch with a local Asian music band and booked a flat top lorry for them to play from on the route of the carnival. Then, the night before the carnival, myself and some comrades spent most of the night decorating the lorry. However, the band members did not take it seriously enough and they were very late to leave Southall in the morning. Consequently the lorry got stuck in a traffic jam, created around London because of the massive turnout, and were unable to reach Trafalgar Square and turned back. But having realised the exceptional opportunity that they had missed, they were extremely apologetic and begged me to let them know of any future similar activities.

In the meantime, although we did not fill all the coaches from Southall, we drove to Ealing Broadway to pick up school students from there who had been waiting for the coaches. While I was expecting only a few dozen of them, to my 'shock and horror' there was a sea of ANL lollipops waiting for us and after filling all the remaining seats in the coaches there were still too many left standing on the pavement. Thus, sadly, I had to ask the adults, especially the comrades, to vacate their seats for the young students and themselves to catch the underground trains.

By the time we got near Trafalgar Square, it was totally packed and also the surrounding areas too. I, myself, had never seen anything like it before, which was totally overwhelming. There were people of all colours and ages; men and women, young and old, black and white, and all seemed very happy and excited. The atmosphere was electric and very colourful; with all those placards and lollipops and people blowing whistles and singing and dancing. Many people also had brought along various musical instruments with them and here and there you saw groups of people surrounding someone playing a violin or a guitar or even a small band playing.

Soon the march began to assemble and we were somewhere in the middle of the march. It was all very lively and excited with people shouting slogans like, "The National Front is a Nazi Front. Smash the National Front", or "Black & White Unite and Fight. Smash the National Front". But we had not walked far when we started to hear the news that the front of the march had already reached Victoria Park and the various bands on the stage had already begun to perform. There were some people who began to rush ahead but others were happy just to take part in the march as there were also a number of lorries from the tops of which some bands were providing entertainment on the move.

When we reached the park, we were too far away from the stage to see anything properly but the atmosphere was great. People were mingling and started to provide their own entertainment in their own little groups. However, I was also responsible for a number of older Asian men and women and some children who had come all the way from Southall. I was quite concerned that they may feel left out as there was no Asian music that they would understand and enjoy. But, to my surprise, I need not have worried as they all seemed to be quite happy to see so many young people enjoying themselves and they were content to just soak up the atmosphere.

It was a great day of solidarity and to see all those young people 'Rocking Against Racism' must have sent shivers down the spines of even the most hardened racists and must have worried them that the end of their project was now in sight. Indeed, I think, that's exactly what happened in practice and I think that day set in motion the end to the rise of racism and fascism in this country during that period.

Jack Robertson

is a member of the SWP and served on its Central Committee between 1976 and 1981. He worked in the Industrial Department at the time of the long-running strike at Grunwick and during the national firefighters' strike of 1977. He also worked on Socialist Worker and was editor of the rank and file paper, *Engineers Charter.* He subsequently worked as a journalist in London, latterly for Thomson Reuters, and is now retired.

Reflections on RAR

My generation was the one that hoped to die before it got old. Most of the bands which emerged in the UK during that period, including The Who, started out playing their own, usually frantic, versions of American blues and R&B classics. The best of the guitarists from these bands – Jeff Beck, Jimmy Page (of Led Zeppelin), Peter Green (of Fleetwood Mac), Dave Gilmour (of Pink Floyd), Keith Richards (of The Stones), Pete Townsend (of The Who) and Eric Clapton (of Cream) – had all copied the guitar licks they played from blues legends such as Howlin' Wolf, Muddy Waters, John Lee Hooker, Willie Dixon and Robert Johnson.

Before they hit the big time, these white British bands all played in venues where black American blues, R&B and soul were the absolute norm. In London this would have been somewhere like The Marquee club in Soho or the Crawdaddy in Richmond. Where I grew up, in Edinburgh, it was The Place, a club where the entrance was at street level and then descended another four levels to the Grassmarket. All of the music played on each floor was either Motown, R&B or soul. Blues-based combo, Jethro Tull, regularly played here live as did the extraordinary Irish blues guitarist, Rory Gallagher. But probably the most popular of the lot were Jimmy James and the Vagabonds and Geno Washington & the Ram Jam Band, two mixed-race bands, with horn sections, which played storming versions of soul classics by the likes of Sam and Dave, Wilson Pickett, Otis Redding and Low Rawls. For a short time, I played in a band which had started out copying the style of the delta-blues exponents, the Memphis Jug Band and Cannon's Jug Stompers. Our crowning moment was to play the warm-up for Arthur 'Big Boy' Crudup, when he came to Edinburgh during his 1969 UK tour. Crudup had written 'That's All Right', a cover version of which Elvis Presley released as his first single in 1954 but, typically, Arthur had never made a penny from this song or any of the others that he wrote.

By the mid-1970's, all of the guitarists mentioned earlier had become rock legends. None of them was as good as Jimi Hendrix, who first came to England in 1966, but Eric Clapton was one of the most popular and he was a fantastic blues guitarist. He plays on two great albums from this period: *The Yardbirds live at the Marquee Club*, with Sonny Boy Williamson, and *Bluesbreakers*, John Mayall with Eric Clapton described on the sleeve notes as 'the most influential blues band in the Western World'. Mayall was already a blues afficionado – he had listened to blues and jazz from his father's collection of 78s and had then been inspired by Alexis Korner's Blues Syndicate when he saw them in Manchester.

● Shop stewards meet inside the boardroom at the Chloride factory occupation in Manchester. Summer of 1976. Me at the back, in the corner, with hair.

The first two tracks on the Bluesbreakers album with Clapton – 'All Your Love' and 'Hideaway' – are cover versions of originals by Otis Rush, Willie Dixon and Freddie King. The others include tracks by Ray Charles, Mose Allison, Memphis Slim and Robert Johnson. When Clapton left to form the super-group Cream with Jack Bruce and Ginger Baker – and graffiti started to appear proclaiming Clapton is God – they became renowned for hugely amplified versions of blues standards such as 'Rollin' and Tumblin', 'Crossroads', 'Spoonful', and 'Born Under a Bad Sign'.

For anyone who knew anything about popular music, then, this made it all the more extraordinary when a decade later Eric Clapton made his notorious outburst backing Enoch Powell. By the time this happened, in 1976, I was working for part of the time as a journalist and sub-editor at the *Socialist Worker* print-shop in East London. The papers were printed overnight on a Tuesday and next morning they were bundled up and dispatched to all parts of the country to be collected by whoever the poor sod was with the job of local *Socialist Worker* organiser. Their task was to ensure that every member got at least one copy of the paper for themselves and that they would sell as many copies as possible either in their own workplace, at factory gates or on street sales.

The political decision to launch the ANL had been taken by the leadership of the SWP at a time when support for the National Front had reached alarming levels. But the logistical aspect of this routine and this network were absolutely essential for the future success of the both the Anti Nazi League (ANL) and for Rock Against Racism (RAR). When I arrived in East London in 1976, I'd been an engineering shop steward in Trafford Park, Manchester, which could be grim. But there were some areas in East London, like Hoxton and Shoreditch, which you would avoid like the plague. We lived in a top-floor flat just off Whitechapel High Street and not far from Brick Lane, where the National Front assembled every Sunday to sell their newspaper. The buildings we were in, Fieldgate Mansions, had been the focus of rent strikes in the 1930s, had been taken over by the squatters rights movement in the early 1970s and were now occupied in the main by junior medical staff from the London Hospital next door and by Bangladeshi families who were beginning to arrive just as the earlier wave of Jewish migrants were moving out and upmarket, to Ilford.

At that time, the tiny synagogue on Fieldgate Street was still there (and still is, next to the East London Mosque); there was a Jewish delicatessen just round the corner on New Road; and, at the Aldgate end of Petticoat Lane, there was a Tubby Isaacs seafood stall and a Bloom's salt-beef restaurant. As we soon got to know, this was exactly the spot – at Gardiner's corner – where Oswald Mosley's fascists had been driven back by an anti-fascist onslaught now celebrated as the Battle of Cable Street. My partner, Mary Edmondson, began her career as a doctor in General Practice in Cable Street. The mural which now decorates the entire side of a building in Cable Street, celebrating the victory over Mosley, was painted by one of her patients, the East End artist, Dan Jones. He also did the illustration for the cover for *Socialist Worker* which celebrated the huge turnout for the first major ANL Carnival at Victoria Park.

Most of this area of East London – in and around Spitalfields and Shoreditch – is now so trendy, it's hard to imagine that it was ever such a dump. The doss-house that used to loom at the bottom of our street was one of the places Jack London had described in *The People of the Abyss*. Now, it's been turned into luxury flats. But, in the '70s, everywhere you went there were NF stickers and slogans on lamp-posts, walls, windows and doors. Encouraged by Enoch Powell's inflammatory 'rivers of blood' rhetoric, the Front had started to get big votes in elections. Asian families and left-wing activists had become regular victims of having shit posted through their letter boxes, occasional firebomb attacks and violent assaults on paper sales. Racist murders were becoming a regular occurrence.

During the course of the 70s, an estimated 35 racist murders were perpetrated by NF members. Altab Ali Park, at the top end of

Whitechapel High Street, was built to commemorate one of these killings, carried out on a garment worker on his way home. Another of these attacks, took place took place in Leamington Spa, where the NF had established a following. One of their members, the particularly revolting specimen, Robert Relf, had put his house on the market, proudly brandishing a placard which read 'For Sale to An English Family'. A few weeks earlier, an Asian man – Gurdip Singh Chagger – had been brutally murdered on the streets of Southall. Now, a similar attack took place on Relf's territory. An elderly woman, Mrs Mohan Devi Gautam, had been dragged from her home in Leamington by two white thugs, shoved into the garden shed and set on fire. This Ku Klux Klan style killing of a 76-year old woman I remember as being the final wake-up call which motivated individuals and organisations on the left to drop whatever differences they might have had and join forces for a common purpose: how to smash the National Front.

Our own offices, at 6 Cottons Gardens, were right in thick of all this, at the Shoreditch end of Kingsland Road. The neighbouring estate of Hoxton had a well-founded reputation as hot-bed of NF activity and for a time, the NF HQ was a few hundred yards away, at the Old Street end of Commercial Street. When I arrived for work one morning, in August 1976, it was to find our entire building ablaze following a petrol-bomb attack by the NF. This revenge attack took place a few weeks after the Nazis had suffered their most humiliating defeat at Lewisham, and shortly after the launch of the ANL.

Like everybody else, I was totally horrified to hear about Clapton's cretinous comments on race. I can remember very clearly Roger Huddle storming into the office to tell us what Clapton had come out with and to read out the letter that he and Red Saunders had written to the music papers, *New Musical Express*, *Melody Maker* and *Sounds* denouncing Clapton and calling for support from like-minded music fans. I can also remember Roger turning up the following week absolutely fizzing with excitement at the overwhelming response there had been.

The three stalwarts in the art-room of *Socialist Worker* at this time were Roger Huddle, Ruth Gregory and the photographer, Syd Shelton. Along with their close friend, Red Saunders, these were the ones who recognised the necessity for an organisation like RAR and subsequently ran it on an absolute shoe string. From what I can remember, they were pretty much left to their own devices. But the resources of the print-shop and its distribution network were absolutely essential for the production of the brilliant ANL posters and placards and for the RAR badges and stickers.

At present, it can sometimes be a temptation to regard the far-right in Britain as something of an irrelevance, especially since the relatively recent implosion of both the BNP and the EDL. But, as we have seen elsewhere in Europe, it cannot be taken for granted that things will stay this way. The great success of both ANL and RAR was that these campaigns were part of a two-pronged attack on the Nazis: one was to isolate them culturally by showing that the vast majority of decent citizens regarded their ideas as totally repulsive. The other was to drive them off the streets and make sure they never showed their faces again.

A climate was created in which one of the ANL's most prominent supporters, Brian Clough, was perfectly happy to describe NF members as the 'scum of the earth'. In an interview for *Socialist Worker*, the front man for the Sex Pistols, John Lyddon, told Dave Widgery that he despised the National Front and that no-one should have the right to tell anyone that they couldn't live here because of their colour, or their religion. The Pistols number one smash hit 'God Save the Queen' had caused an absolute furore when it came out to coincide with the Queen's Silver Jubilee and was immediately banned by the BBC. But its chorus 'No Future' also became the template for innumerable ANL and RAR leaflets: NF=No Future; Nazi Front; No Fun; No Freedom.

Tom Robinson

Winter of '79

Nearly all of us who grew up in 50s Britain inherited a casual thoughtless racism, homophobia and misogyny as part of the national culture. We weren't aware of it at the time any more than fish are aware of water. We had Eeeny Meeny in the playground, golliwogs as toys and songs taught in school such as Polly Wolly Doodle and Uncle Ned. Women still needed their husbands' permission to open a bank account while homosexuals were treated as mentally ill or sent to prison. At school I actually taunted other kids as 'queer' even though they weren't and I was. My early teens were not a period I'm proud of, for many reasons.

What changed the attitudes of my generation towards race more than anything was the new and amazing music we began to discover by the likes of Muddy Waters, Otis Redding, Aretha Franklin, John Lee Hooker, James Brown, Stevie Wonder and Bob Marley. It was daft – how could you love this music and continue to look down upon the kind of people who created it.

In my own case, getting involved with the Gay Liberation Front in the early '70s also made a major difference. GLF believed freedom was indivisible: you either lived in a fair and just society or you didn't – and at that time the oppression of minorities was much more overt. The Met were harassing gay men in Earls Court and black youth in Brixton under the same 'Sus' laws – and opposing them was all part of the same struggle. Once you looked at where rock came from, the proposition of Rock Against Racism when it came along was blindingly obvious.

Eric Clapton's comments came against a background of racial unrest – embodied by rise of the National Front. But they were at wide variance from most music fans at the time – and caused such widespread dismay. Red's founding Rock Against Racism letter in *Melody Maker* offered both hope and a focal point for those of us who embraced the

more culturally diverse society that was slowly emerging.
RAR managed to square the circle – in a way that had previously been thought impossible – by being genuinely of the Left, yet achieving a mass appeal with the general public. It used ordinary language instead of alien political jargon and featured well designed graphics as a central part of its identity.

● Tom Robinson Band on cover of *TH4*

The most refreshing thing about RAR in those early days was its grassroots nature – the way unknown reggae and punk bands could be found sharing stages at small venues. And, unlike almost every political gig staged before or since, RAR always made sure every band got paid at every gig they promoted. Fair wages for work done was a point of principle – rather than exploiting the goodwill of any struggling musicians prepared to support the cause.
In crude capitalist terms, the founding team had a grasp of branding, marketing and message that was no progressive political group in this country ever matched before or since. Since the word "branding" itself is the pure essence of Saatchi-speak, that's perhaps not so surprising. Live Aid built on these techniques (with logos and slogans galore) and got into bed with capitalism unequivocally. But each to their own – given the outcome that many thousands of lives were saved at the time – fair play to Ure and Geldof too.
It's true that the Brexit vote of 2016 risks plunging our country back into 1970s levels of racism and intolerance – and every one of us, young and old, needs to battle against that happening. But it's also easy to forget just how far we've come since then. The sheer ugliness of the cultural landscape we all inhabited back then would be unrecognisable for today's teenagers and twenty-somethings. For them the RAR carnival must now seem as remote as Cable Street did to us at the time. Their turn to show mass solidarity for justice and humanity will come. And the job of us oldsters will be to spot it when it does, and help make it happen with every drop of strength we can muster.

Keith Rusby

In 1976 Keith had left North London Polytechnic after being Social Secretary of the Students Union. He began working in Honky Tonk Records in Kentish Town, before running it with Mike Bettison and Nigel Wilkinson. He helped set up Camden Anti Nazi League and was involved with RAR. Camden Libraries, Community Arts, Street Entertainment, Pyrotechnics, Greenwich Festival, and Greenwich Housing Department occupied his time until retiring in 2014. Kept involved with music through Sidmouth and Towersey Festivals. Still Loves music, Hates racism.

Folk Against Racism

I was running a record shop with two others in Kentish Town, north London at the time. We specialised in punk, reggae, soul and anything leftfield. We loved music, hated racism.

Looking back, it seemed to happen in an instant. The growth of the NF, Eric Clapton's support of Enoch Powell. I remember seeing Muddy Waters at Dingwalls, and half way through his set he introduced Clapton on stage with him. A large section of the audience met his arrival with boos and shouts of 'racist'. I was involved in the setting up of Camden ANL. Our shop displayed the ANL and RAR logo's, sold the badges and on one occasion had windows and doors covered in NF slogans.

I loved punk and reggae, and loved the RAR Carnivals. I also loved folk. From when I first heard Bob Dylan, Irish music in the pubs of Wandsworth and Hammersmith, then discovering singers such as Martin Carthy, The Watersons, Shirley Collins, Anne Briggs, and that traditional songs and ballads from England and Scotland had resonance, power and beauty.

For me, and just about everyone else I got to know on the 'folk scene', folk was never about Arran sweaters and twee songs. It was about a living oral tradition. Sung by ordinary working people, songs told of hardship, appalling working conditions, struggle against oppression ballads sung by soldiers and farmers during the Napoleonic wars telling of war-weariness or high grain prices. Songs telling monumental stories (if you're in any doubt, just listen to 'Tam Lin', amongst thousands of other songs)), humour, songs that just entertain, of love, death and everything else in between! Simply, folk song gives us a social history. It's worth mentioning that Topic Records (Britain's oldest independent record label) was established by the Workers Music Association, part of the general movement 'to encourage international solidarity in the struggle to contain the menace of fascism and to provide the workers with a home to express their hopes and wishes through music' (Topic

Records *The Voice of the People* – 7 cd and book celebrating 70 years of the label. It's first release in 1939 was 'The Man That Waters The Workers' Beer' by Paddy Ryan, backed by the Topic Singers singing 'The Internationale'. Humour and politics on one 78rpm record!)
One of the people in the record shop was Mike Bettison, melodeon player with an English dance band Flowers and Frolics, also residents at the Islington Folk Club, which was run by Bob Davenport, singer from Gateshead who sang with Flowers, lifelong socialist and one of the most powerful singers you're likely to hear. I knew lots of performers who supported the ANL and RAR, and I wanted the 'folk scene' to make it's contribution and show that racism plays no part in our music and our lives. So, what to do. I still had contacts at North London Poly Students Union where I had once been Social Secretary. Bob Davenport's wife Jean ran a folk agency from the shop, so it was obvious. Organise a RAR concert. I recall, there was a modicum of doubt about the gig, questioning the genre of the event. RAR gigs usually took a specific form, punk and reggae.
The Student Union at NLP gave the use of the big hall on Holloway Road and supplied the posters and leaflets. I can't remember who supplied the PA. Flowers and Frolics and Bob Davenport immediately gave their services, and brought in Taffy Thomas, street entertainer, dance caller and story teller, to MC. Then who to get. Pulled a bit of a fast one here. I contacted Martin Carthy, one of the best known, if not the best known folk singer in the country, and John Martyn. John said he'd do it if Martin does it, and Martin said he'd do it if John did it! Well that's how I remember it, but time creates it's own version of things. A bit like folk song really.
Now we had the line up: Bob Davenport & Flowers and Frolics, Martin Carthy, and John Martyn, the hall, PA, publicity and stewards. Everything in place. All we needed to do now was sell the tickets. And tickets we sold. I think the venue held about 1,000 people.

We sold out days before the gig.
And what a fantastic night it was. Everyone performed brilliantly. I know people who were there, remember it as being as great as I remember it. I feel proud that I organised that concert, and that the music I have always loved played it's part. And by the way, it raised the most money RAR ever made from an indoor gig.
Folk music fitted in to RARs aims, and still does. The legacy lives on. In 2010, Show Of Hands song 'Roots' appeared on the compilation album *The Best of British Folk*. But it was also used, without permission, by the BNP in a campaign video. The band successfully had their music removed from the campaign video. Show Of Hands and other performers and people involved in the folk scene set up the campaign Folk Against Fascism. Yes, Love folk, Hate racism!

Nina Saunders

Artist

I remember being a young Danish woman at Heathrow airport in the Mid '70's, black people were being singled out and held up at passport control... hours... little children crying.

Although I didn't feel particularly Danish, I knew then that I would never become a British citizen.

RAR was very open; it didn't feel like I needed some special knowledge to join in, it was very equal.

There was always loads of people round the house... enough pots of tea brewed to break the Guiness book of records, the oven was always full of baked spuds for evening volunteers.

So on top of all this energy us young mums, with babies started to make food for the RAR stalls, at the carnivals and gigs to raise extra money for the campaign.

I remember Red coming home exhausted one night to find the bath tub full of lettuce soaking in water.

Jackie, Patsie and myself organised a rota of helpers, buttering, filling, and wrapping baps ready to go to the carnival (see page 198)... house full of kids, lots of reggae music (a kind of mad family Xmas feeling)... then later we'd go to a Misty in Roots gig at the Hope and Anchor, a local pub. I found myself right in the middle of the explosion of music, art and fashion going on at that time... Also it was a great time to have kids, we all had a common cause, none of us were isolated. We seemed to share everything.

● Nina outside her London studio.

They were scary times as well and serious threats to us, and a lot of violence at gigs and on demos both from NF skinheads and the police... and then a bullet in the post!

Even though I was scared, I was also young, naive. My mum back in Denmark had never seen an avocado, and I had never seen a woman in twin set and pearls with a turban screaming 'oh bondage up yours' they were truly amazing times.

I remember being at the opening of Camerawork Disability Access Centre in East London by Ian Dury. There was a set by the Japanese feminist punk group the Frank Chickens – not an everyday event in Jutland, Denmark.

All these things were the most important exploration of life and culture that inspired me to become an artist, it gave me the rock to stand on.

RAR Letter

When we read about Eric Clapton's Birmingham concert when he urged support for Enoch Powell, we nearly puked.

What's going on Eric? You've got a touch of brain damage. So you are going to stand up for us and you think we are being colonised by black people. Come, you've been taking too much of that *Daily Express* stuff, you know you can't handle it.

Own up. Half your music is black. You are rock music's biggest colonist. You're a good musician but where would you be without the blues and R&B?

You've got to fight the racist poison, otherwise you degenerate into the sewer with the rats and all the money men who've ripped off rock culture with their cheque books and plastic crap.

Rock was and can still be a real progressive culture not a package mail order stick-on nightmare of mediocre garbage.

Keep the faith, black and white unite and fight.

We want to organise a rank and file movement against the racist poison in rock music – we urge support – all those interested please write to Rock Against Racism, Box M, 6 Cotton's Gardens, London E2 8DN.

p.s. Who shot the Sheriff, Eric? It sure as hell wasn't you!

Signed:

Peter Bruno, Dave Courts, Angela Follett, Roger Huddle, Red Saunders, Mike Stadler, Jo Wreford.

September 1976

Red Saunders

All power to the imagination

Rock Against Racism: A rebel musical movement broke down fear and took on racism. Forty years ago this month (November 2016) music fans fought back against racist comments from top musicians by launching an anti-racist movement in music. One of the founders of Rock Against Racism, Red Saunders, spoke to Ken Olende, from *Unity* Magazine about what happened.

In the summer of 1976 the fascist National Front (NF) was growing and there was a general rise in racism across Britain. But it was a rant from guitarist Eric Clapton, who had just had a hit with a cover of Bob Marley's 'I shot the Sheriff' *that got Rock Against Racism started. How did that happen?*

We were sitting around in my photographic studio in Great Windmill Street, Soho, in the August 1976. I was in a radical theatre group called Kartoon Klowns and that was where we rehearsed. Someone came in all angry with the new issue of *Melody Maker* and said "Have you seen this about Eric Clapton?".
During a concert in Birmingham, he'd said that he supported top racist Enoch Powell and foreigners should get out of the country.
What we read was terrible, but since then I've heard a tape of what he said. It was far worse. He said, "Throw the wogs out! Keep Britain white!" He kept going on about "wogs".
I was shocked. I was a fan. I'd bought the albums and I'd seen him play. I'd watched him in the supergroup Blind Faith.

The same summer David Bowie said in an interview with Playboy magazine, "I think Britain could benefit from a fascist leader. After all, fascism is really nationalism... I believe very strongly in fascism, people have always responded with greater efficiency under a regimental leadership...Adolf Hitler was one of the first rock stars...You've got to have an extreme right front come up and sweep everything off its feet and tidy everything up".

Yes. I think Bowie was stoned out of his head at the time but we had to stamp on him. He couldn't get away with that stuff. At least he later retracted it and went on to make a donation to the Anti Nazi League. But I don't believe Clapton ever apologised for what he said.

I'd been in political theatre groups since 1964, performing about racism and apartheid and against war.

We had a group of friends who'd come to rehearsals including the Royal Group of Dockworkers shop stewards' committee. That introduced me to another level of ideas.

I was a mod. I was really into black music—more R&B than the blues. In the 1960s I used to work at the Marquee Club collecting empty glasses. You only got paid two and six a night, but it got you free entry. You could meet the musicians. We had a wonderful evening in the pub once with the blues singer Jimmy Witherspoon. I was just this 17 year old kid.

Photograph: Red Saunders

When I was an apprentice photographer one of my closest friends was a Caribbean motorcycle dispatch rider.

There was that whole sixties progressive anti-racist angle. We thought Clapton was part of that. That's why it was such a shock to hear him coming out with the foulest rubbish. That's why we exploded when we heard about it.

I don't want to try and get inside his head to work out how he could say that while he was playing that music, but people have muddled, mixed up, alienated ideas.

I've never been one for writing letters, but after a day of thinking I sat down and wrote a letter. It was signed by me and my friend the graphic designer Roger Huddle and some of the theatre group.

We sent it to all the music press—like *Black Echoes, NME, Melody Maker, Sounds*—and the socialist press—including the *Morning Star* and *Socialist Worker*. We got letter of the week in *Melody Maker*—they sent me an album token. We'd put a PO Box number and, to our amazement, within a few weeks we had 400 or 500 replies.

It was completely bonkers, but we thought, "Now we've got to do something". Don't ever think writing letters is a waste of time. Rock Against Racism wouldn't have happened without that.

We decided we'd better put on a gig. I was doing a lot of photographs for the music press then. At that time "pub rock" was a big thing and I was a fan—bands like Bees Make Honey and Ace. They were exactly what the name says—they played rock in pubs.

The first gig we did was with Carol Grimes. She was pub rock. In fact she was benefit rock. She did more benefits than anyone I knew. She'd

● Top: Red's design montage for final *TH*14. Below: Nina Saunders, Patsy Galvin and RAR stalwart Robert Galvin, ready to feed the dancers.

say she was a blues singer.
Roger Huddle said we need to do gigs in east London where the NF were. So we booked the Princess Alice pub in Forest Gate. We'd organised things before so we weren't frightened. We got some socialists from the dockers' union to do security. I remember putting up the banner on stage. The banners came from the other side of our sixties background—Agitation. We loved artists from Alexander Rodchenko and Andy Warhol.

So the gig was a success and it snowballed quickly.

As soon as the responses started coming in to the letter I went "We need a logo", before thinking about a magazine or a manifesto.
I was a freelance photographer for the *Sunday Times* magazine, which David King designed. He was one of the top designers in the country and a good anti-racist.
He came up with that star. And a year or two later he came back with the Anti Nazi League arrow.
The RAR star soon appeared on everything – posters and badges. I think badges are so important. Show what you think on the tube. Have an argument even though that's frightening. You might get your head whacked in, but it works.
That October, I was asked by *NME* to do some pictures of punk rock. I said, "What's that?" It was the ICA, in central London, which was an art venue, so I didn't know what to expect. I took a picture of some woman biting the ear of Shane MacGowan, who went on to be in the Pogues. There was blood everywhere. I could only vaguely see what was going on. The Clash were on and it was incredible. They were wearing amazing clothes. I went backstage and met them. Before long we'd be asking them to play for us.
It very quickly became our thing to mix up the bands. We had to have black bands on stage. That was a more important priority than having black people in the audience because we were fighting racism among white people.
But putting the black and white bands together broke down the fear. One of the most wonderful gigs we did was at Hackney Town Hall. We had the reggae band the Cimarons on with the punk act Generation X. Everyone jammed together at the end. It became the blueprint.

How did RAR's magazine Temporary Hoarding relate to this?

The first issue of *Temporary Hoarding* said what we were about, "We want rebel music, street music. Music that breaks down people's fear of one another. Crisis music. Now music. Music that knows who the real enemy is. Rock Against Racism. Love Music Hate Racism".
We thought it was important to have some kind of publication to say what we were about. Now as the punk rock movement grew, all these fanzines appeared.

I'd seen the most famous one, called *Sniffin Glue*. We mixed that with Chinese wall posters that I knew about. These were newspapers designed to be pasted on a wall. They were a temporary hoarding, just intended to last for a bit.

So that's what we based our magazine on and why we called it *Temporary Hoarding*. And quite often we literally designed it as a poster so you could paste it on a wall. We wanted lots of visual images. The left is too wordy sometimes.

I'm 71 now and to this day, if I go to an anti-racist rally or a trade union meeting and there are nine speakers on the platform, I think, "Give me a break! Put on two speakers and a DJ, please".

We wanted to do something that looked good and got our message across quickly.

Luckily we had a lot of people who were very good at visual images. Ruth Gregory and Syd Shelton were earning their living as graphic designers. So was Roger Huddle. I was a photographer. David Widgery was writing for Oz.

● Red and Nina Saunders, with daughter Lisa 3 weeks old at Victoria Park Carnival 1978

There was no internet. We relied on posters and stickers. The city was covered in posters.

On top of that we relied on the music press. Journalists such as Vivien Goldman would always tell people what were up to. And the *NME*'s editor Neil Spencer was a supporter. It was so cool to be in *NME*. It was the bible.

How did RAR grow?

We got letters from all over. They'd say something like, "I'm Tommy and I live in Aberystwyth and we've got an NF teacher. I hate racism and I like RAR. Can you please help us?" I'd write back and say, "That's fantastic Tommy. You are RAR Aberystwyth. We've got nothing to give you. All the luck!" We sent those letters all over.

In the big cites we found some brilliant people, like Paul Furness, who set up Leeds RAR club. That was an area where the Nazi National Front were really strong. Then you had Manchester where I met a wonderful working class woman in Hulme.

And the whole thing built up over a couple of years. And you can't talk about it all without talking about the anti-Nazi demonstration in Lewisham a year later and the launch of the Anti Nazi League (ANL). Until that we'd been small and local. After that it went really national. But really that's a story that deserves to be told in more detail, so I'll save it for another day.

When we decided to have a Carnival in 1978 that was a whole new adventure. We thought it had to be in the heart of NF territory—that's why we held it in Victoria Park in east London.

Some people like Dave Widgery felt we didn't need the ANL, but I thought it was important. If there was a carnival, who was leafleting the local factory? Who was booking the coaches? Who was getting trade union money? Suddenly we had money and that let us book huge venues. Where are you going to get £10,000 to book the PA?

At first we were expecting 10,000 but we got closer to 100,000. We marched from Trafalgar Square. The police said no one would do that.

My favourite moment was at the Blade Bone pub on Bethnal Green Road, which was a big NF haunt at the time. They came out and were all sieg heiling as we went past. But we just went on going past for 10 minutes, 20 minutes—thousands and thousands strong—so the fascists lost spirit and went back inside.

But the old Jewish lady from the tobacconist stayed to watch all the time we went by—so pleased to see us.

What do you think all this time later about what you achieved?

After we had RAR, when Thatcher and Reagan came they were triumphant and we were knocked back. That is mirrored. At the tail end of RAR we set up Rock Against Thatcher. That is what happens to united fronts when the clear and present enemy dissipates. But it's also like a rock group with all those young people running everything—people split and there are differences.

What can someone who is 17 and wants to fight racism learn from RAR?

It's up to them. But I still support the old 1960s slogan, 'All power to the imagination'. You've got to do it yourself with your own culture. It's got to be bottom up and DIY. Punk was great for that. We beat the NF out on the streets and with the power of music and culture. RAR was a shooting star that lasted six very frenitic, hetic and amzing years of my life. And here we are forty years later talking to people not even born then who still want to hear about those RAR days.

This resistance is in our history and our tradition. But it is really hidden. That's why I've been doing a series of photos recreating hidden bits of our history. I call them Hidden to remind people, we're not mad for thinking things can change.

● Red, Lorraine, Jessica, Felix and Roger, along with 4,000 others confronting the EDL in Walthamstow 2012

David Seymour

Keeping pace with Rock Against Racism

I remember Rock Against Racism from my days at Art College in Taunton. It was a bit off the beaten track, but was on the circuit of most touring bands and, like many art colleges, it was a place of political activity. In those days this meant joining RAR in opposition to the far right racist group the National Front and their hate campaign against non-whites. Our source of information was the music press – the *NME* and *Melody Maker* – and getting involved was a simple matter of calling RAR and getting sent a box of badges. It's the badge that really sticks in my memory; it must be one of the design icons of the 70s. That was from '78 to '80. The music scene was really vibrant then, with punk rock and British rhythm and blues still going strong, reggae turning more dub, the development of new wave, the ska revival, the first goths and romantics emerging onto the streets and an incipient kind of thrash metal. Rock Against Racism was the political soul of much of this; it gave a political direction to punk rock, which otherwise would have gone completely down the path of nihilism. It was a mystery to me at the time how punk and reggae became so intertwined, because the music was so different. But the Clash made sense of it, and RAR helped different styles to combine by bringing together diverse musicians and fans at events that included some of my favourite bands: Aswad, Elvis Costello, The Slits, Graham Parker & the Rumour, X-Ray Specs and the Tom Robinson Band. This was the environment that paved the way for ska. In fact, The Beat first met at a Rock Against Racism rally in Victoria Park, East London, where 80 000 people gathered in 1978. That event put a big nail in the coffin of the National Front as a political force. 20 years later I ended up in a pub cricket team in Victoria Park with Red Saunders, the rock photographer and agitprop activist who instigated Rock Against Racism when he sent a letter to the music press in 1976 exhorting musicians and music fans to raise their voices against fascism. I don't remember if Red was a batsman or a bowler, but I do recall his running between the wickets – like a supertanker that picks up a good head of steam but takes a long time to slow down again on the other side of the stumps. Our team, the Caledonian Conquerors, was a friendly mix of white squatters, Cockneys, Pakistanis and West Indians (but, despite the name, no Scots!). We had the kind of open-minded and multi-cultural mindset that came directly out of punk rock and Rock Against Racism. In my job as a teacher of ESOL (English for Speakers of Other Languages) at Hackney College I have also collaborated with Red to help the students create a magazine, the *Hack*. I think things like RAR, community cricket and ESOL have all helped to develop London into a fantastic global city. And, of course, the arrival of people from all over the world is what makes London work as a great melting pot of cultures. Which leads me to believe that now is the time for a revival of Rock Against Racism, faced as we are with a resurgence in anti-immigrant discourses throughout post-brexit Britain. As Heaven 17 sang in 1981: Brothers, sisters, we don't need that fascist groove thang.

Michael Shann

Thirteen

Summer of '81: The Specials, The Jam,
the older lads dancing to northern soul
in a blur of gleaming brogues. We were all coy
till they closed the curtains, then we'd dance too
and later we'd pair off in the dark,
discovering the sweet taste of lip-gloss,
and all mixed up with the music and heat,
what we'd eventually come to call love.

Small town incendiaries

Hurrying home through the old ordinary,
my first album burned through its carrier:
toxic vinyl, corrosive, flammable,
a calling from London, Belfast, blasted
from my bedroom when Mum and Dad were out.
Of course I went back, thumbed through the records
with a thumping heart, seeking sounds that pushed
me further, over the edge of myself.

Neil Spencer

Music journalist and editor of *NME* during RAR days.

RAR Reflections

The Cimarons/Generation X
Hackney Town Hall
August 1977

It was an evening when, to quote a ballad from the English Civil War, the world was turned upside down, an evening of brief but delicious disorder. As much started with the venue. Hackney Town Hall was absolutely not on London's music circuit, which was served by pub rock venues like Fulham's Nashville Room and Islington's Hope and Anchor. Live reggae music was way scarcer, confined to clubs like Dalston's Four Aces, a mere half mile from Hackney's civil headquarters but in cultural terms, a light year away.

Hackney Town Hall belonged to neither tribe. The Mare Street monolith was where you married and paid taxes, not raved. Built in the 1930s, its interior paid homage to previous generations of public servants with oil paintings of bewhiskered aldermen and upright Labour councillors lining its walls. Tonight they gazed down on a scene that would have been incomprehensible to them, a crowd of ramshackle youth garbed in denim and ripped t-shirts (if white), and tams, dreadlocks and earth shoes (if black). The crowd was not all trend-conscious by any means, but the bands onstage were. In the wake of Bob Marley, reggae musicians and followers had turned militant and rootsical. Rastafarian red gold and green was everywhere. In the wake of the Sex Pistols, still soaring on 'God Save the Queen' in this Silver Jubilee summer, rock had likewise turned spiky and mutinous.

The Punky Reggae Party, as Marley had dubbed it on disc only the previous month, would become a familiar event in the years ahead, but this was one of its earliest manifestations and sent shock waves round the place.. The council staff manning the event, not least those guarding the stage, looked stunned but stoical; where had this mixed bunch come from? They coped nobly. There was no hint of aggravation or trouble among the crowd, just electrified enthusiasm. It was an unsophisticated setting; there were no spotlights, just playing, just energy.

Most of the punters were there for Gen X. Though the band hadn't yet issued a record – debut single 'Your Generation' was a few weeks away – they had a reputation built on a year gigging and putting Billy Idol's sneering good looks on the pages of the music press. They blasted into 'From The Heart' and moved up the gears through 'Kleenex' and 'Wild Youth' to a frenzy of pogoing. The group were never scratchy punk hardliners, always retaining a link to rock past as a title like 'Ready Steady Go' suggests, but it was still a surprise when they broke into a pedal-to-the-floor version of Lennon's 'Gimme Some Truth', Idol spitting out the words with venom. The ex-Beatle would have been proud.

Following a high energy set like that would pose a problem for many bands, but the Cimarons were coming from another place entirely, one perfectly suited to the warm summer night. In any case they were way too accomplished to doubt themselves; they had arrived from Jamaica a decade earlier and as one of the UK's few self-contained reggae bands had backed visiting JA stars and toured internationally while racking up modest hits of their own. Though they had started out with pop reggae, the Cims had long brandished a militant edge, there on a slow, opening 'Ship Ahoy', their take on The O'Jays' chilling account of the slave trade from '73.

Then they rocked, JA style, through 'Harder Than The Rock', soon to become a theme tune, covers of of The In Crowd's 'Born In Ethiopia', Ras Ibuna's 'Diverse Doctrine' and Sparrow's 'How You Jamming So'. For much of the audience, this was their introduction to live reggae, a winning one.

It was not the first rock/reggae culture clash – Aswad had played alongside label mates Eddie and The Hotrods, and The Cimarons had shared a stage with The Jam at the Royal College of Art, but the chemistry that night was incendiary, spilling over into a long finale where the two bands jammed together exuberantly, swapping roles through the warhorse of Them's 'Gloria' and The Slickers' 'Johnny Too Bad' before a radical talk-over exchange on Tapper Zukie's 'MPLA'. The mood was euphoric, ending with the singers of the two bands clasping upraised hands while the crowd chanted 'Black and White Unite'. Afterwards you could smell change on the East London breeze, the taste of the world turned upside down.

Virginia Turbett

Rarmories: Photography

My memories of the gigs are getting hazy now but I do remember well the feelings; the long hauls to gigs in Edinburgh, West Runton and Cambridge. Train journeys with Garry Bushell as we were covering the RAR scene for *Sounds*. Hard to believe now that Garry, with his *Socialist Worker* background, was possibly the first music journalist to pick up on the importance and excitement that the ANL/RAR gigs were generating.

Huge bands and individuals from huge bands travelling to little places like West Runton Pavillion – as far East Coast as you can get in the UK. The hardcore fans who appeared at every gig – how did they do that? The gigs closer to home: Crisis playing, possibly the last ever gig at the Acklam Hall, under the Westway where we hid in the toilets while skinheads broke all the windows around us with lead pipes, waiting for the police who took about 30 minutes to arrive.

The Brixton Carnival, my second only music photo shoot where the sun shone and I can still today feel the pulsing from the front of the stage through my dm's. The Rainbow, where The Clash and Pete Townsend played to support those arrested and injured at Southall.

Sham 69 and the Angelic Upstarts, who are remembered for having a dodgy fan base played at Ally Pally. Jimmy Pursey in tears, saying he felt ashamed, when the NF and British Movement skinheads trashed their final gig at the Rainbow.

Somebody said recently how lucky we were to have lived on this earth at the same time as David Bowie. I agree but feel I am also lucky to have been a very small part of a movement that felt massively important and had the energy of a hundred juggernauts thundering around the country. I got to see Alex Harvey on stage with The Ruts, Tony James, Aswad, Misty, Jimmy Pursey and Tom Robinson – where else but a RAR event would that happen?

I still meet people who have spotted their younger selves in my photos of RAR gigs and tell me how they spent all day hitching to a gig or painting their school blazer with the names of bands in day-glo paint (not caring how mad their Mum would be…that's proper dedication to the anti-racist cause), to see the best bands who were donating their time; the Scottish punks including Dennis who had a political education that exceeded many on the left I worked with – all of them saying loudly and proudly that there was to be no tolerance of facism in our music. RAR gave all of these people a badge (I still have my actual badge) to wear that identified the masses against the facist minority who were at the time trashing and intimidating at, and after, gigs and the importance of that cannot be over estimated.

● The Ruts at West Runton Pavillion, 20th March 1979

● Malcolm Owen, The Ruts, Rainbow Theatre Southall Benefit, 13th July 1979

● Fans at the front Alexandra Palace, 14th April 1979

● Crisis play RAR gig at Acklam Hall – ended after 20 mins when skinheads attacked and smashed through doors and windows, 24th June 1979

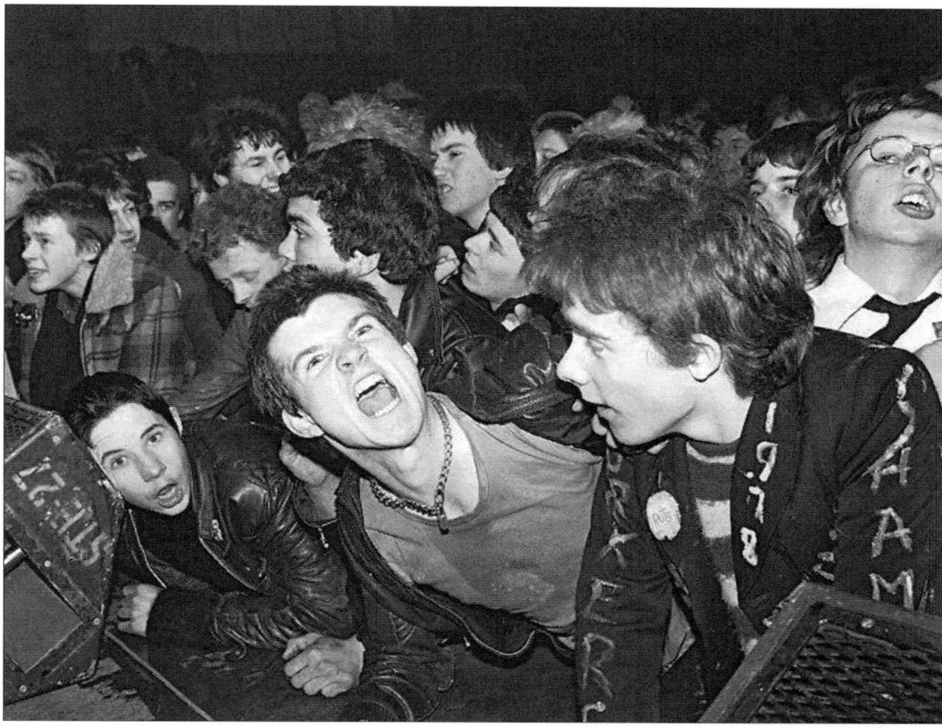

● RAR hits Cambridge Corn Exchange. 17th March 1979. (The bloke in the blazer nearest camera is now my friend and neighbour!)

Militant Entertainment at Alexandra Palace, 14 April 1979

Alexandra Palace 14 April 1979. Fan joins Tom Robinson, guitars Jake Burns and Tony James.

Virginia now

Kate Webb

Songs of Freedom

Forty years later, among all the theories advanced about its origins and politics, one glaring fact about Rock Against Racism is often forgotten: at its root was the shared love of music. Thinking about the performers who appeared on our stages, and the music they played there, seems like a good way to cut through the arguments and get to the heart of RAR. At an event to celebrate the publication of Syd Shelton's photographic history of RAR, Syd, Paul Gilroy and I each selected three tracks that in some way epitomized the era. What follows are some reflections on the music I chose, and on my involvement with a movement that interrogated the past, prefigured the future of networked politics, and celebrated the turbulent era we were living in, with – as Syd's photographs attest – passion, style and commitment.

Track 1.**Winter of '79—Tom Robinson Band** (1977, There are many songs that convey the apocalyptic imagination of the late 1970s and early 1980s in Britain – the pervasive sense of urgency and danger, of state violence and fascist threat – but Tom Robinson's 'Winter of '79' differs from others in treating the moment historically. Written in 1977, the song predicts an uprising in 1979 and then looks back at the insurrection from a time in the future when a world-weary activist addresses a new generation: "All you kids who just sit and whine, you should have been there back in '79, You say we're giving you a real hard time, you guys are really breaking my heart". Robinson's prophecies weren't far off the mark: the next few years would see tanks in Belfast, bombs in London, and riots in cities up and down the country. Like many of the period's best songs, his catch the jittery mood on the streets. You can hear it especially in 'Long Hot Summer', which was inspired by the Stonewall riots, and in the shifting allegiances of 'Up Against the

Wall', where he confronts his audience with the question: "Just whose side are you on?"

Robinson wasn't alone in his sense of foreboding, further warnings of collapse can be heard in the songs of many other bands who played for RAR: in The Clash's 'London Calling', Aswad's 'Judgement Day', the Ruts' 'Babylon's Burning', Stiff Little Fingers' 'State of Emergency', and, most potently perhaps, in the weird atmospherics of the Specials' 'Ghost Town'. On the verge of Thatcherism and the neo-liberal takeover of the world, much of the music of this pivotal moment records the sound of a country breaking apart, of old communities dying and new ones struggling to be born. And it's important to remember that pop music hadn't yet been fully assimilated into capitalism: it was a playground the young still had largely to themselves, which meant these songs rang out like warning shots fired across a radio that no one in authority was listening to.

●Tom, top, Kate below on left, then Karen, Scruf and Scruff and Jo. Photograph for *TH* by Syd Shelton

Tom was the first person who made me think about how you could link people together under the radar. Something of a graphomaniac, he wrote long letters to his fans, connecting them to one another. In the winter of '77 I was seventeen, working in the hat and glove department of Debenhams on Oxford Street, and looking for people to share my anger with. He put me in touch with two Jewish schoolgirls from Camden who called themselves Scruf and Scruff; Karen, a stylish secretary, the daughter of East European immigrants; Alan, who was serving in the army in Northern Ireland and being tormented by other soldiers for his love of punk; Patsy, the daughter of West Indian immigrants who was working as a back-up singer; and a razor-sharp Irish girl who went by the name of Anna Gram, and lived on the estate behind my mum and dad's house in Clapham. Anna approached me on the Northern line one day, my badges giving out a signal,demanding to know if I was the Irate Kate that Tom Robinson had written to her about.

Not long after this happened, decanted early from work one evening because of another IRA bomb threat, I walked out of Debenhams and made my way over to the East End where RAR were a holding a meeting. I remember being embarrassed by my work clothes as I descended into a basement of noisy punks, socialists, writers, photographers and graphic designers, most of them a decade or so older than me. By the end of the evening I was so fired up by their heady talk (they discussed Toussaint L'Ouverture, Alexandra Kollontai and Kurt Weill as if they were old friends), that I chucked in my job and volunteered to become RAR's first full-time worker.

Red Saunders, the man who dreamed up RAR after Eric Clapton's racist outburst in Birmingham, donated desk space I could use in his Soho photographic studio. Every morning I'd walk up Great Windmill Street as elaborately painted women pushed chairs out in front of the sex shops, smoked and drank espressos, and waited for the day's punters to slink in. At the studio, the photographers put out their paraphernalia – maybe a wind-machine for a glossy *Sunday Times* portrait of Kate Bush – and I'd set to answering the letters that had begun to pour in from across the country. We quickly outgrew our spot in Soho and with the money coming in – school kids' pennies sellotaped together, the odd fiver from a supportive vicar, tenners from the anarchist bookshop stocking RAR's poster-magazine, *Temporary Hoarding* – we could afford a room in Clerkenwell, not far from the Marx Memorial library. Here the operation got a little more sophisticated: the RAR office became the hub and contact point for a much larger group of people and activities.

By day I'd liaise with the newly-elected RAR committee and the rapidly increasing number of RAR groups in the UK and abroad, communicate with bands and their managers, send out press releases, gestetner newsletters, order new badges and stickers, encourage people to write reviews and reports for *Temporary Hoarding,* pay bills, draw up agendas, and talk to other groups with whom we often collaborated (the campaign against the Corrie anti-abortion Bill, the Right to Work marchers, and CURB, who organised against violent bouncers). By night we'd run letter-writing sessions, often working into the dawn with a gang of volunteers – teenagers, like my sister Jo and her friends, skiving from school; shop assistants, machine operators and secretaries bunking off work. We'd all squeeze into RAR's tiny office, sackfuls of mail strewn around the floor. From the letters flooding in it was evident that there was a nation of kids out there, bored out of their minds, and horrified by the spectre of the National Front marching on their high streets. They described living in nowhere towns and suburbs that closed down at seven o'clock, aching for a life less parochial. What they wanted was the glamour of dissident art and radical ideas – a new world they tried to fathom by listening to John Peel late into the night or reading James Baldwin under the covers by torchlight.

RAR became a network before we knew what a network was. We told these kids: here are the addresses of other music fans in your area, set up a RAR group, design a poster, put on a gig, write your own fanzine, and challenge the local National Front. We told them anyone could do it and wrote step-by-step Gig Guides showing them how. And in *Temporary Hoarding*, The Mekons published an article explaining how to build your own PA system, while the Au Pairs described how they recorded their first single by borrowing their mum and dad's holiday money. The explosion of punk and reggae meant that there were bands all over the country hungry for gigs. And there was massive energy and frustration everywhere you turned, which RAR tapped into and transformed into action.

As well as organising our own gigs, tours and carnivals, RAR took a stall round the country when the TRB went out on the road. The band dressed like the school kids they sang about, "sullen, unhealthy and mean", and Tom had 302.0 stencilled on his shirt. This was the code for homosexuality in the World Health Organisation's classification of diseases – something he'd been alerted to by Paul Furness, a key RAR activist, who worked in the Records Office of Leeds General Infirmary.
One of the characteristics that marked Robinson out from many of his contemporaries was that along with his irony in songs like 'Glad to be Gay' ("The British police are the best in the world..."), he also understood, instinctively, the importance of bringing people together. It was not enough to complain about discrimination against gays if you ignored what was happening to your "brothers in Brixton, backs to the wall". Racism, sexism and homophobia – these things were all part of the same problem, and we would sink or swim together.
For RAR, too, solidarity was the watchword. As David Widgery, the East End doctor who wrote so passionately for *Temporary Hoarding*, argued in an article on colonialism: 'there's no *us* without *them*'. This is why Robinson was so important to RAR, a movement dedicated to routing racism, but also to exploring a much broader cultural politics. He understood how to express and channel anger, but he was also hugely charismatic and convivial – something you can see in Syd's great shot of him at the first RAR carnival in Victoria Park. Tom is facing the audience, back to the camera, his arms wide open, embracing the crowd.

Track 2. **Oh Bondage, Up Yours!—X-Ray Spex** (1978). This was the moment when women got bored of being fans or groupies and started taking to the stage. There were all-girl bands like The Slits, The Raincoats, 15.16.17, and The Bodysnatchers; women who fronted otherwise male groups such as The Selector; or mixed groups such as the Au Pairs. Many of these were tribal, slotting into the already-established indie, ska or lovers rock scenes. But X-Ray Spex's singer, Poly Styrene, couldn't be pigeon-holed. Part Somali, part Scottish-Irish, she was like the advance party for the new self that was going to reinvent Britain. And her music was equally idiosyncratic. She captured the spirit of the time like no one else. Poly got started, as many others did, after seeing a shambolic, end-of-the-pier Pistols gig, and deciding she'd like to have a go herself. That was the basic punk DNA—an egalitarian anyone-can-do-it, but you had to have swagger. It was a defiant attitude that boasted (as Angela Carter once said of Louise Brooks): "This is me. Now show me what you can do."
In 'Oh Bondage, Up Yours!', Poly moves between two voices: the masochist "Bind me, Tie me", and the refusenik "Up Yours!". She begins by talking in an excruciatingly coy voice: "Some people say that

little girls should be seen and not heard", then yells out, "but I say, Oh Bondage, Up Yours!", and the music kicks in. It was a declaration of war: and whether you read this as a women saying she was tired of the sexist shit and wasn't going to take it any longer, or more broadly as a cry against all the ties that bind, Poly was here to tell us she had something to say and was going to be heard. But her sense of herself as a performer also says a lot about the aesthetic of punk. As she indicated repeatedly in interview, she didn't think of herself as a tortured artist writing about her own suffering, but as someone who was playing with ideas and words, sending up clichés and unexamined dogma. So when X-Ray Spex played at the first RAR carnival, Poly appeared sartorially resplendent in a twinset, as if in pastiche of Margaret Thatcher. But she refashioned the archetypal English look, combining her tweeds with dayglo socks and an African headscarf.

● Poly Styrene

Punk is often been characterized as angry or nihilistic, and there are still arguments about its origins and purity: were you early enough on the scene, were you authentically English or, as John Lydon accused others, singing in an American drawl, imitating Jamaican patois? In fact, like some of the best reggae, its main mode was reportage of under-reported lives and places. RAR acts like The Members vividly evoked 'The Sound of the Suburbs', Steel Pulse announced a 'Handsworth Revolution', while John Cooper Clarke, appearing at the Northern RAR Carnival in Manchester, was scathing about the misery and tedium of much everyday life: "The bloody train is bloody late, You bloody wait you bloody wait, You're bloody lost and bloody found, Stuck in fucking chicken town".

But as Poly Styrene demonstrated, anger wasn't the only mode; there was parody, too. The Clash had a nice line in skewering capitalist commodification in songs like 'Lost in the Supermarket', as did the Gang of Four in 'Damaged Goods' ("I can't work, I can't achieve, Send me back"), and X-Ray Spex in 'Warrior in Woolworths', or the sweetly melancholic, 'GermFree Adolescents'. Other bands dragged up in the clothes of the oppressor: Robinson sometimes appeared on stage dressed as a policeman, while Steel Pulse donned long white robes for their protest song, 'Ku Klux Klan', which they played in an electric performance at the first RAR carnival.

When Poly sang about 'Identity' she wasn't talking about her own, but the idea of it as something manufactured: "Did you do it before you read about it?", she mocks. There's a sophistication here which was evident among many of the bands who played for RAR and RAS (Rock Against Sexism): groups like the Gang of Four, the Mekons and the Au

Pairs. RAS was the brainchild of another *Temporary Hoarding* writer, Lucy Toothpaste. She was also a member of the RAR committee, alongside Syd, Red, Widgery, *TH* editors and designers, Ruth Gregory and Roger Huddle; photographer and banner-maker, Robert Galvin; myself, John Dennis and Wayne Minter – who both joined me at the RAR office. (After death threats and a letter bomb, our operations moved to Cable Street and then to Finsbury Park.)

RAR had been keen to put women on our stages but Lucy rightly saw this wasn't enough: the aim of RAS was to challenge sexism throughout the music industry. And this meant challenging the bands, too. In the Au Pairs interview she and I conducted for *TH*, and in another we worked on with the Gang of Four, she's particularly interested in ideas of power, in dissecting the aggression that then characterized so much music, asking: what did it mean, was it necessary, and how might a woman utilize the power invested in her when she walks up to the microphone and takes control of the stage?

Track 3. **Sonny's Lettah – Linton Kwesi Johnson** (1979). In one of the finest examples of the reportage song, Linton Kwesi Johnson brought us news from the front line, conveying just what it felt like to be an immigrant or the child of immigrants living in Britain. RAR supporters had seen how thuggishly the police behaved at Wood Green, Lewisham and Southall, where Blair Peach was killed, and at a succession of anti-NF demos, and these had been widely reported. But this LKJ song, or dub poem, described something the TV and newspapers weren't talking about: attacks on individual black people, the casual, everyday assaults and insults meted out on the streets and in the back of police vans. 'Sonny's Lettah' is about SUS – the stop and search tactics the police started to deploy at this time under the cover of a nineteenth century law, the 1824 Vagrancy Act. Nearly forty years before the #BlackLivesMatter campaign, it revealed a commonplace cycle of police violence, followed by black people's self-defence, then their criminalisation.

The singer, Sonny, finds his brother, Jim, picked up by the police and roughly handled: "Jim start to wriggle and the police start to giggle". Sonny responds angrily and the incident ends with Jim charged with SUS and Sonny charged with murder. The whole thing, immaculately produced by Dennis Bovell, is told in epistolary form, in a letter sent from Brixton Prison to the brothers' mother back home in the Caribbean. The song is notable for the way that it contrasts the deference and respect Sonny shows to his mother with the brutality of the British police when someone challenges their authority. To this brutality, LKJ answered with militancy. 'Fite Dem Back', he proposed in another song, and, more pointedly, "We don't rock against racism, we fight against it."

The demand for respect, even in the midst of disobedience and insurrection, was something that the black community kept insisting on. Black people were not, as the police or politicians said, or the gutter press frequently reported, aliens or savages, but people with cultures and histories of their own. And reggae musicians often extolled their culture, expressing a determination to resist those who would deny or eradicate it. Dennis Bovell's band, Matumbi, who performed at RAR's first official gig, made just this point in a song called 'Black Civilisation'. For many alienated white kids this was a new idea. If black people had a culture in which they took pride, what was white culture? What was whiteness? It made legible to them something that had previously been invisible. At the first RAR carnival the Clash sang a furious version of 'White Riot', their response to this sudden realisation. They were abetted in this by Jimmy Pursey, the Sham 69 singer – a band with a significant National Front following. Pursey was incredibly loyal to his largely working class supporters and reluctant to tell them what they should think. But his appearance at the carnival confronted the racism among some of his fans, a stand underlined in a song he released shortly after, 'If the Kids are United': "Understand him, he'll understand you, For you are him, and he is you".

● Ruth Gregory and Syd Shelton, *TH* designers at the RAR office

Slowly these values of respect, and of cultural curiosity and appreciation, injected something new into the anger of punk, shifting the way that a whole generation learned to talk to, listen to and live with one another. The moment when black and white musicians came together at the end of every RAR gig was nearly always achieved with a reggae jam, something celebratory and uplifting – sentiments largely unavailable in the disaffected vernacular of punk. This coming together, and the ecstasy of the crowd at many RAR gigs and carnivals – the joy in celebrating a togetherness that politicians from Enoch Powell to Margaret Thatcher kept denying – was most frequently orchestrated by one of England's finest live bands, Misty in Roots. Misty often performed with the Ruts, stable mates on their co-operatively owned Southall record label, People Unite; with the TRB; with Elvis Costello at the second RAR Carnival in Brixton; but also, crucially, with Pursey and Sham 69. And when Clarence Baker, the singer from Misty was brutally beaten by the police during the anti-NF demonstration in Southall, putting him in a coma, RAR responded with two benefit concerts at the Rainbow called Southall Kids are Innocent, at which Aswad, the Clash, Misty, the Ruts, the Members, Bongo Danny, the Pop Group and Pete Townshend all played.

The final RAR Carnival at Leeds in 1981 featured the Specials. Like The Beat and UB40, they were a mixed-race band who had come up playing through the RAR clubs. Together on stage, they embodied everything RAR stood for. And in songs like 'Doesn't Make it Alright', their lyricist, Jerry Dammers, addressed head-on the way that poverty and alienation led to prejudice and violence, telling their audience "it's the worst excuse in the world", but also suggesting a way out of the trap racism set for working class kids: "Just because you're a black boy, Just because you're a white, It doesn't mean you've got to hate him, It doesn't mean you've got to fight."

● Kate on RAR's Militant Entertainment Tour, 1979 © Syd Shelton

On the thirtieth anniversary of the first RAR carnival Jimmy Pursey expressed what many people involved in RAR and the music of this critical moment felt: "We are still depressed by the government, but we are not confused by our culture. Britain is a multi-cultural society and it always will be if I have anything to do with it." But by the summer of 2016, bigotry went unchallenged on the BBC, Britain voted to turn itself back into an insular little country, and the blood of foreigners ran on our streets. Perhaps this winter we should be remembering the architect of punk, John Lydon, a man inspired and educated by his love of reggae, singing to us in 'Rise': "I could be black, I could be white", and then repeating insistently, as if trying to instil the message: "Anger is an energy". Forty years on from RAR, when the country is sleepwalking back into fantasies of racism and separation, we could do, once again, with some of that galvanising spirit.

● After Rock Against Racism, Kate went on to work in film, television and publishing. She has a doctorate in literature and politics from the University of East Anglia, and now works as a literary critic. Her writing appears in the *TLS, Spectator, Al Jazeera*, and the *Guardian*; she writes a blog at katewebb.wordpress.com.

Lucy Whitman

In 1977, Lucy called herself Lucy Toothpaste, produced 3 issues of her fanzine *JOLT*, graduated from university, and joined Rock Against Racism. Main contribution to RAR was as a writer and member of the editorial collective of *Temporary Hoarding*. Later got involved in Rock Against Sexism, and wrote about popular culture for feminist mag *Spare Rib*. For the last ten years she has been collecting stories of people affected by dementia, resulting in two anthologies, *Telling Tales About Dementia: Experiences of Caring* and *People with Dementia Speak Out*, both published by Jessica Kingsley Publishers.

Fun versus fascism / Lucy Whitman aka Lucy Toothpaste

The backdrop

In the late 1970s, we were genuinely scared that the National Front might be about to gain real political power and influence. The reason they didn't was because enough people up and down the country saw the danger and got together to stop them.

Rock Against Racism and the Anti Nazi League are the best known of the organisations which sprang up to defend us all against this threat, but there were lots of other groups dedicated to the same aim. For example, in London there was Women Against Racism and Fascism (WARF), the Campaign Against Racism and Fascism (CARF), Southall Black Sisters, Southall Asian Youth Movement, the Gay Activists Alliance, and so on; there were hundreds of other groups all over the country.

We were rising up not just against the threat of future fascism but also against the reality of racism in the present day, both individual and institutional: racist murders such as that of Gurdip Singh Chaggar in 1976 and Altab Ali in 1978; the Sus law; police violence at the Notting Hill carnival in 1976 and at numerous anti-racist demonstrations – notably Southall 1979 where Blair Peach was murdered and many others, including Clarence Baker from Misty in Roots, were severely injured. All this at a time when British TV was still broadcasting the Black and White Minstrel Show and comedies like It Ain't Half Hot Mum – shows whose crude racism is genuinely astonishing to young people today. Apartheid was alive and kicking in South Africa and Zimbabwe was yet to break free.

The reason RAR was so successful in this mighty endeavour was because it made politics fun. Rock Against Racism entered stage left at almost exactly the same time as punk and home-grown British reggae bands appeared. Was this just a happy coincidence or was it all part of the zeitgeist? The irreverent, do-it-yourself ethos of punk and the fiery militancy of the emerging reggae bands were the perfect match for the "Don't just sit there, DO something!" message of RAR.

In the early days, some punks who knew no better had flirted with Nazi regalia in a naive attempt to be "provocative"; they were soon slapped down by those who had a better grasp of what the Nazis actually stood for. Wearing swastikas as a fashion statement is always a stupid thing to do, but all the more so at a time when a neo-fascist party is gaining popularity.

One of my favourite RAR badges was the small one which read "Nazis are NoFun" (pun on NF, geddit?) (Though I did feel quite threatened when a burly man at the bus stop stared at me menacingly and read the badge aloud in a sneering voice.) Just going out of the front door – with my jagged hair and my black plastic jacket festooned with anti-racist and feminist badges – made me feel like a walking target, especially during the time I was living in Hoxton, east London. Hoxton is now achingly chic, but back then it was a wasteland, full of boarded up shops covered in NF graffiti. There were NF stickers everywhere – and we warned each other to be careful when tearing them off as they sometimes had razor blades behind them. One day when I changed trains on the tube, a stranger and I stood together scratching out the words scrawled on a poster: "Jews make good lampshades".

The battle of Lewisham – 13 August 1977, when fascists met their match on the streets of south London – has eclipsed similar battles in folk memory, but I will never forget the time the NF marched through Wood Green, much closer to my home turf, a few months earlier. I remember it as terrifying and thrilling. Terrifying to see the NF marching through our neighbourhood and the vast numbers of policemen who were there to protect them. Thrilling to see that they were totally outnumbered by the motley collection of anti-fascists who had turned out to greet them. The fascists were totally taken by surprise at the response, and must have realised they had no chance of winning local people over to their point of view.

I also remember encountering a man trying to sell National Front News in Crouch End (an unfashionable suburb in those days, unlike now). He offered me a copy of the paper and nearly jumped out of his skin when I bellowed at him to fuck off. I can't say it was entirely down to me, but never again did I see anyone trying to sell *National Front News* in Crouch End Broadway.

One of the great strengths of RAR was that from the outset it attracted an incredibly talented team of writers, designers, photographers and amateur impresarios, who were united both in their dedication to the anti-racist cause and in their genuine enthusiasm for the music. It would have fallen flat on its face if it was just a bunch of well-meaning lefties who had no interest in the cultural explosion that was going on at the time. However, the roots of some of the founder members in the organised left (primarily the International Socialists, forerunner of the Socialist Workers Party), though scoffed at by some, was advantageous in many ways: there was a bedrock of experience in organising events and demonstrations; there was a network of contacts which made it possible to protect our events from the very real danger of attack by fascist thugs, and to link up eventually with the Anti Nazi League for the carnivals; there was a knowledge base about the history of political and cultural struggles which informed our whole approach, especially the look, feel and content of our fanzine, *Temporary Hoarding*; and last but not least, there was the use of the SWP print shop in Hackney, without which it would have been a lot more difficult to produce all our wonderful artefacts.

It hardly needs saying that Rock Against Racism also thrived because it attracted the most exciting bands in the land to perform at its gigs. Everyone will have their favourite list. My personal top ten would be: The Clash, Steel Pulse, X-Ray Spex, Aswad, Buzzcocks, Matumbi, the Au Pairs, the Cimarrons, the Specials, and Misty in Roots, who probably played more RAR gigs than any other band.

Where did I come in?

I got into punk early in 1976, and in 1977 I called myself Lucy Toothpaste and gave birth to my fanzine, *JOLT*, where I wrote about women in punk bands and ranted against sexism, racism and fascism. I was excited when I went to a couple of RAR gigs and realised that there were lots of other people thinking along the same lines. I joined the *Temporary Hoarding* editorial collective, and got the chance to write for a much wider audience.

Punk appealed to me because it split conventional culture open. All of a sudden there was space for ideas which had previously been regarded as outlandish or taboo – for example, we ditched the rule that girls had to look pretty, feminine and harmless.

Much-reproduced photos of the highly sexualised images promoted by some on the punk scene, such as Vivienne Westwood and her shop assistant Jordan (the punk Jordan, that is, not the other one) have tended to obscure the fact that the dominant aesthetic of punk was androgynous, and often quite asexual. Girls could and did wear exactly the same clothes as boys. Out on the streets, I was frequently mistaken for a boy at the time. If any of us did decide to wear a party frock, it would be garnished with a pair of Doc Marten's – a combination which was literally unthinkable before this era.

Collage – mashing up unconnected images and ideas which seemed to contradict each other, to make a new message – was the order of the day. Juxtaposing the sweet harmonies and hypnotic rhythms of reggae with the ugly cacophonies of punk, two contrasting art forms united by the urgent demand to "Question authority!" was RAR's masterstroke.

Temporary Hoarding combined fabulous graphics, brilliant photography and incisive writing. The fanzine gave people something to take home and think about after a gig – giant posters to put on the wall, letters from supporters, tips on how to set up a RAR group or put on a gig of their own, adverts for RAR badges, photos and write ups from RAR events round the country, and lots of chunky interviews and articles, all written in a spiky, exuberant style – with deadly serious intent. We basically had a Reithian mission – to inform, educate and entertain – with the added twist that we wanted to excite, and incite our readership to get involved.

The list of musicians, bands and other cultural icons who we interviewed, and sometimes crossed swords with, is pretty impressive and includes: Johnny Rotten, The Clash, Aswad, Carol Grimes, Tom Robinson Band, Poly Styrene, Patrik Fitzgerald, Adam & the Ants, Peter Tosh, Jimmy Pursey, Mark Perry, Tony Wilson, The Fall, The Mekons, Alien Kulture, Au Pairs, Gang of Four, The Ruts...

Articles with titles such as 'Out with apathy!', 'No more normals', 'I seen the world – I didn't like it', explored topics such as the growing menace of neo-Nazi groups, the Sus law, what was going on in Northern Ireland and in Southern Africa, scary predictions (which all came true of course) about what would happen if Margaret Thatcher came to power, sex and sexuality, why we needed to resist attempts to restrict abortion rights, history lessons on racism, fascism, colonialism and the culture wars of previous generations.

We were unabashed about the educational side of things. Nowadays, most schoolchildren in Britain learn about the Holocaust and the slave trade in their history lessons, but that wasn't the case back in the 70s. My geography textbook, circa 1968, blithely referred to the "natives" in South Africa. We all had to educate ourselves and each other about the history of racism and fascism, about the horrors of the concentration camps and the battles on the streets of Britain between Mosley's Blackshirts and the anti-fascist campaigners of the 1930s. Most of this education took place in the cultural sphere, through fringe theatre groups, independent films, radical magazines, posters and of course through the lyrics of reggae artists who had set the history of slavery, racism and resistance to music. *Temporary Hoarding* was part of this massive wave of consciousness-raising activity.

The many tentacles of oppression

Throughout the 1970s, women had been raising our own consciousness of the ways in which we were oppressed both individually and institutionally within society. However, when RAR began, feminist insights which are now taken for granted had not filtered through to society at large.

There was a lot of sexism both within the music business and within the traditional left. It turned out that people who were totally committed to anti-racism might have a very low level of awareness about sexism, and this sometimes led to tension. You couldn't take it for granted that either musicians or activists or, crucially, music journalists who supported RAR necessarily recognised that the oppression of women was real, or was in any way relevant to the struggle against racism and fascism. (I was taken aback when, in a largely sympathetic article about RAR in the *New Musical Express*, I was characterised as "perilously sallow and pretty uptight". My offence? To have pointed out, in what I thought was an enthusiastic, not aggressive, tone of voice, that RAR was committed to challenging sexism as well as racism.) In the early days, one or two bands with quite sexist attitudes had been booked for RAR gigs and some people didn't understand why this caused an uproar. It was maddening to have to confront sexism within our own movement, but on the other hand it gave us the chance to start a dialogue about the ways in which women are oppressed and the connections with other kinds of oppression.

Tom Robinson's involvement in RAR from the earliest days had also helped to put lesbian and gay rights on the agenda. I am sure that lots of people who became involved in some way with RAR because of their anti-racist beliefs, but who had never thought about sexism or gay oppression before, learned a lot through coming into contact with anti-racist feminists and gay activists, who challenged sexist and homophobic attitudes wherever they found them.

The example of Rock Against Racism also inspired the formation, in 1979, of Rock Against Sexism, but that's another story...

Did RAR make any difference?

Yes, it did. Rock Against Racism helped to politicise a whole generation of young people, and to educate them about racism and the growing threat of fascism. It didn't reach everyone, but anybody who was interested in the live music scene at the time, who went to gigs and who read the music press, couldn't fail to be aware of RAR and be affected by it. RAR also encouraged a whole generation of young activists to do things for themselves, which was very different from the traditional model of left-wing parties trying to "organise" the workers. RAR is remembered for the huge carnivals, but it drew its strength from the scores of RAR groups up and down the country who put on local gigs, and all the bands who played at those gigs.

Lots of people joined in, people who did not consider themselves to be "political" at all, and got their first taste of being part of a cultural resistance movement. Lots of people found their own voice through RAR, to speak up not just about racism and fascism but also about other kinds of oppression. RAR also got a huge amount of coverage in the music press, so anti-racist and anti-fascist ideas were reaching all sorts of people who were unlikely go to a political meeting or join a political party.

Rock Against Racism was vital to the success of the Anti Nazi League and the anti-fascist movement in general because it added a cultural dimension to the politics. This captured people's hearts and minds in a way that political meetings and ordinary demonstrations never could, and reached out to far more people.

The RAR carnivals were a fantastic experience for all the thousands of people who were there, but they also attracted enormous media coverage. This meant that the message the Anti Nazi League and all the associated groups were trying to put across reached millions of people. I firmly believe this helped to turn the tide of public opinion. Rock Against Racism was a key part of the wider anti-racist and anti-fascist movement, and definitely contributed to the downfall of the National Front as a serious force in British politics.

TEMPORARY
HOARDING
ROCK AGAINST RACISM
20p.
We want rebel music, street music. Music that breaks down people's fear of one another. Crisis music. Now music. Music that knows who the real enemy is.
Rock against racism.
LOVE MUSIC
HATE RACISM
ROCK
AGAINST
RACISM

● *TH* number 1

David Widgery

1947-1992. RAR's philosopher and writer

What is Racism

Racism is as British as Biggles and Baked Beans. You grow up anti-black, with the golliwogs in the jam, the Black and White Minstrel Show on TV and CSE dumbo history at school. Racism is about Jubilee mugs and Rule Britannia and how we won the war. Gravestones, bayonets, forced starvation and the destruction of the cultures of India and Africa was regrettable, of course. But without our Empire, the world's inhabitants would be rolling in the mud still, wouldn't they? However lousy our football team or how broken down our Health Service, we've got this private compensation that we're white, British and used to rule the waves. It would be pathetic, if it hadn't killed and injured and brutalised so many lives. And if it wasn't starting all over again.

Most of the time British racism is veiled behind forced smiles, charming coppers and considerate charities. But when times get hard, the newest arrival is the first to blame. Once they kicked out the Protestant French settlers, and then tormented the Irish construction workers who built our roads and railways, for the crime of being Micks. From the 1880s until 1939 it was the Jews turn, refugees from terrible brutality in East Europe who became the victims and scapegoats again in London and Leeds.

Racism is beaten back by the solidarity of ordinary people. Then emminant people say it will never happen again. Low and behold, times get bad and jobs are hard to find and wages are washed out and life gets lousy. And then the junk images of racialism, the remains of 500 years or 'our' Empire surges up again and the Beast begins to stir. They need a racial problem to distract people from the real ones. They need an answer for people who don't want to think. In 1977 the answer is; BLAME THE BLACKS.

Last year in Britain saw racial violence worse than the height of the Mosley anti-Jew campaign in the Thirties, Gurdip Chagger, Dinesh Choudry and Ribbi Al Hadid were stabbed to death in openly racial murders. Dozens of black people have been injured by the racialists, egged on every morning by the *Mail* and the *Express*'s screaming headlines that make their acts of hatred respectable. Fascists, their spiked Union Jacks and slow military drums under heavy police protection forced their way through Hackney, Bradford, Leicester, despite active and forceful protest. In north London, the police boasted openly that they were using snatch squad techniques to pick out anti-NF demonstrators, 'that had been perfected in Northern Ireland'. Repatriation, which means forced deportation, which means the rounding up and hunting down of blacks is informally supported by the Tory Party. And the Labour Party has no answer, except to cringe. It has created the political conditions in which the fascists flourish. From the wire cages in Heathrow Airport's immigrant compounds to the gleaming Alien Registration Computer in Holborn, a new colour bar now stretches. Every retreat by officialdom inflames the appetite of the Right. Once again racialism is back. And challenged it must be. For when racialists rule, millions die.

In the 50ies and 60ies, British employers courted black labour, sucking in skills and muscle from the Caribbean and Asia. Black workers filled the jobs that no one else fancied, shift work in the hospitals, sweeping the airport corridors in the early morning, in the blazing heat of the foundries and the twilight shifts in the mills. They saved for back-to-backs in streets where the refuse somehow never got cleaned up by the Council or got pushed into the old council blocks that no one else wanted. Promised the sky, they were slotted in at the bottom. Chapeltown, Manningham, Southall, Brixton; crowded houses, dismal pubs, wet plimpsols, dogs licking dustbins. No fault of the people who had to live there but they got the blame. Black workers were never thanked. They were tolerated...as long as they knew their place and kept to it. And worked their heart out.

Now the economic furnace which sucked them in is faltering. Prices soar, wages sink. The economic system is at odds with itself. The more it tries to untie itself, the deeper the knots of inflation and unemployment cut in. To sell your labour now is a privilege, now the economy can't use the workers it's got.

Blacks, no matter most are British born, suddenly become a 'problem'. Forced into the decaying bits of the big cities, they are accused of causing that decay. Out of work they are called lazy. Half educated in overcrowded, bullying schools and they are called sub-normal educationally. They are blamed for the conditions they endure and Government Offices make a living producing books of statistics about how terrible things are. The youth are told on all sides they are worthless. If they fight back, it's proof of their savagery. If they remain passive to the taunts, that testifies to their inferiority. For everyone who feels fear, gloom, guilt, despair; there is a simple answer. If the buses arrive full up, if they don't bother to repair the lifts anymore, if Casualty is closed; it's because of the blacks. Racialism is an antidote to thought that offers, easy pointless action; a blanket in your head to hide under.

The problem is not just the new fascists from the old slime, a master race whose idea of heroism is ambushing single blacks in darkened streets. These private attacks whose intention, to cow and brutalise won't work if the community they seek to terrorise instead organises itself. But when the state backs up racism its different. Outwardly respectable but inside fired with the same mentality and the same fears, the bigger danger is the racist magistrates with their cold sneering authority, the immigration men who mock an Asian mother as she gives birth to a dead child on their office floor, policemen for whom answering back is a crime and every black kid with pride is a challenge. Because of the changes in the immigration laws, just to be black is to be half illegal. You become a permanent suspect, always you can be stopped and asked for your passport. The police insist they are impartial but contrast their zeal to force a way through unwelcome streets for the Front and their attempt at Notting Hill Gate last summer to smother a peaceful and joyous music festival held by the people in their own neighbourhood, with imported riot-trained police. How can we take the police's claim to be impartial seriously when their evidence at the Mangrove, the Metro, the Leeds Bonfire Trials, and others is thrown out by the juries... when they accuse an 18 year old girl for assaulting 8 policemen or charge the Islington youth with an unnamed crime at an unknown time. How long before they start on white 'undesirables'...the Reds and the Queers in the same way?

This new legal viciousness is even more sinister when the hardened fascists return to the streets. But they can be resisted. But only when people who realalise what's going on come together, and show their strength, As a parent of one of the Islington 18 said: 'We parents should start thinking we've worked too damm hard all these years... if black parents stand up and say "we are with our kids", we will win'. Another said, 'When ordinary black working class parents start working with white people on a case like this, that's what the police are afraid of. We can go further'. Together we can make it.

● *Temporary Hoarding*: 1 (1977)

Reprinted with permission of David Widgery's partner Juliet Ash. This piece will also be reprinted in *Against Miserabalism: Writings of David Widgery 1968 - 1992*.

● *TH*8 1979

David Widgery

The Rising Of The Neon Star

From a letter to the music press to a national organisation and a radical culture roadshow in two and a half years isn't bad going. So Red Saunders – tour toaster, socialist impressario and co-author of the famous letter that founded RAR in August '76 – could be forgiven his scorn at the petrified, Heinekened, baggy-flared steward screaming 'You've got to stop them' as the Bradford gig reached yet another climax of crashing speaker towers, abducted singers, skins dancing on their heads and militant mayhem. 'Stop them? Why?' Red asks, ever the honest Ted. 'It's like this every night, Guv.' He returns, dirty raincoat, dimple and brilliantined DA to conduct further choral anthems of 'Mash the Nazis', 'Punk Lives' and 'Wipe out the racists with our culture'.

For though the political aim of the tour is deadly serious – to confront the National Front's bid for youth support – the method is fun, riot and rhythms: the politics of free emotions and musical unity against the racialist Big Fear. Castro Brown, UK Reggae big wheel, has never seen anything like it either. 'There's an election coming up,' he confides. 'You lot could win it easy.' Geoff Dene of the Leyton Buzzards who has changed the words of their enchanting evocation of a misspent London musical youth to 'Saturday Night Underneath the Painted Rhino' thinks RAR are 'lovely people to work with. I mean, without them, there'd be nuffin', would there?' As the Buzzards jam away with the Barry Forde Band, their bass player is in tears with emotion. The kids feel it too. They don't talk of Good Vibes anymore. Just 'Really good feeling tonight. All together like.'

The 'Militant Entertainment' tour has been six months in the planning.

It results from a decision at RAR's second national conference to scale down from the open-air Carnivals of '78 and get back to the roots, what *Temporary Hoarding*'s Lucy Toothpaste calls 'the real anarchy in the UK' – the RAR clubs. These local clubs now exist in over 30 towns, putting on small scale gigs and run by a mixture of culture-conscious lefties and punk and Rasta kids. Like any successful youth outfit, they are informal, a bit anarchic and depend on friendship networks rather than membership cards. Which means they are sometimes shambolic and can create headaches for RAR Central. So for RAR itself, the tour is part of 'firming up'. 'Getting to know the faces behind the telephone numbers' as Wayne Minter, the RAR gig scout, who goes round the country, checking out venues and liaising with the local groups, sees his job.

With personal loans from various rock and roll angels, RAR borrowed the money for 100,000 anti-racist advance rhino leaflets, 30,000 posters, 20,000 rhino badges, 15,000 copies of a special tenth issue of *Temporary Hoarding*. The 30 or so bands permutated on the tour were approached on the basis of good music and commitment rather than Big Name. But since the bill was arranged, so good was RAR's finger on the musical pulse, that nearly a third of the bands involved have been offered major signings and outfits like The Ruts, The Gang of 4, The Mekons, Stiff Little Fingers, and the Buzzards are officially certified by the music press as 'soon to be famous'. 'In two years time, people just won't believe you could see Misty in Roots, The Ruts and the Gang to of 4 on the same bill,' thinks Kate Webb, RAR's first full-time organiser and a full 15 years younger than some of RAR's more balding punk pates.

On tour went four and a half tons of PA and Lighting, a militant lightshow scudding images of Biko and Notting Hill Gate and Her Majesty with 'Scrounger' etched on her Royal Forehead, and a mobile RAR stall of badges and anti-racist propaganda. RAR's advice to the electorate – pinched from Surrealist Mimi Parent – is 'Rock hard, life is deaf'. And the local groups responded to the energy and the momentum the rhino picked up. (A rhino? Well one reason is that when it gets going, it's very hard to stop.)

In Middlesborough, where Sid Vicious is still big, punks with neck padlocks and scars were out leafleting the local football stands the previous week; in Norfolk bus drivers volunteered to drive convoys from all over East Anglia; in Edinburgh where an emergency second night was put on when Stirling University cancelled at short notice, new posters were designed, silk-screened and fly-posted within hours of the news. And at Manchester, one of the four gigs RAR Central had to cancel, two girls in the Moss Side RAR pulled together a last-minute local bill, packed the poly on a Tuesday night and produced what Wayne judged one of the best gigs of the tour.

Between gigs at their garret in Finsbury Park, how do the RAR crew assess the tour's impact? John Dennis, schooled at the RCA, educated at a Notting Hill Gate adventure playground, was pulled in full time to handle tour administration. 'As promoters, there is now no doubt at all that we can deliver the goods. But people also understand why we are different from the regular commercial promoters. We did the carnivals when no one else was doing things on that scale. Now we've done the tour. There is an alternative and it works.' But looking ruefully at the office pocket calculator he admits that the financial losses on the tour look 'terrifying'. 'If anyone has been thinking of helping us out, now is most certainly the time.'

Kate sees the tour in terms of better understanding between the bands and RAR, the unity expressed in the end of gig jams, the musicians helping out on the RAR stall, Red's agit-pop toasting. And the way RAR can perhaps help the new generation of groups from falling into silly gestures and short-sighted cynicism about everything, which was the fate of too many of the pioneer punk bands. And in the process undermine racialist support where it matters most.' When I see kids at gigs who were NF and aren't any more, then I know its all worthwhile. We're connecting,' says Kate. 'You see these beery bearded types with their socialist newspapers outside the gig. And then inside there is Geoff from the Buzzards – who's an East Ender – arguing it out with some Geordie punk. He's doing it.'

Red's just received Today's Catastrophe, the *NME* have somehow printed the closely guarded secret that Tom Robinson and friends are joining the soul-meeting at the Ally Pally...a week before RAR was authorised to release the news. The office braces itself for the TRB's management's phone call. 'What will I do? I'll grovel, that's what I'll do,' says Red. 'Christ, this tour has made me do such terrible things. Like breaking it to Carol Grimes, who played RAR's first ever gig, that we just could not afford to get her and the band up for the Scottish leg. That really hurt. And the body blows.' He grasps his ample abdomen and mimes falling to the floor. 'Like Aswad getting ill and having to pull out of the Midlands dates. But that's the difference between us and all those NW3 experts on Marxism and Popular Culture. We're out there giving our souls for the kids and the culture. We've always had to fly in the face of reality. If we'd been "realistic", we wouldn't have started RAR, wouldn't have played reggae to punks, wouldn't have got through to Johnny Rotten and Elvis Costello.' But will RAR's favourite slogan, 'All Power To The Imagination', impress the bailiffs?

Politically, the tour is the biggest thing to happen in the election so far and the Ally Pally Rally on Easter Saturday might just be the largest gathering of the low-energy hi-security parliamentary contest. RAR sees the climax of the tour as 'a show of anti-racist enthusiasm aimed at racist candidates in whatever party'. But they have a particular interest in turning the National Front's biggest election effort yet into a

catastrophe of Lost Deposits.
Judged by the tour, while the Front is not out, it's following is down among young people. And it's completely lost the 'underdog' glamour of two years ago. The Front's January membership bulletin admits that new recruitment among young people almost dried up last year. Kids seem much more aware of the NF's fascist cadre nestling under the patriotic veneer and the implications of their No Fun philosophy. And there is no great love for the middle-aged politicians of the major parties endlessly plotting for the carpet slippers vote. 'However you vote, Babylon win' a dread accurately informed me at Manchester.
RAR's special success is that it has become a positive focus, not just the endless anti-this, anti-that. An expression of militant, multi-racial solidarity against whoever is in charge. For The Ruts, playing for RAR is 'well, The Obvious'. As Paul Rut puts it, 'We grew up with Southall RAR. We're growing up together. I'm no politician and I wouldn't spout a load of anti-racism. But we grew up multi-racial and it's okay that way. It's a practical thing. We listened to a lot of reggae but when you're gigging with a band like Misty, you can work out how to actually do it.'
Without being big headed, RAR can claim some credit for a sea-change in music. Two years ago it was still, despite the punks, considered very unfashionable not to be cynical. The music business was still in the world of the Permanent Putdown and the Great Swindle. Indeed a slightly sardonic eye is still essential equipment. But now mega-stars like Elton John and Joan Armatrading go eloquently out of their way to support RAR's aims, and musicians are showing maturity and compassion which puts to shame the 'show biz celebrities' who jumped on the Anti Nazi League platform and then jumped off again when the going got a little rough.
It's not 'only rock'n' roll' and never was. You can have principles and not be boring. Certainly the music weeklies are nowadays better written and more socially responsible than the ever-deteriorating Fleet Street productions. If you want to read exciting political prose, take *NME* not the *New Statesman*. Bands like the TRB have weathered the hail of put-downs about being 'preachy' and 'po-faced' and 'too-nice' because they wrote about politics, not with a capital P but as how you are messed about in life and what to do about it. It's the musicians in the '70s showing the commitment associated with the poets of the '30s. Hopefully they will avoid making the same mistakes.
So the rhino arrives, having weathered mysteriously cancelled music licenses, elitist College Guardians, nervous breakdowns (literally) and a mid-tour cash crisis. It apologises to anyone and missed on its roots route and will see them at the alley family. And racists beware, a four and a half ton rhinoceros takes a lot of stopping.

From listings magazine *Time Out* published week of 13-19 April 1979.

Bernie Wilcox

Manchester RAR organiser in 77/78. Still a committed socialist and anti racist and non-executive director of various private companies.

It's early September, 1977 in Wigan. Hundreds of young people mostly recruited from outside dole offices are marching from Liverpool to the TUC Conference in Blackpool on a Right To Work March and Manchester RAR are organising the nightly entertainment. Tonight it's at the famous Mecca of Northern Soul, the Wigan Casino. The Sex Pistols are banned from performing in most council areas and are doing gigs under fake names like SPOTS (Sex Pistols On Tour). Somebody has spread a rumour that the Pistols will be playing in Wigan and the town is awash with Punks from all over the country. No matter how many times we tell them that the Pistols won't be playing, they just don't believe us. The final band start playing just as the Northern Soul crowd are coming in for their all-nighter. The travelling Punks realise that Ed Banger and the Nosebleeds aren't quite what they'd hitchhiked up the M6 for and suddenly everything kicks off with Punks scrapping with Northern Soul kids and Ed Banger getting his head banged with cans of lager. It's not a great beginning for the Manchester RAR gang. We were hoping to unite the youth and they'd ended up punching each other's lights out.

Despite our intentions of getting young people together, things quite often kicked off at Manchester RAR gigs but only between the white kids. We obviously had the issue of the National Front turning up causing trouble but quite often it was just Saturday Night's Alright For Fighting stuff. We had a policy of trying to avoid preaching to the converted in student venues or liberal areas like Chorlton where lots of middle class lefties would undoubtably turn up but we wouldn't really achieve much other than the equivalent of organising an SWP social evening.

We preferred to go to the areas where racism was rife and where live music was never heard outside of the working men's club but that did mean that things wouldn't always be genteel affairs. Punks and Teds ended up scrapping at a RAR gig with Shaking Stevens and the Sunsets (their manager was a great RAR supporter) playing with Mick Hucknall's Frantic Elevators but undoubtably the worst was the 1977 RAR Christmas Party at Stretford Civic Theatre with The Fall, The Worst and John Cooper Clarke. Stretford had been hit hard by the decline of the huge factories in nearby Trafford Park and it was an area on its way down with the inevitable emergence of right wing politics and racism. I'd asked the steward at the theatre to use plastic glasses but he insisted that he'd never had any trouble before and didn't expect any on the night. Of course, the local boot boys didn't often go to see Cinderella or My Fair Lady which was the usual sort of entertainment at the gaff.

JCC got a really good reception (it was groundbreaking stuff that John was doing in taking his revved-up poetry to a music crowd) but The Fall's Mark Smith managed to wind up the audience, something that he was pretty good at. A pint pot went sailing through the air and landed on the stage just near bass player Tony Friel's feet and that was the trigger for a hailstorm of pots and glasses raining down on the band.

● Manchester RAR team at Kelly's, L-R: DJ, Militant Frank Manley; Chris Griffin (Manchester Mekon); Anita Waters; Tony Jawando.

Photograph: Phil Painter

We dropped the safety curtain but Mark insisted that the band kept on playing from behind it with glasses thudding against the cloth. The gig'd be stopped immediately these days but it didn't seem that abnormal back then.

The PA supplier Chris Hewitt taped the gig on a C90 cassette and gave it to me at the end. I passed it onto Mark a few months afterwards and he released it years later as an album, The Fall 1977. You can still hear the broken glass on it.

RAR in Manchester had started by getting together with Dick Witts who ran the Manchester Musicians Collective. The Collective bands were very supportive of RAR. Loads of Manc musicians started at the Collective including, The Fall, Mick Hucknall, Joy Division and Burnley-based Boff Whalley from Chumbawamba. Ian Curtis actually borrowed the haunting melody for 'Love Will Tear Us Apart' from fellow Collective band, Manchester Mekon's song, 'Cake Shop Device'.

We'd hit a real musical sweet spot in Manchester with all these bands

Steel band on truck during the march to Alexandra Park. Photograph: Phil Ramsell

inspired and energised by the Pistols' iconic Lesser Free Trade Hall gigs, all desperate for an audience to play to at the same time as demonstrating their opposition to racism.

We were well-established by the time of the April 78 Carnival in London. It was a revelation and a massive shot in the arm to me personally. I just never imagined that there'd be so many people who cared so much about racism to travel all the way to London and march for miles. I'd been at Grunwick in '77 when Arthur Scargill led thousands of Yorkshire miners to join the picket and also in Lewisham that same summer, but these were tiny compared with the Carnival and to see such huge numbers felt like we were making enormous progress and we were! A lot of this was down to the ANL, which had an immense broad support across the Labour movement and of course, these people were good at getting lots of people out onto the street. How crucial the ANL were in the success of the Carnivals cannot be underestimated.

I'd missed my coach back and blagged myself onto the Manchester ANL train where I sat with Geoff Brown. Geoff was the Manchester organiser for the ANL and we'd been fellow SWP comrades for a few years. As I sat down we both said "Wow. We've got to do this in Manchester"

It seems pretty incredible now but we gave ourselves just 10 weeks to put it all together. We had a lot of initial opposition from London RAR and

ANL who didn't think we could do it, but we just knew that there were loads of people all over the North that would love to come along. People living in London often don't understand the North, something that has been the case for years. Even in David Widgery's wonderful book on RAR he didn't quite get the correct venue of the Northern Carnival.

The date was effectively set by Chris Hewitt, the guy who made the The Fall tape. Chris ran the Deeply Vale free festival every year and as we were using the Deeply stage and PA it had to be the weekend before Deeply. The ANL's Gerry Fitzpatrick and Paul Holborrow were brilliant at cutting through the red tape and winning over the local council. Geoff had organised the ANL team to do everything from putting together thousands of yellow lollipops to renting flat back wagons and generators so that loads of bands could entertain the crowd as they snaked their way from Strangeways Prison to the beautiful Alexandra Park in Manchester's predominantly-black, Moss Side.

The two bands we wanted to play more than anyone else were Steel Pulse and Buzzcocks. Steel Pulse had done the April Carnival and agreed to it right away. Despite being a Manchester band, Buzzcocks proved more of a challenge. Aside from the Pistols and The Clash, they were the UK's biggest Punk band and had organised those famous Lesser Free Trade Hall gigs back in '76. Their manager didn't like the SWP and viewed RAR and the ANL as SWP fronts. I always suspected that despite his anarchist sympathies at the time, he was worried about the political overtones impacting on their TOTPs appearances. He wouldn't give me any encouragement about the Carnival at all and time was pressing because we needed to get the publicity out.

Fate's a great thing isn't it? I was walking along Manchester's Oxford Road and out popped Buzzcocks' Pete Shelley from a musical instruments shop. It was too good an opportunity to miss and I immediately collared him and persuaded him to do the gig. To be fair, Pete didn't take that much persuasion and I was dancing a jig when their manager called me the next day and confirmed it.

We had a big crew sleeping backstage on the Friday night to protect it in case the NF came to wreck it. As it happened, it was us that got wrecked. Local TV personality and colleague of Tony Wilson, Trevor Hyatt, came along with Manchester's answer to Billy Connelly, Bob Williamson, and a big bag of weed. By the end of the night, we couldn't have protected the place if we'd have tried.

The day itself was superb. In the weeks before, Market Street and Piccadilly were like Badge City, Arizona with almost everyone wearing one or two or ten. We just knew that the Carnival would be a big one but we were absolutely gobsmacked when 40,000 turned up and they weren't just from Manchester. As we'd predicted, people from all over the North who might not have schlepped all the way to the capital, made their way to the world's first modern city for a day of diversity and

Photograph: John Sturrock

fun. Those weeks leading up to the Carnival became the weeks when it became cool to be anti racist in Manchester.
We had now-deceased SWP comrade Pete Ridley on the backstage gate and he told a superb human story of the day.
"An older woman came up to the gate and said she urgently needed to speak to Pete Shelley. I politely explained to her that if she didn't have a pass, she couldn't come in but she told me she was Pete's mum. I said that I didn't care if she was the Queen, if she didn't have a pass she couldn't come in. She then produced a Tupperware box out of her bag and said, "Listen, I'm Peter Shelley's mum and I've got to see him because he's left home this morning without anything to eat and I've brought his sandwiches." I had a word with Bernie and we united an embarrassed looking Pete Shelley with his mum and his lunch."
Unfortunately, hiring council-owned halls wasn't always without problems. The spaces quite often lacked atmosphere and the management wanted all sorts of forms completing and needed proof of insurance that we didn't have. In Manchester city centre, the music venues for Punk bands were getting a bit scarce and so we decided to start our own club night at a small club called Kelly's on Amber Street where the Printworks is now situated. Tommy, the owner was part of Manchester's legendary Quality Street Gang and although he didn't have a stage, he'd promised me he'd have one in good time for the first gig.
The Fall opened for us. Tommy, as good as his word, didn't provide a stage but the band wasn't bothered. He said that they'd just play on the dance floor and this they did, with Mark wandering through the audience doing his bit. What a night that would have been for those legions of devoted Fall fanatics nowadays. The week after we had Joy Division playing and despite his many promises, Tommy still hadn't brought a stage. One of the RAR gang was the social secretary of the students union and he had a collapsible stage if someone could go and collect it and return it at the end of the night. Joy Division's Peter Hook and Steven Morris immediately offered to do just that and away we went. They picked it up, erected it, played on it, dismantled it, returned it to the student union and then put their own gear in their van and went home for the night. If only all rock stars could be so nice and normal

Opposite: part of the march to Alexandra Park. Above: Bernie, 2020.

● Next page: Jo Wreford's *How did race-hate happen?* from *TH* Northern Carnival special 1978

● I left Manchester to live in Holland at the end of that month and I'll leave it for Debbie Golt (page 97) to pick up the story from there.

1950 START HERE
1958
BOOM!
BOOM!
BOOM!
AND THEY GOT THE AGRO
Meanwhile.. in East Africa...
RIVERS OF BLOOD
1969
BIOLOGICAL
1968
WHITE WORKERS OF IMPERIAL TYPEWRITERS
1974
THE 1974 GENERAL ELECTIONS SAW THE OFFICIAL ARRIVAL OF THE NATIONAL FRONT ON THE NATION'S T.V. SCREENS. THE FRONT LOST ALL 54 DEPOSITS IN FEBRUARY AND ALL 90 IN OCTOBER BUT IN BOTH CASES THEY GOT BROADCASTING TIME AS OF RIGHT. THE UGLIER FACE OF THE FRONT WAS SEEN AT RED LION SQUARE WHERE AN ANTI-FASCIST DIED IN A BATON CHARGE BY MOUNTED POLICE
IMPERIAL
THAT'S THE ONE!

HOW DID RACE-HATE HAPPEN?
1962
but then came...
SMETHWICK
PETER GRIFFITHS
VOTE
THIS PARLIAMENTARY LEPER...
WE HAVE ALWAYS FAVOURED CONTROL
WHITE PAPER
REMOVES ALL STAINS
1965
INDUSTRIAL RELATIONS ACT 1971
THIS IS A HIGHLY OBJECTIONABLE BILL...
IMMIGRATION ACT 1971
1971
IT RESTRICTED RIGHT OF ENTRY TO PEOPLE CALLED 'PATRIALS', BRITISH PASSPORT HOLDERS WHO WERE BORN IN THIS COUNTRY OR WHOSE PARENTS WERE. THE ACT OPENED THE DOOR TO IMMIGRATION WIDER THAN ANY TIME BEFORE — WHITE IMMIGRATION THAT IS. IT SLAMMED THE DOOR ON MOST COMMONWEALTH BLACKS.
THE TORY ANSWER? THEIR INDUSTRIAL RELATIONS ACT 1971 — IN THE SAME YEAR THEY PASSED THEIR IMMIGRATION ACT. WORKERS' ACTION GOT RID OF THE INDUSTRIAL RELATIONS ACT, BUT LEFT THE IMMIGRATION ACT INTACT. THE ACT WAS THE MOST SEVERE YET....
1973
3 DAY WEEK
PROPERTY & PRICES BOOMED, WAGES FROZE, & HEATH'S GOVERNMENT BUST ITSELF IN ITS ATTEMPT TO BREAK THE MINERS' STRIKE. PRODUCTION NEVER RECOVERED, AND UNEMPLOYMENT HIT THE MILLION MARK......
ANGRY AT THEIR FALLING LIVING STANDARDS. LABOUR'S ANSWER? BARBARA CASTLE STARRING IN 'IN PLACE OF STRIFE' — OTHERWISE KNOWN AS THE INDUSTRIAL RELATIONS BILL — IT FLOPPED.
BLACK WORKERS MOVEMENT
We Will Drive You Racists into The Sea
WHITE PHILOSOPHY IS DESTROYING HUMANITY
STOP POLICE ATTACKS ON
CRISIS!
1976
BLAME THE BOSSES NOT THE BLACKS
1977-8
THESE ARE THE LIARS!

Polly Wilson

lived in Walthamstow from 1972 til 1986. Went to Warwick Junior High and Walthamstow High School for Girls. Worked on a stall down the market every Saturday selling mohair jumpers, ska ties and braces, belts and ting!
I moved back to Australia in 1987 but visit London regularly. I teach migrants and refugees English and help them with settlement issues. Sad to say that recently in the suburb where I work an anti-racist rally was provoked by a 'Reclaim Australia' rally organised by the United Patriots League. As usual they were outnumbered by anti-fascists. NEVER AGAIN!

When I came to live in Walthamstow as a 12 year old, having come from Australia I naturally gravitated towards others who came from different backgrounds, still do, This was in the 1970's and there was still such a thing in comprehensive schools as the Commonwealth kids. So all of us students who came from, or whose parents came from, countries that were part of the commonwealth got to go out together on excursions like to the Natural History Museum. I was the only white girl as all the other countries were Caribbean, Pakistan, India etc. It was great actually and although politically it's very dodgy, sending 'the kids who come from countries that were invaded by Britain' off for a school excursion, I remember it clearly and loved being part of that group. The first time I became aware of racism was at that same school, Walthamstow Junior High. Pakistani girls were really ostracised by all the other students. They were bullied and alienated and it was horrible. I made a point of making friends with one girl from Pakistan in my class to stop her getting picked on and got her to bring me in some of her mum's food which I would sit and eat in front of the other students. Smart move eh? This opened up for me a lifetime love of naan and curries etc.

● Me selling *SKAN*

Outside of school I would also come across racism when I was with my mates. We were often pulled up by the police just walking down the high street in the evening and it was always my black friends who were hassled just that little bit more. I remember once though when a copper pulled me aside and asked what I was doing hanging around with black blokes!! Once on the underground some members of the National Front got on and stared at us all, we were 16 or something and these guys were much older and looked absolutely terrifying. Luckily I think they decided that we were too young to beat up so they just intimidated us instead. The fear that I saw on my mates faces has always stayed with me. The NF or members thereof were responsible for petrol bombing a Pakistani family's house in Walthamstow around that time as well killing a mother and children. The funeral was huge and forlorn of naturally, but the march on the walk back to the station was full of fury.

● Walthamstow SKAN at the Victoria Park Carnival 1978

When Rock Against Racism was set up we all just jumped aboard. At last we could fight back. Some of us at school set up a group called SKAN, School Kids Against the Nazis. We were spurred on due to our school renting the hall out to the NF for a meeting. Our school was multi-cultural and we felt it was a right smack in the face. We quickly organised leaflets and leafletted the other schools in the area telling them to come to the school if they disagreed with our schools actions. It didn't take much to get a lot of people there because if you were black or had black mates you knew or had already had encounters with the NF. We got a chant going. "we are black, we are white, we are fucking dynamite".

A lot of friendships were made and a lot of us became politicized that evening. It still gives me goose bumps when I think of the feeling of unity.

SKAN held meetings once a fortnight and made some pamphlets advertising gigs run by RAR as well as attacking the NF's politics. We got badges made as well. It was a time of great unity which was absolutely relevant and warranted as the NF were literally terrorising sections of the community and spreading their filth around the East End.

Jo Wreford

Forty years and counting

It was 1976 and the National Front
Stoked the stinky fires of white supremacy
So easily fanned with talk of alien swamps
That re-kindled Enoch Powell's rivers of blood rant
Then Eric Clapton – his reputation casually built
On the legacy of black American enslavement
That is 'the blues' –
Drunkenly parroted this poison
On stage in Birmingham England
And a different fire was lit
Sparked by revulsion
As Rock Against Racism
Gave a voice to the joyful diversity
That is the best of this small island

It's 2016 now and
You kip if you want to
But I'm wide awake
It's time to
Get up stand up
And drown the latest firestorm

Rememorising KK and RAR at the Roundhouse, May Day 1977

We sat round a broad and rather battered pine table. Picked up for next to nothing at a favourite second hand shop off Hackney's busy 'waste' market in Kingsland Road, Hackney, it had doubtless already served a long and useful life. In its latest incarnation it had been the hub of long into the night discussions and bouts of intense creativity that were the engine of Kartoon Klowns (KK for short), a radical and fiercely independent and unpaid theatre group that had broken away from the iconic Cartoon Archetypical Slogan Theatre (CAST).

But this night in 1976 the table was not to be witness to the writing of a script and the sorts of improvisations that had brought into being KK's latest play 'Yes, but – Socialism or Barbarism'. This night in 1976 the table would see the creation of a totally new social movement that would to be wholly unusual in its inclusivity, its youthfulness, and its refusal to be typecast or boxed in by political sloganeering.

For on this night Red Saunders paid an unexpected visit to fellow KK members Pete Bruno and Jo Wreford, to vent his fury over a story printed in that week's *New Musical Express*. The article described a drunken Eric Clapton on stage in Birmingham in a rant that was uncomfortably close to the drivel then being spouted by Enoch Powell.

How could this be? Was this not the very same Eric Clapton whose music and reputation had been built unashamedly on the back of the music of black American slavery that was 'the blues'? This was a gross betrayal, not just of the legacy of black music on which Clapton depended, but of those, like us, who loved that music. Our previous involvement in CAST, and its involvement in the Anti Apartheid struggle had already sensitized us to the horrors of racism. And now bigotry was growing in the UK, the National Front was mobilizing and it seemed that the same poison was infiltrating the music industry. Something had to be said and done.

So round that lovely old table we composed a letter to the *NME [MM]*, protesting Clapton's racism and demanding that he recant. We called on music fans everywhere to join together to fight racial prejudice wherever and whenever it appeared. It was a potent piece. But how should we sign it? Individual signatures were all well and good but this seemed to demand something more significant. It was Red who came up with the answer – "How about 'Rock Against Racism'?"

The very next day the letter was sent, and RAR was born.

At the time we had no idea of just what an impact the letter would have. Yet within the week we were to find out, as our letterboxes were inundated with mail from young people and older, music lovers all, and all demanding to know how they could get involved, how to join Rock Against Racism, how to get in touch, what they could do to help. The RAR letter proved to be the snowball that rapidly turned into an avalanche, a spontaneous uprising against the offence that is racism.

RAR grew rapidly, and grew again.

We leave the pine table behind now, and jump to the near future and preparations for the first major RAR gig, on May Day in 1977, at the Roundhouse in Camden Town, London. The evening represented perfectly the eclectic mix that was always the foundation and strength of RAR. Diverse bands had agreed to appear, and there was no headline feature. The night would also be unique in presenting what was (although we did not know this at the time) the very last appearance of the Kartoon Klowns. By now RAR had blossomed into a loosely tight organization able to attract and rely on a raft of unpaid professionals who together had designed a brilliant logo, and the now iconic fanzine *Temporary Hoarding* (which made its first appearance at the Roundhouse gig), the posters and leaflets essential to publicity, and a vast number of volunteers to distribute them.

Others were cajoled into persuading the bands (all performing for free) to get involved, others to sort out the lighting and stage mechanics and so on. Nonetheless, to this day, just how we managed to get this event together remains something of a mystery. Remember, it was organized without mobile phones or email and internet; everything was done hand to mouth, face to face, by letter stamp and post, and all by people most of whom were holding down full time day jobs at the same time. It seems now nothing short of miraculous.

For members of Kartoon Klowns the Roundhouse event represented an additional challenge. It was certainly one of the biggest venues we'd ever performed in, and regardless of whether some of us had been there before – Pete and Red as part of CAST and the anti Ian Smith 'Psychodelphia' event with the Pink Floyd in December 1966, and later, again with CAST, at the gig when I made my very first (rather reluctant) appearance with the group – it was still a huge space to fill.

The one previous experience on a comparable stage was perhaps KK's performance at the beautiful old Theatre Royal Stratford, East London, a gig organized to celebrate the 25 April 1974 revolution in Portugal. But that had been before a home crowd as it were. Like ourselves the audience were trades unionists, members and supporters of the radical left and of the new spirit of revolution that events in Portugal seemed to represent. We received a tremendous reception, and the applause at the end brought the house down. I can only speak for myself, but I left the stage walking on air buoyed up by the deafening clapping and shouting. Even Roland Muldoon – the founder and leader of CAST with whom we'd shared a testy relationship since splitting from him to set up KK – appeared backstage to pronounce the performance "fucking amazing!" Praise indeed.

And it was deserved. 'Yes, but – Socialism or Barbarism' was like all KK productions a simple play to put on. It was designed to be performed almost anywhere, so it didn't need much: a wooden ladder, a chair, a few props, some decent lighting, probably a screwdriver – someone always needed a screwdriver – and provided we were ready with our white face make up and blues jeans and t-shirt outfits, we were set to go. Yet the play laid out a complex and remarkably prescient critique of the state of the trades unions, the Labour Party and their increasingly uncomfortable relationship with government and big business. It foresaw the rise of Blairism and its sycophantic embrace of an increasingly powerful corporate capitalism – "Worker character to Labour party apparatchik "does that mean when we've got capitalism working at its best we've got socialism?" Labour party apparatchik to worker "You've got it!" – The play didn't pander to the audience, it wasn't simplistic. It was funny and tragic, and it was designed to make people think. It was, indeed, a 'fucking amazing' piece of theatre.

But playing the Theatre Royal gig to rejoice in the fall of the repressive regime in Portugal was one thing, playing the RAR gig at the Roundhouse felt like quite another. We had no idea how the play would go down with a RAR audience whose youthful diversity was always its greatest strength, and made it unique. Skinheads, punks, dreads, hippies, gays and a host of others come together to protest racism and its emergence in the music they loved, and to mark that protest with an alternative line up of bands that featured Aswad, The Slits, Pete Townshend and Ronnie Lane. [other bands?] There was no headline band, and everyone had to muck in. There was a very funny scene when Townshend entered the long shared 'dressing room' and clocked Pete Bruno – one of his biggest fans at the time and with whom he shared a particular facial profile – and as Red put it later 'did the organ stop of all organ stops'.

In the midst of this stellar bill was a slot for Kartoon Klowns. How would theatre, no matter how dynamic, be received? Would they get it? Would they laugh? Walk out? Wander about and barrack us? – Nervous? – You bet we were.

But we need not have worried. The performance went perfectly, people were engrossed. They laughed when it was funny (and it often was – what are clowns for after all?) and they were quiet when it wasn't. 'You could hear a pin drop', as someone said afterwards. The play was applauded to the Roundhouse rooftops – and – that was that. The Klowns never performed again.

Jo today

It is always easy to be wise after the event, but the truth is that in the mayhem of being in the middle of the sudden and totally unexpected explosion that was RAR, we had no time to dwell on the implications of this rapidly growing movement for Kartoon Klowns. And apart from photographs and some notes taken at those nights around the big old pine table, we had never thought to record KK. And no one at May Day gig in 1977 did so. There were no selfies then, remember, no Twitter or Facebook or Instagram.

And even had we foreseen that the commitment of time and energy required to get RAR on the road and keep it running would inevitably overwhelm Kartoon Klowns, would we have chosen KK over RAR? Certainly not. But the loss of Kartoon Klowns, of its particular style and energy, its political nous, and perhaps above all the sense of family that it embodied, was in hindsight, a minor tragedy.

It was a loss that should have been marked then, but only long after the event, when it had become clear that we simply could not continue to keep RAR growing and carry on the Klowns, could we step back and regret the passing of what had been such a dynamic and intense collective. So in the absence of a memorial we present this piece:

As a celebration of the early days of the unique experience that was Rock Against Racism certainly, but also as a rememorising of Kartoon Klowns – a great theatrical collective, and their play 'Yes, but – Socialism or Barbarism'.

Sarah Wyld

The three photographs I sent you together were taken on the same occasion in Lavender Hill, opposite Battersea Town Hall (now the Battersea Arts Centre). The people in the pictures were protesting against the National Front which was about to hold a meeting in the town hall. There were many police lining the street and it seemed that they were there to protect the NF. That was the feeling I got. The young people demonstrating were optimistic and good humoured, as the pictures show. I believe that this was the day before Blair Peach was killed in another part of London.

Stop
Nazis!
HAROLD

Mike Simons

Racism and resistance in the UK: A partial timeline

● 1 May 1974: Asian workers at Imperial Typewriters in Leicester strike against a multinational firm and a racist local union that was influenced by members of the National Front. The strike, although a significant step forward for Black and Asian trade unionism in Britain, ended in bitter defeat in July 1974.

May 1974: Robert Relf puts a 'For Sale to an English Family' sign outside his Leamington home in 'protest' against race relations law. The media treat him as the 'voice of middle England'. In fact, Relf was a hard-core Nazi, a member of the British Movement and the Ku Klux Klan who had been jailed for racially motivated crimes.

15 June 1974: Police kill Kevin Gately during a protest against the NF in Red Lion Square London.

● 3 May 1975: Brian Hosie, a member of the NF and the Ulster Defence Association, is jailed for the murder of Jamaican-born Hector Smith in Glasgow. Hosie boasted of the murder, 'Niggers mean nothing to me. It's just like shooting a dog. Niggers make good fertiliser.'

24 May 1975: Glasgow Police launch a savage attack on 300 socialists and trade unionists protesting outside a NF rally in Glasgow's Kingston Hall. Prominent members of the trade union and socialist movement in the west of Scotland were arrested and beaten. Glasgow City Councillor Andy McMahon says, 'I saw the most savage brutality by the police, something I've never seen before. I saw a woman kicked to the ground and punched in the face and members of the Sikh community with their turbans ripped off.'

July 1975: Some 400 Asian catering workers at Heathrow Airport strike for pay parity with other ground staff.

5 November 1975: Mounting anger at police harassment of Afro-Caribbean youth in Leeds boils over into running street battles on bonfire night.

December 1975: NF thugs armed with bricks and bottles attack a National Council for Civil Liberties meeting in Manchester.

● May 1976: Asian refugees expelled from Malawi arrive in Britain to hysterical racist abuse from the newspapers. A *Daily Mail* headline declared, 'We want more money. say £600 a week Asians'. The *Daily Telegraph* declared 'Migrants here just for welfare handouts'.

22 May 1976: Racists in South Woodford, east London, stab to death Dinesh Choudhri and Riphi Alhadidi.

4 June 1976: Racists murder Gurdip Singh Chaggar in Southall. Asian youth break from their community elders and take to the streets in protest. Kingsley Read, chairman of the National Party, a split from the NF, declares "One down, a million to go". A year later Justice McKinnon acquits Read of charges of incitement to racial hatred and tells the Nazi, "I wish you well".

5 August 1976: Guitarist Eric Clapton makes his notorious racist outbursts at Birmingham gig.

23 August 1976: Start of the Grunwick strike – the most significant Asian strike in British history – begins in north London.

31 August 1976: Notting Hill Carnival erupts into riots after mounting provocation by police.

September 1976: Mohan Dev Gautam, a 60 year old woman, was murdered by a racist gang who dragged her from her home in Leamington Spa and set her alight.

September 1976: *New Musical Express, Sounds, Melody Maker* and *Socialist Worker* publish letter calling for formation of Rock Against Racism.

12 November 1976: Rock Against Racism's first ever gig, featuring Carol Grimes, in the Princess Alice pub in east London.

10 December 1976: second RAR gig at London's Royal College of Art, featuring Matumbi, Limousine and Carol Grimes.

● 23 April 1977: Anti-fascists attack a NF march in Wood Green, north London.

April 1977: Tory-run Gravesend Council in Kent bans a Sikh festival.

May 1977: NF attract 119,063 votes in the Greater London Council election and almost 15,000 in Leicester. In Blackburn, the breakaway Nazi organisation, the National Party, field eight candidates and win an average 40% of the vote.

May 1977: RAR produces its first copy of *Temporary Hoarding* for a May Day gig at the Roundhouse.

May 1977, police launch an 'anti mugging' campaign in Lewisham, south London. The operation is recorded internally as 'Operation PNH' – Police Nigger Hunt. More than 60 black youngsters were detained, and 18 of them charged.

13 June 1977: Start of a week of mass pickets at Grunwick.

23 June: Arthur Scargill leads thousands of Yorkshire miners to the Grunwick picket line.

13 August 1977: The battle of Lewisham sees 5,000 local people smash a NF march through a multicultural area of London.

8 October 1977: Greater Manchester police mobilise 9,000 officers to protect NF march in Levenshulme. Some 3,000 officers escort NF National Organiser Martin Webster on a 500 metre 'one-man march' in Hyde, where the Nazis had been banned from demonstrating.

November 1977: Launch of the Anti Nazi League.

December 1977: Chief Constable of Durham Police invites National Front leader Martin Webster to address officers on the subject of 'Law and Order'.

● January 1978: Margaret Thatcher, her opinion poll ratings falling, makes a direct play for the racist vote, saying on ITN's World in Action programme, "people are rather afraid that their country might be rather swamped by people with a different culture."

21 April 1978: 10-year-old Kenneth Singh stabbed to death yards from his East London home.

30 April 1978: First RAR/Anti Nazi League carnival in Victoria Park, East London with X-Ray Specs, Patrik Fitzgerald, The Clash, Steel Pulse, and the Tom Robinson Band. Some 80,000 march 7 miles from Trafalgar Square to the gig.

4 May 1978: Asian textile worker Altab Ali murdered near Brick Lane on his way home from work.

14 May 1978: 18,000 demonstrate against the racist murder of Altab Ali.

11 June 1978: Nazi gangs rampage down Brick Lane in the heart of east London's Asian community.

18 June 1978: Around 7,000 join protest at racist attacks in East London.

30 June 1978: Some 500 march in silence after murder of Ishaq Ali.

14 July 1978: Grunwick strike committee, abandoned by their union and the TUC, calls off the strike.

14 July 1978: Albany Empire in Deptford, the scene of many south London RAR gigs was torched by Nazis and destroyed,

15 July 1978: Rock Against Racism Northern Carnival at Alexandra Park, Manchester: Steel Pulse, Buzzcocks, Exodus and China Street play to 35,000 crowd. Graham Parker and the Rumour play a RAR gig in the city as a warm-up, two days before.

24 September 1978: Second London RAR/Anti Nazi League carnival in Brockwell Park, south London, with Aswad, Sham 69, Misty in Roots, Elvis Costello & the Attractions.

10 December 1978: Racist murder of Michael Ferreira, an 18-year-old Guyanese mechanic, in Stoke Newington.

December 1978: The number of RAR events organised since launch tops 300 local concerts and five carnivals.

● March 1979: Militant Entertainment Tour launched, involving 40 bands at 23 concerts.

14 April 1979: Militant Entertainment Tour climaxes at Alexandra Palace with Aswad, Angelic Upstarts, John Cooper Clarke, Dambala, The Ruts, Leyton Buzzards.

20 April 1979: Police deploy 2,000 officers, including 60 mounted officers, to 'protect' an NF election rally in Islington Town Hall, north London, from 300 counter demonstrators. Police refuse non-National Front members access to the meeting.

21 April 1979: Police deploy 5,000 officers from 21 forces in Leicester to protect 1,100 Nazis who hold a march to a NF election rally in a girls' school. Police with dogs chase 2,000 counter-demonstrators onto a university campus.

23 April 1979: Police deploy 2,700 officers to protect NF election meeting in Southall, West London, and run riot in a predominantly Asian area. ANL supporter Blair Peach killed by police in Southall during the ensuing protest. Clarence Baker, manager of Rock Against Racism stalwarts Misty is savagely beaten in the band's headquarters, left with a blood clot on the brain and hospitalised for 15 days. Rampaging police trash the band's equipment. Some 345 people arrested during the protest.

25 April 1979: Metropolitan Police deploy 4,000 officers (with 3,000 held in reserve) to protect a NF election rally at Newham Town Hall, East London, attended by 400 Nazi supporters.

28 April 1979: Police deploy 5,000 officers to protect NF election meeting in West Bromwich.

28 April 1979: Metropolitan Police refuse permission for anti-racist march to pass the NF headquarters. Some 8,000 officers deployed to marshal a 4,000-strong protest.

30 April 1979: Police deploy 1,000 officers to stop 200 protesters disrupting NF election rally in Bradford

13 & 14 July 1979: Southall Kids Are Innocent gig at London's Rainbow theatre with Misty, The Ruts, The Pop Group, Pete Townshend, Bongo Danny, Aswad, The Members and The Clash.

● January 1980: Major internal split in NF between traditional Nazis and 'modernisers'. NF would-be Fuhrer John Tyndall says 'unfavourable publicity' generated by the Anti Nazi League and Rock Against Racism were key reasons for the NF's decline and he resigns from the organisation.

2 March 1980: Thousands of anti-Nazi activists force police to reroute NF demo in Lewisham

15 March 1980: NF march in Glasgow banned after mass pressure from anti-racists and the Labour movement. 100 Loyalist NF supporters try to march. Nazis burn down a Labour movement social club and bookshop in revenge.

20 April 1980: NF 'secret' march in Lewisham met by 2,000 anti-Nazi opponents.

26 April 1980: 300 NF supporters attempt to march in Corby, called under the slogan British jobs for British workers. Protected by 2,000 police, they are harassed by protestors shouting 'where were you when they closed the steel works', as local youth throw bricks at the Nazis.

30 April 1980: Anti Nazi League march in Bristol against police violence attracts 700.

27 May 1980: Inquest into the death of Blair Peach returns a verdict of misadventure, resulting in a public outcry.

21 June 1980: A series of racist attacks in Small Heath Birmingham, prompts a 500-strong protest march.

June 1980: Hard core Nazi British Movement start organising in Rochdale

July 1980: Metropolitan Police station 150 Special Patrol Group officers, its elite 'heavy squad'. in Brixton. SPG officers harass local unemployed youth and threaten civil servants on a picket line fighting victimisation of shop stewards.

17 July 1980: Four racists stab to death Ali Atab Beg in East Ham High Street, London. The murder followed a speech by Enoch Powell in nearby Hornchurch and a spate of attacks on black students and teachers at the local Plashet School. The murders prompt the foundation of the Newham Youth Movement, spearheaded by militant local Asian youth. The death of Ali Atab Beg is the fifth murderous attack on black and Asian youth in east London in five years.

17 August 1980: NF plan to march in West Bromwich under the slogan British jobs for British workers thwarted by mass mobilisation. Small Nazi march eventually takes place in Nuneaton after ANL mobilise thousands.

25 October 1980: 300 members of the British Movement march through Welling, south east London, shepherded around the back streets by police in the face of a large counter demonstrations.

November 1980: Nazis make concerted drive to attract football supporters. At Chelsea home games, several hundred thugs chant 'there's only one Adolf' to the tune of Rod Stewart's Sailing.

November 1980: Anti Nazi League relaunched in wake of rising racist violence in UK and wave of international Nazi terror attacks, including the Bologna station bombing that killed 85, attacks on a Paris Synagogue which killed 2, and a fascist terrorist attack in Munich, which killed 14 people.

23 November 1980: British Movement calls its first national demo, near Paddington station. Promising 2,000 the new Nazi organisation get 500, protected by 3,000 police. Rival Nazi marches take place elsewhere. The NF mobilises

200 in Bolton, protected by 2,000 police. In nearby Chorley, 80 New National Front also march, protected by police.

● January 1981: Tories' racist Nationality Act becomes law.

18 January 1981: New Cross Fire kills 13 young black people in a party. Police indifference to the tragedy turns grief into rage.

2 March 1981: Some 15,000 march from Deptford to central London to protest at both the deaths and the police and media handling of the New Cross fire. The march ends in clashes with the police on Westminster Bridge.

28 March 1981: Enoch Powell – then an Ulster Unionist MP, but still an influence on the Conservative Party – gives warning speech of a "racial civil war" in Britain.

2 April 1981: Police harassment in St Pauls area of Bristol finally provokes backlash when they raid the Black and White Café to arrest its owner. Rioting forces police to withdraw from the area.

10 April 1981: Rioting in Brixton begins after mounting anger at policing – particularly targeted at Black youth in what the Metropolitan Police officially called Operation Swamp – a reference to Margaret Thatcher's notorious 1978 statement. In Brixton, over six days, 120 plain-clothes officers stopped 943 people, arresting 118 – predominantly black youths.

10 April 1981: Malcolm Chambers, a young black man, murdered in Swindon in what was described as an 'anti-black riot'.

11 April 1981: Brixton rioting intensifies. Local youths deploy petrol bombs extensively. Some 279 police injured, along with uncounted numbers of protesters, 30 buildings destroyed.

12 April 1981: More violent confrontations in Brixton between police and local black and white youth.

18 April 1981: Racists murder Satnam Singh Gill, a 20-year-old student, in broad daylight in Coventry city centre.

June 1981: Racists brutally attack Lynval Golding, guitarist of the Specials, outside a London gig.

2 July 1981: Home of Kahn family in Walthamstow set ablaze. Mrs Kahn and three children die. Mr Kahn is severely burned.

3 July 1981: East London fascists March through Southall, West London, smashing Asian-owned shops on their way to a gig by Nazi supporting bands at the Hamborough Tavern. Asian youth fight back, driving the Nazis into the pub and setting fire to it. Police respond by attacking the Asian community.

3 July 1981: Liverpool police harassment of the black community flares into confrontation that escalated over the following days.

4 July 1981: The Specials, Misty, Aswad and the Au Pairs play the RAR-ANL Northern Carnival Against Racism, in Potternewton Park Leeds.

7 July 1981: Police in Toxteth, Liverpool, fire CS gas at unemployed rioters. It is the first ever use of tear gas in mainland Britain.

10 July, 1981: Ghost Town by The Specials is number one single.

11 July 1981: The 'Bradford 12' – a group of Asian youths, members of the "United Black Youth League" – are arrested for manufacturing petrol bombs. At the subsequent trial, the jury acquits them on grounds of self-defence.

12 July 1981: Rioting which began in Toxteth spreads across the country to include Handsworth in Birmingham and Moss Side in Manchester, as well as serious disturbances in Bedford, Bristol, Edinburgh, Gloucester, Halifax, Leeds, Leicester, Southampton, Wolverhampton and elsewhere.

26- 28 July 1981: Rioting erupts again in Liverpool. Police use tactics from Northern Ireland and drive at speed into crowds. Disabled 23-year-old David Moore dies after being crushed by a police van on waste ground in Toxteth.

Autumn 1981: Final edition of *Temporary Hoarding* published.

● *Leeds Carnival: 300 NF 30,000 anti-racists*

NO!

Khadijah Ibrahiim

Rock Against Racism

In our back-to-back and through-terraced houses,
working-class black and white
youth played Snap!
Sex Pistols latched onto this white heat,
graffitied Elizabeth's head,
stuck two fingers up, wore safety-pins
and spat on the Union Jack.
We watched them pogo dancing up and down
to The Clash's *white riot* of reggae-snatched rhythms,
while Maggie snatched milk,
brought recession and the poll tax.
And then The Specials rocked against racism,
they marched right past my street
up to Potternewton Park
'til it was *like a zebra crossing, black and white,*
black and white as far as you can see.

Part of the audience at the Leeds Carnival in 4 JUly 1981
responding to The Specials. Photograph: John Sturrock

Poem: Taken from the poets collection *Another Crossing*
Published 2014 by Peepal Tree Press